tails

BOOK ONE

HERMES
PRESS

neshannock, pennsylvania

D1307050

Published by Hermes Press, an imprint of Herman and Geer Communications, Inc.
2100 Wilmington Road
Neshannock, Pennsylvania 16105
(724) 652-0511
www.HermesPress.com; info@hermespress.com

Cover image: Ethan Young
Cover and book design by H and G Media and Troy Musguire
Daniel Herman, Publisher
Louise Geer, Vice President

First printing, 2012
LCCN 2012934894
ISBN 978-1-61345-015-4

Printed in China

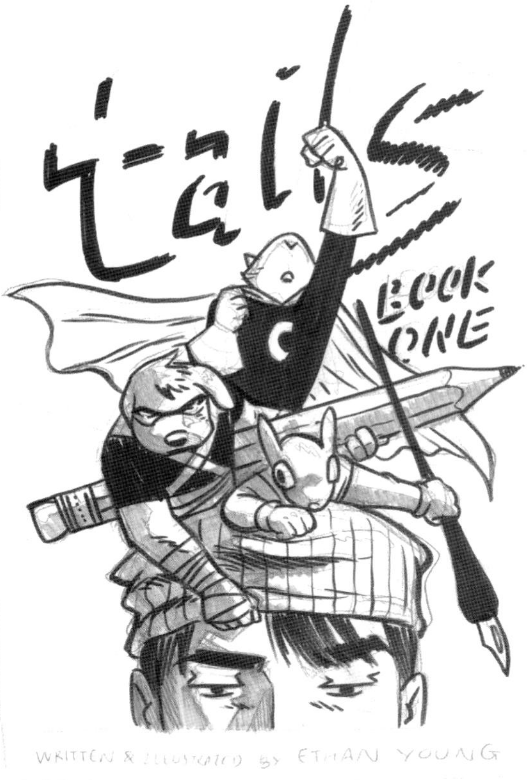
tails
BOOK ONE
WRITTEN & ILLUSTRATED BY ETHAN YOUNG

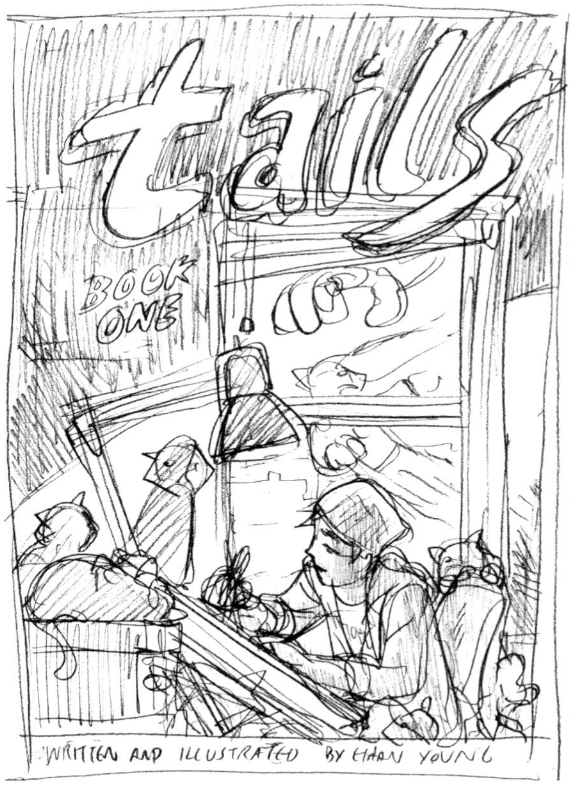
tails
BOOK ONE
WRITTEN AND ILLUSTRATED BY ETHAN YOUNG

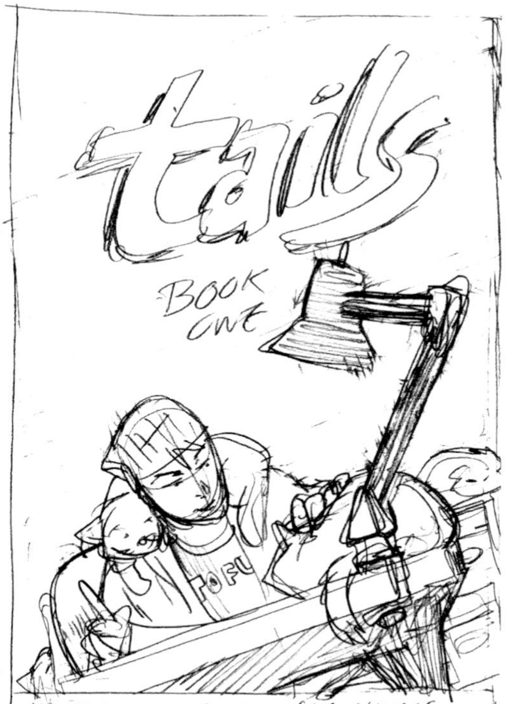
tails
BOOK ONE
TOFU
WRITTEN AND ILLUSTRATED BY ETHAN YOUNG

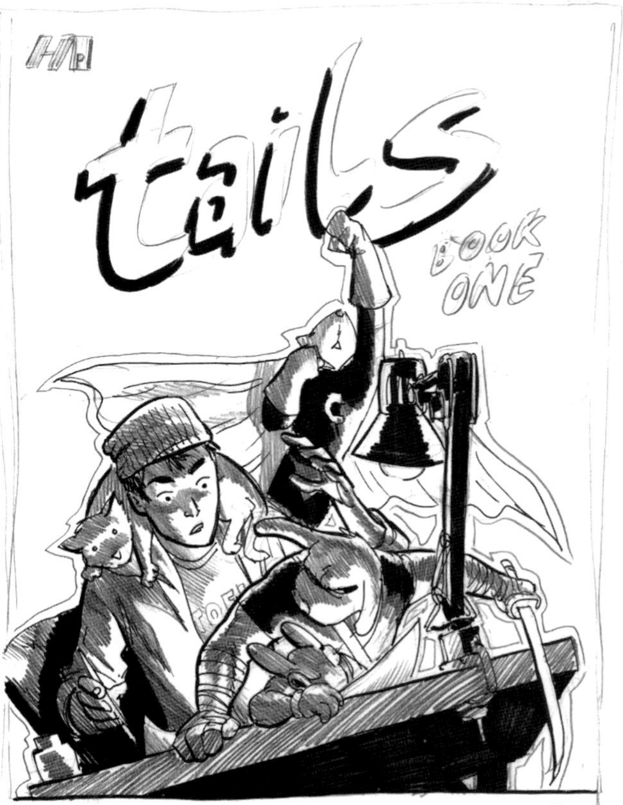
tails
BOOK ONE
WRITTEN AND ILLUSTRATED BY ETHAN YOUNG

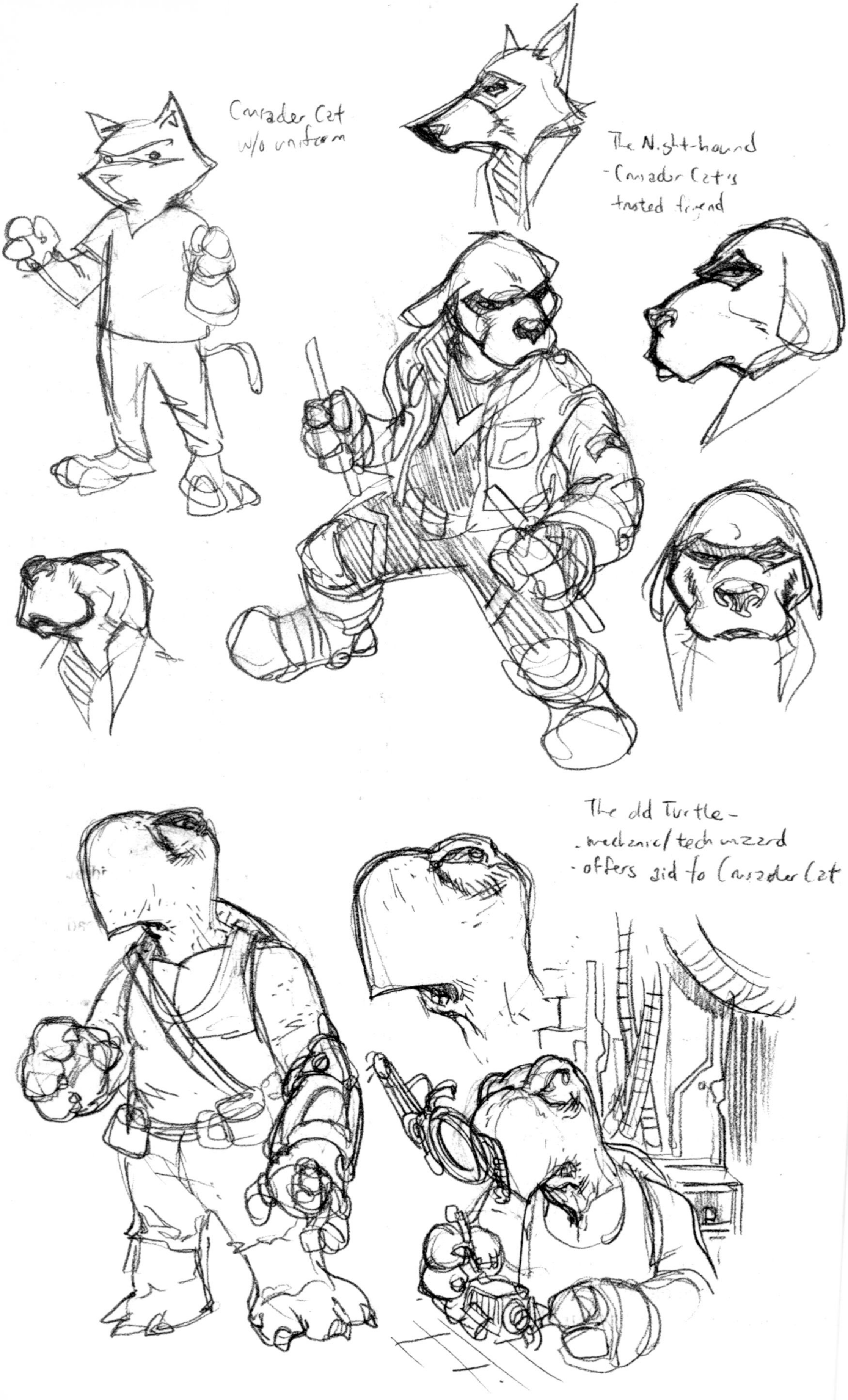
Crusader Cat
w/o uniform
The Night-hound
- Crusader Cat's
trusted friend
The old Turtle -
- mechanical/tech wizard
- offers aid to Crusader Cat

Introduction

I FIRST MET ETHAN (THE REAL PERSON)– Ethan, the sometimes emotionally-flawed and ever-growing comic book character who grows within these pages) when I was doing a website called Graphic NYC. Now, when you handle a blog or website, the amount of e-mails you get by aspiring cartoonists can get annoying, and range everywhere from spammy to entitled (one cartoonist, in particular, once sent me an email demanding that I review the second issue of his comic -- because we'd reviewed his first months prior). Also, when you write/edit a blog, some guy named "Anonymous" always wants to tell you how to do your shit (which is why I killed the comments field), but that's another story…

Ethan, who had been doing his webcomic, *Tails*, in weekly installments, sent an uber-polite email asking if Graphic NYC would be interested in reviewing it. And that was it: a polite, personable communication from what turned out to be a damn good cartoonist.

We (meaning my reviewer, Jared Gniewek) covered *Tails,* and it kicked my friendship with one Ethan Young, who I now consider one of my favorite people in this crazy thing we call the comics industry.

Flash forward years later, while I'm working for Dan Herman at Hermes Press, found out that Ethan was ready to publish *Tails*, and here we are.

To read *Tails* is to mark Ethan's evolution from a good cartoonist to a great one, from his actual drawing to storytelling. While this volume is only the start of something much bigger, Ethan was sure that this would serve itself well as a done-in-one reading experience.

And I promise, the shit gets a good kind of weird from here on out, much weirder than even I'd have seen back in '08 when Graphic NYC first reviewed *Tails*. I know what happens, because Tails has become my honest-to-God first comics-editing gig. Now, it may start off as a little High Fidelity, but it soon gets into metaphysical territory which, ironically, can sometimes seem as Quixotic as the dating scene itself is.

That's what I love about *Tails*: Ethan the comic character's trials and tribulations hit really close to home with me – if you've ever been a single creative type struggling to make it through life, especially in a place like New York, Tails will speak to you. Many of the inevitable frustrations I faced through several of my own projects, be it Graphic NYC, a comic book story, or one of the books I've written, can be reflected through Ethan's own experiences.

Even the weird make-believe (or is it?) fantasy element to *Tails* has that truth as its nucleus, which makes it that more palpable and relevant.

So of course, I'm going to tell you to grab the nearest cat or dog (what, you're not an animal lover!? At least go out and buy a goldfish; they're not as cuddly, but they do make great company), curl up, and read the kind of make-believe/real exploits of one Ethan—frustrated cartoonist, Vegan, New Yorker, honorary crazy cat lady, and something much more…

– Christopher Irving

To my wife, Carol.

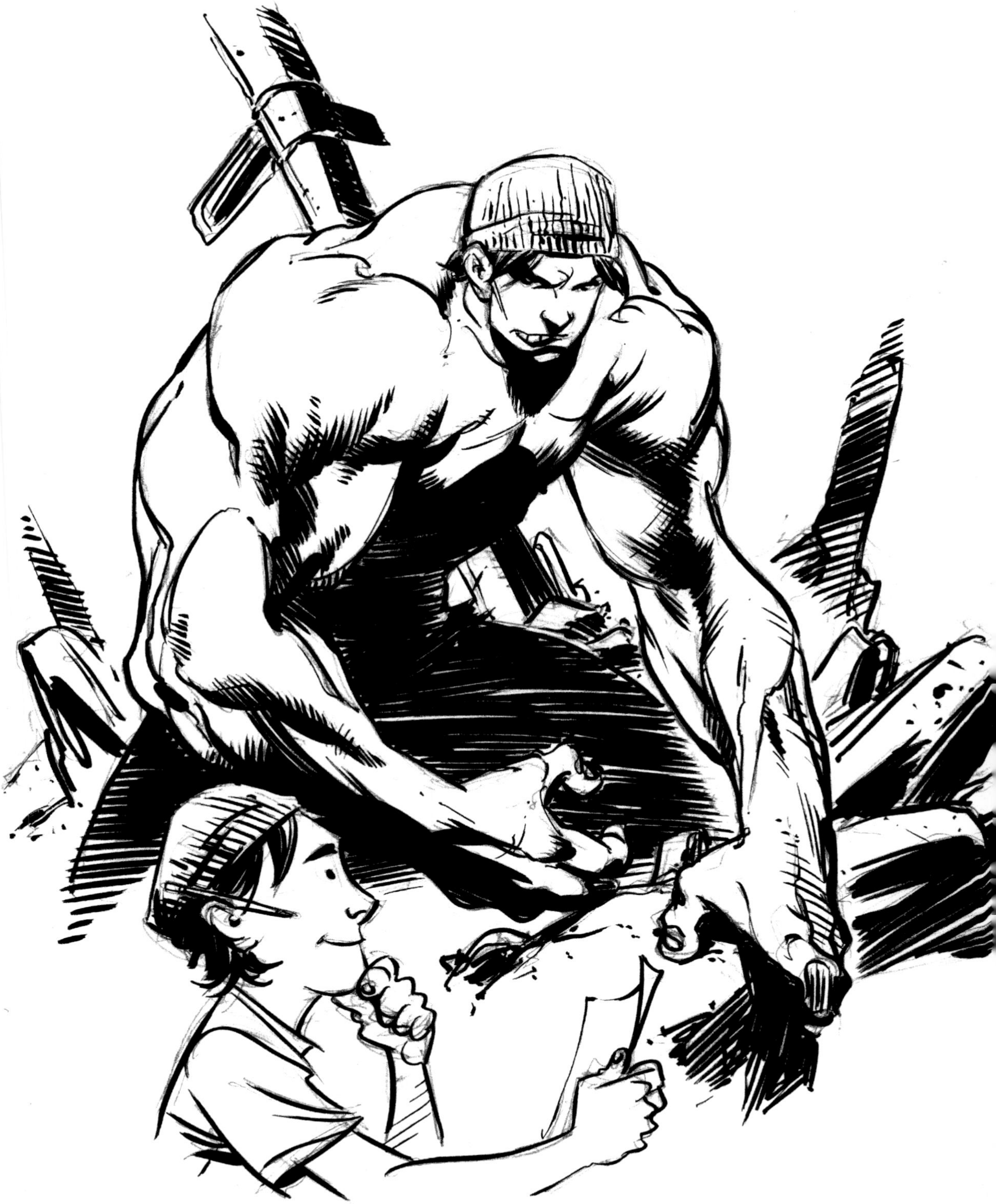

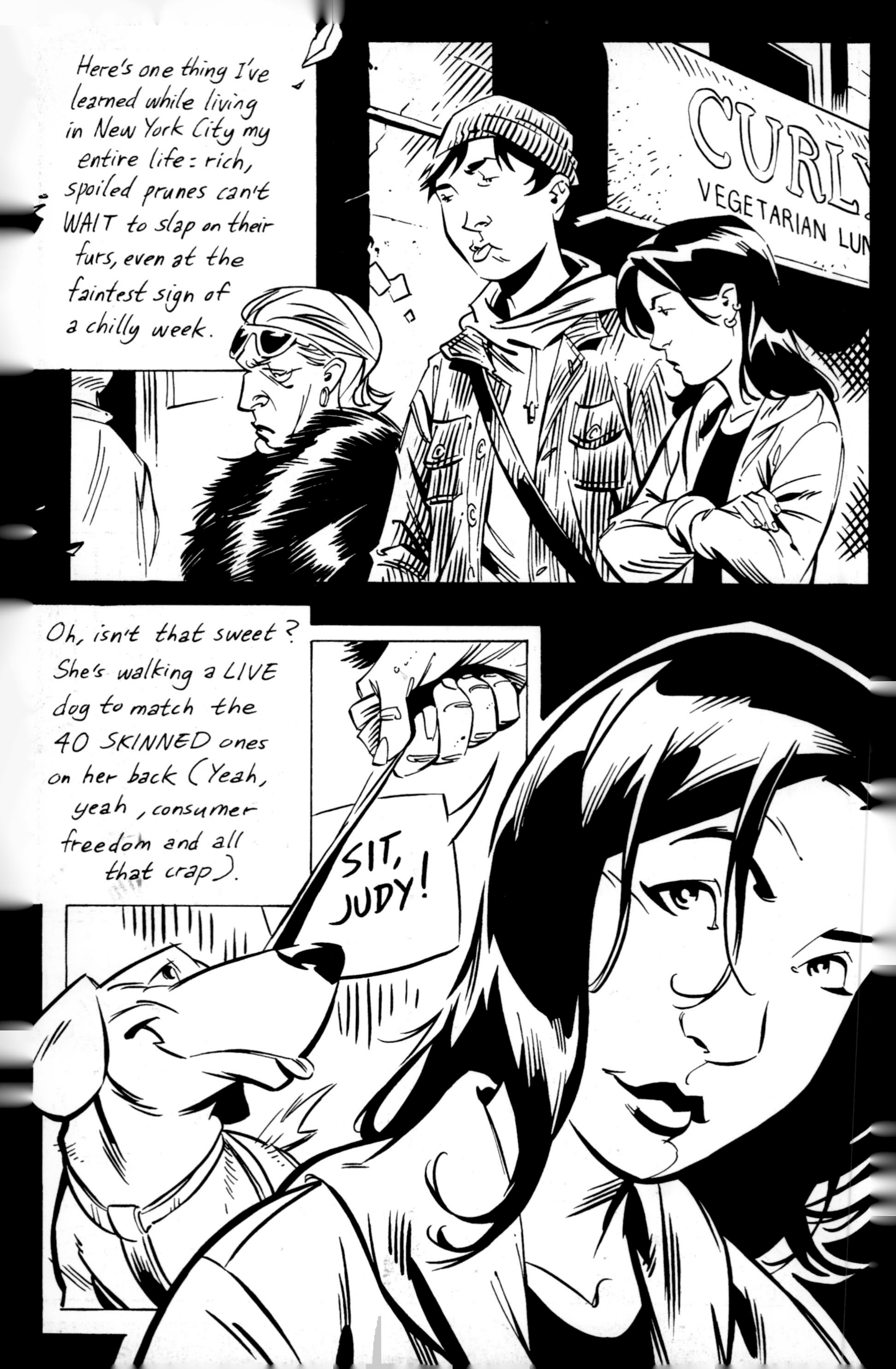
Here's one thing I've learned while living in New York City my entire life: rich, spoiled prunes can't WAIT to slap on their furs, even at the faintest sign of a chilly week.
CURLY
VEGETARIAN LUN
Oh, isn't that sweet? She's walking a LIVE dog to match the 40 SKINNED ones on her back (Yeah, yeah, consumer freedom and all that crap).
SIT, JUDY!

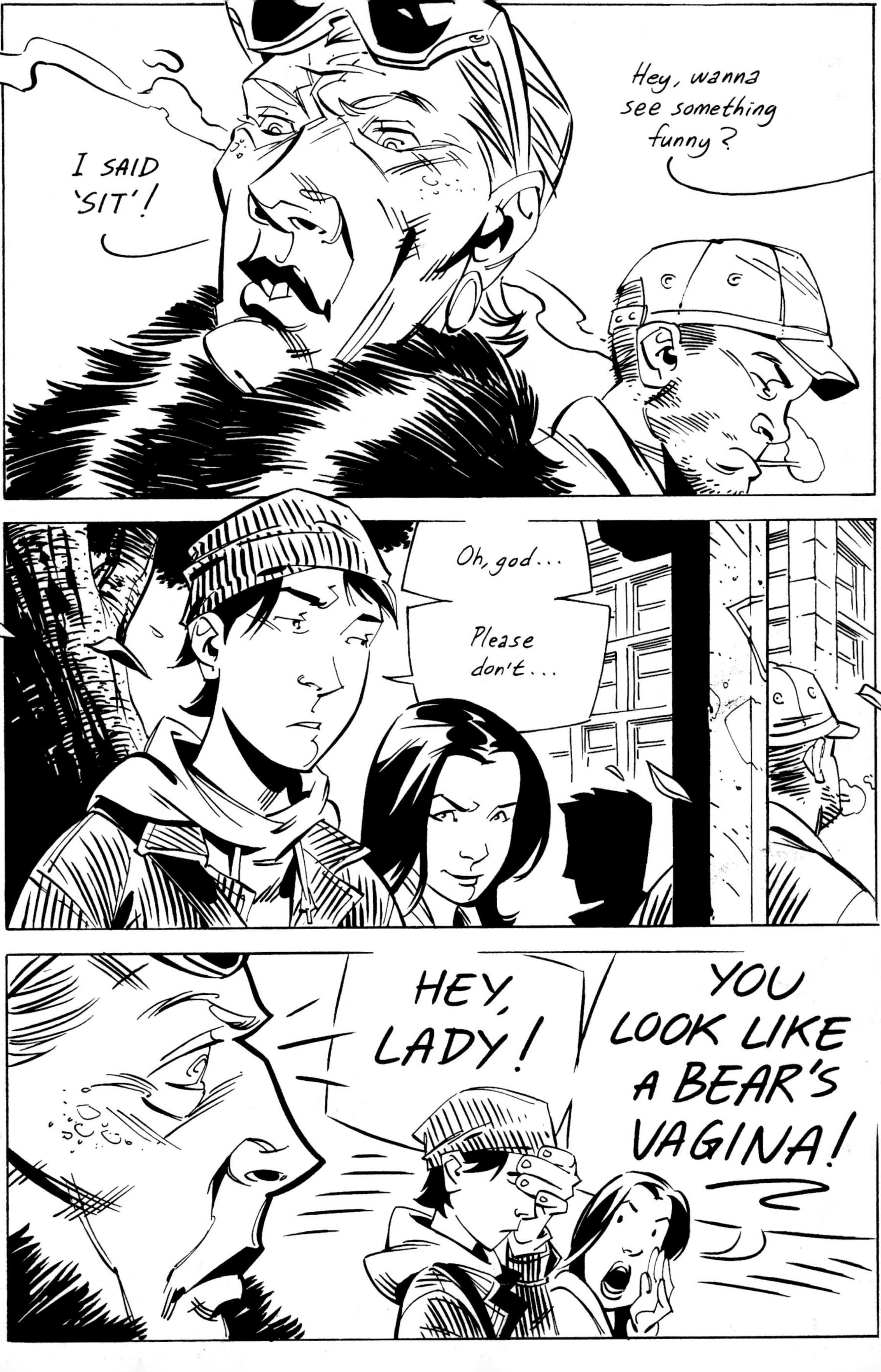
I SAID 'SIT'!
Hey, wanna see something funny?
Oh, god...
Please don't...
HEY, LADY!
YOU LOOK LIKE A BEAR'S VAGINA!

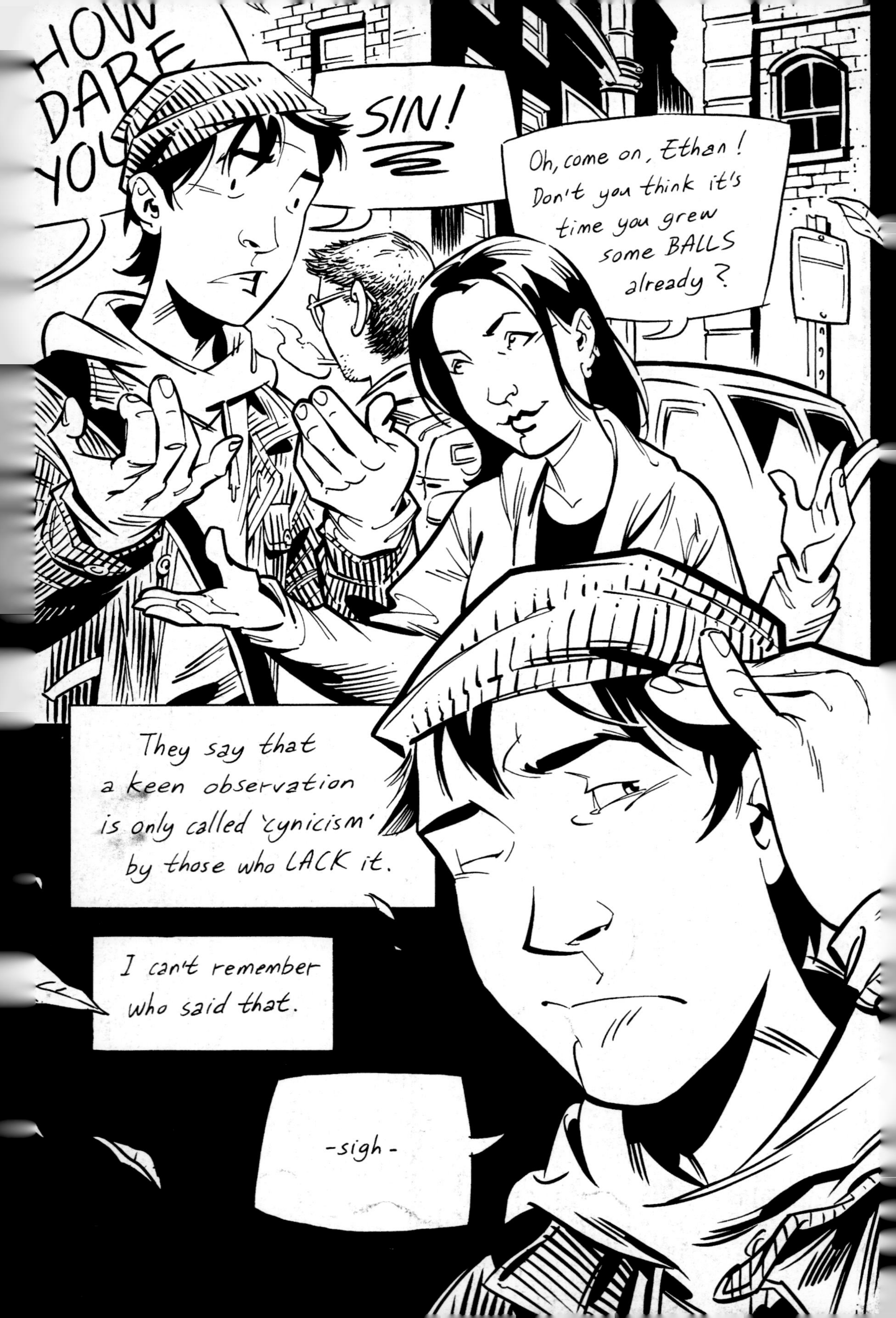
HOW DARE YOU
SIN!
Oh, come on, Ethan! Don't you think it's time you grew some BALLS already?
They say that a keen observation is only called 'cynicism' by those who LACK it.
I can't remember who said that.
-sigh-

LIFE IN PROGRESS

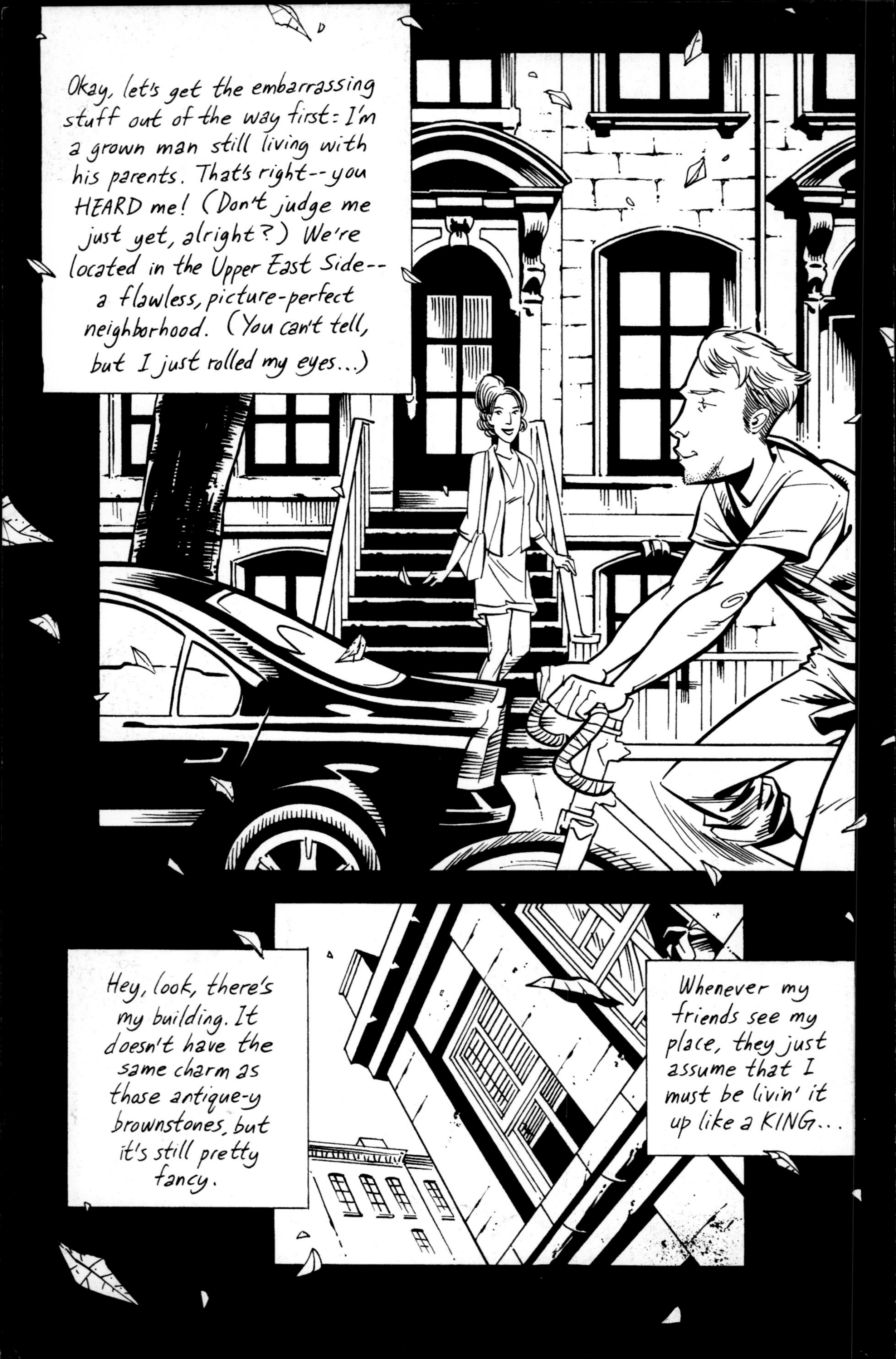
Okay, let's get the embarrassing stuff out of the way first: I'm a grown man still living with his parents. That's right--you HEARD me! (Don't judge me just yet, alright?) We're located in the Upper East Side--a flawless, picture-perfect neighborhood. (You can't tell, but I just rolled my eyes...)
Hey, look, there's my building. It doesn't have the same charm as those antique-y brownstones, but it's still pretty fancy.
Whenever my friends see my place, they just assume that I must be livin' it up like a KING...

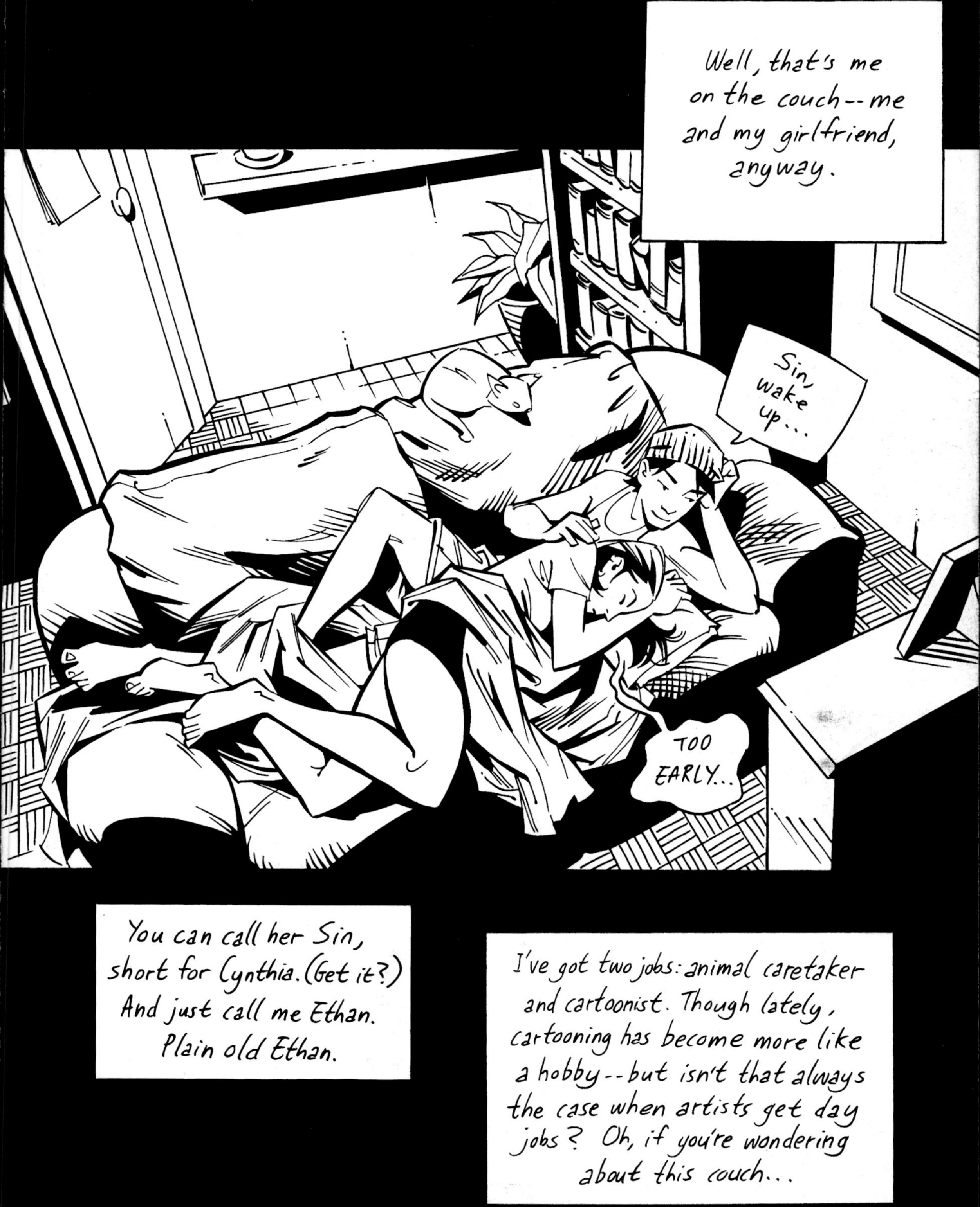
Well, that's me on the couch--me and my girlfriend, anyway.
Sin, wake up...
TOO EARLY...
You can call her Sin, short for Cynthia. (Get it?) And just call me Ethan. Plain old Ethan.
I've got two jobs: animal caretaker and cartoonist. Though lately, cartooning has become more like a hobby--but isn't that always the case when artists get day jobs? Oh, if you're wondering about this couch...

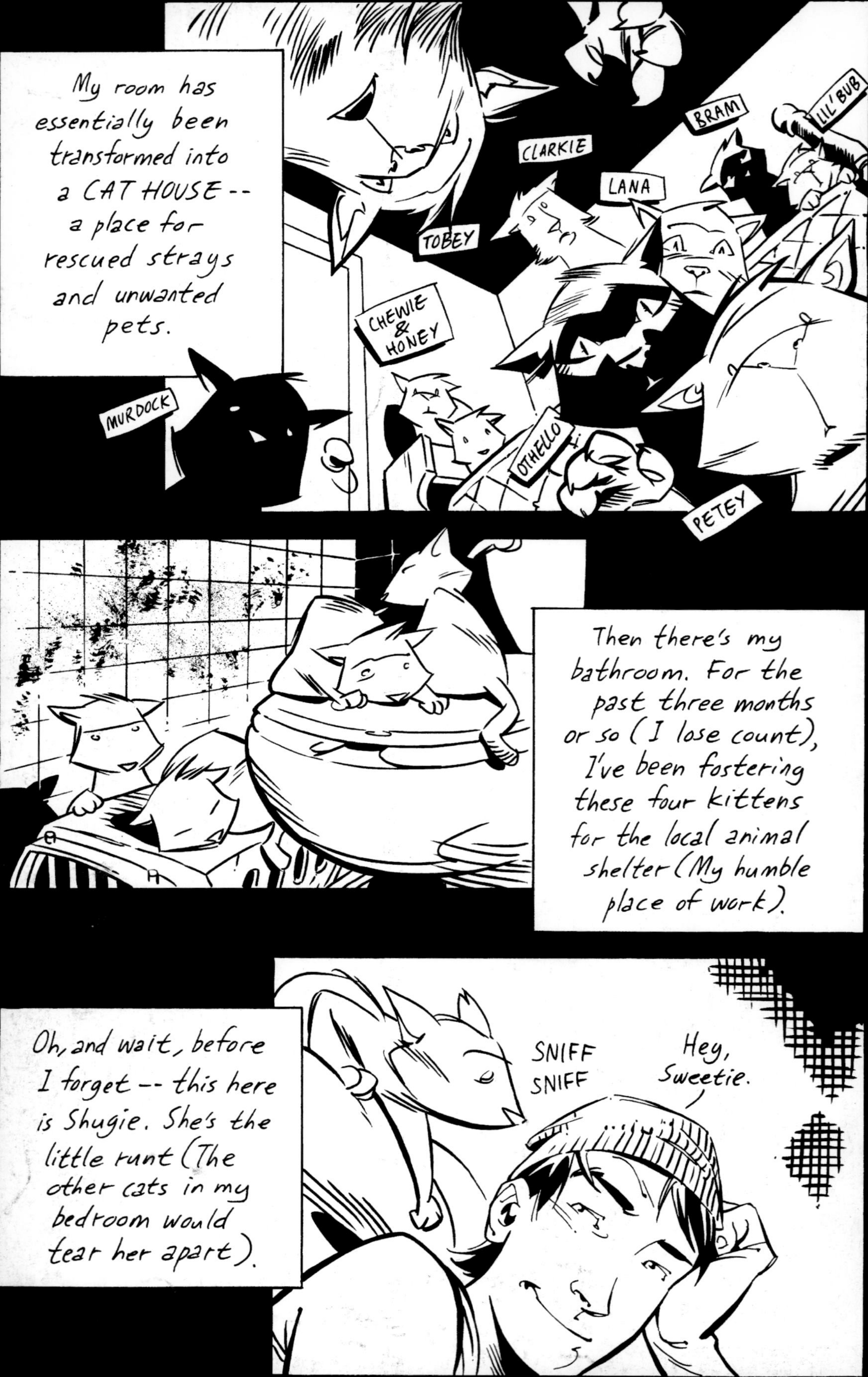

My room has essentially been transformed into a CAT HOUSE -- a place for rescued strays and unwanted pets.
BRAM
LIL' BUB
CLARKIE
LANA
TOBEY
CHEWIE & HONEY
MURDOCK
OTHELLO
PETEY
Then there's my bathroom. For the past three months or so (I lose count), I've been fostering these four kittens for the local animal shelter (My humble place of work).
Oh, and wait, before I forget -- this here is Shugie. She's the little runt (The other cats in my bedroom would tear her apart).
SNIFF SNIFF
Hey, Sweetie.

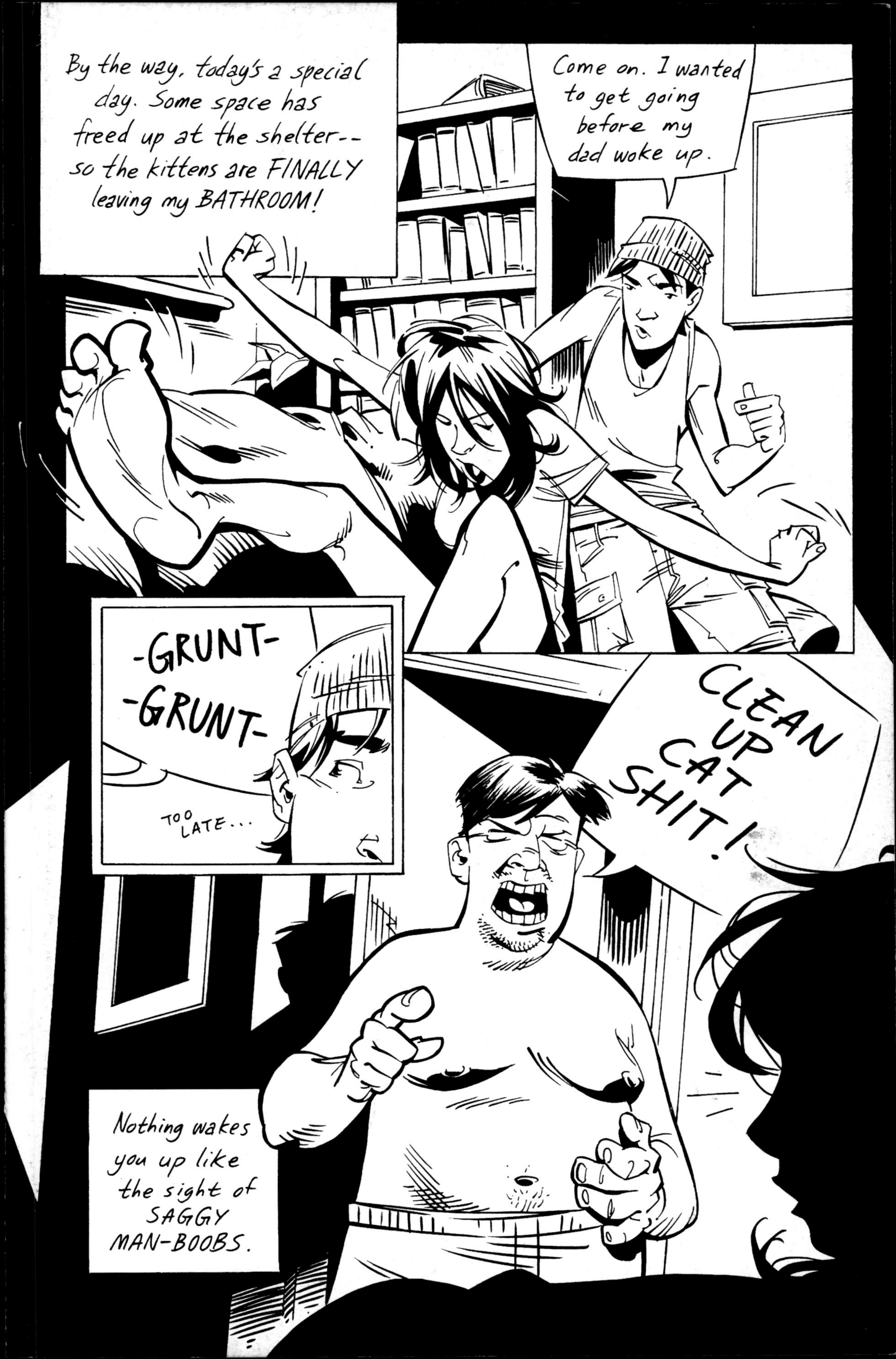
By the way, today's a special day. Some space has freed up at the shelter-- so the kittens are FINALLY leaving my BATHROOM!
Come on. I wanted to get going before my dad woke up.
-GRUNT-
-GRUNT-
TOO LATE...
CLEAN UP CAT SHIT!
Nothing wakes you up like the sight of SAGGY MAN-BOOBS.

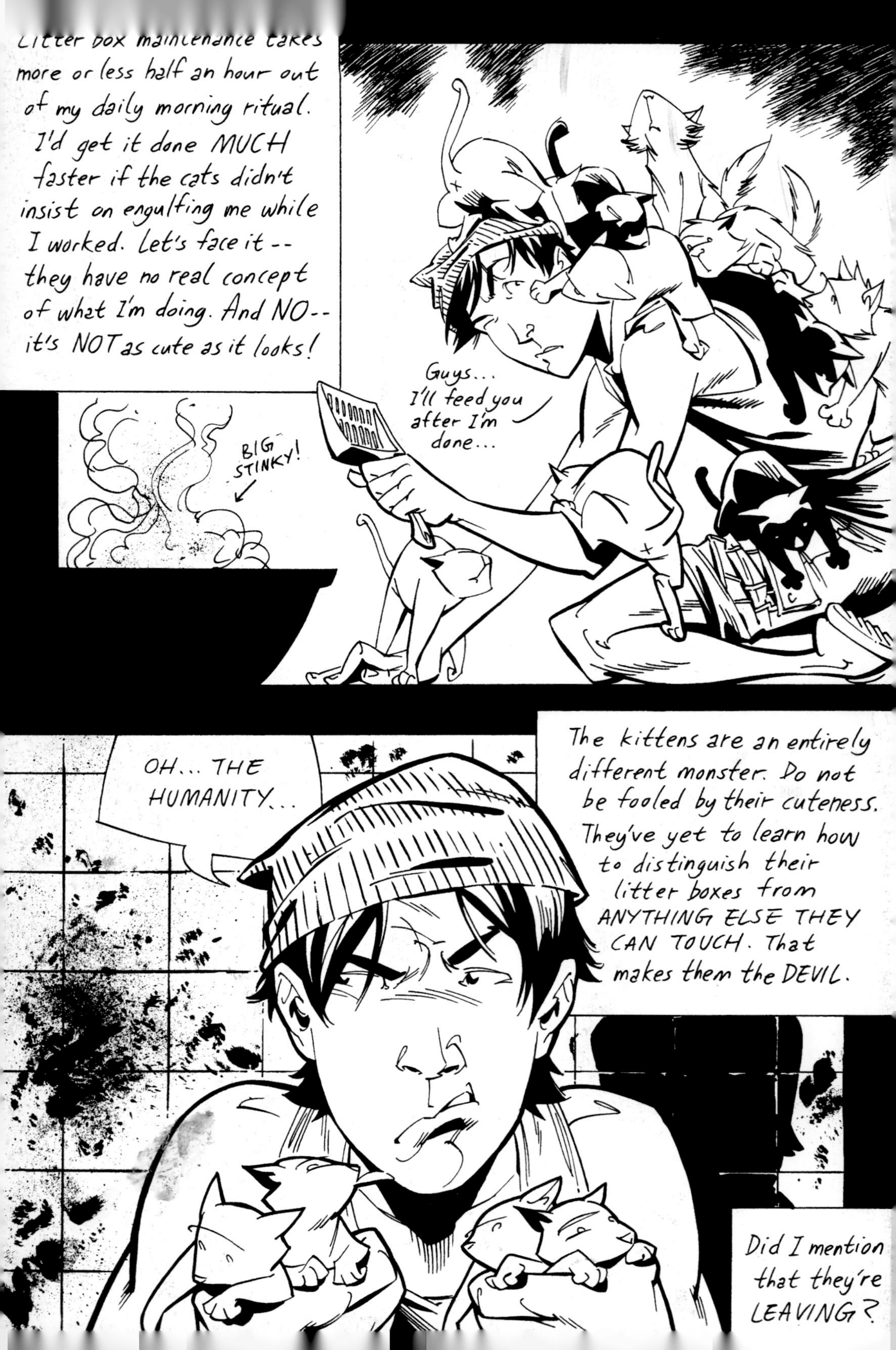
Litter box maintenance takes more or less half an hour out of my daily morning ritual. I'd get it done MUCH faster if the cats didn't insist on engulfing me while I worked. Let's face it -- they have no real concept of what I'm doing. And NO-- it's NOT as cute as it looks!
Guys... I'll feed you after I'm done...
BIG STINKY!
OH... THE HUMANITY...
The kittens are an entirely different monster. Do not be fooled by their cuteness. They've yet to learn how to distinguish their litter boxes from ANYTHING ELSE THEY CAN TOUCH. That makes them the DEVIL.
Did I mention that they're LEAVING?

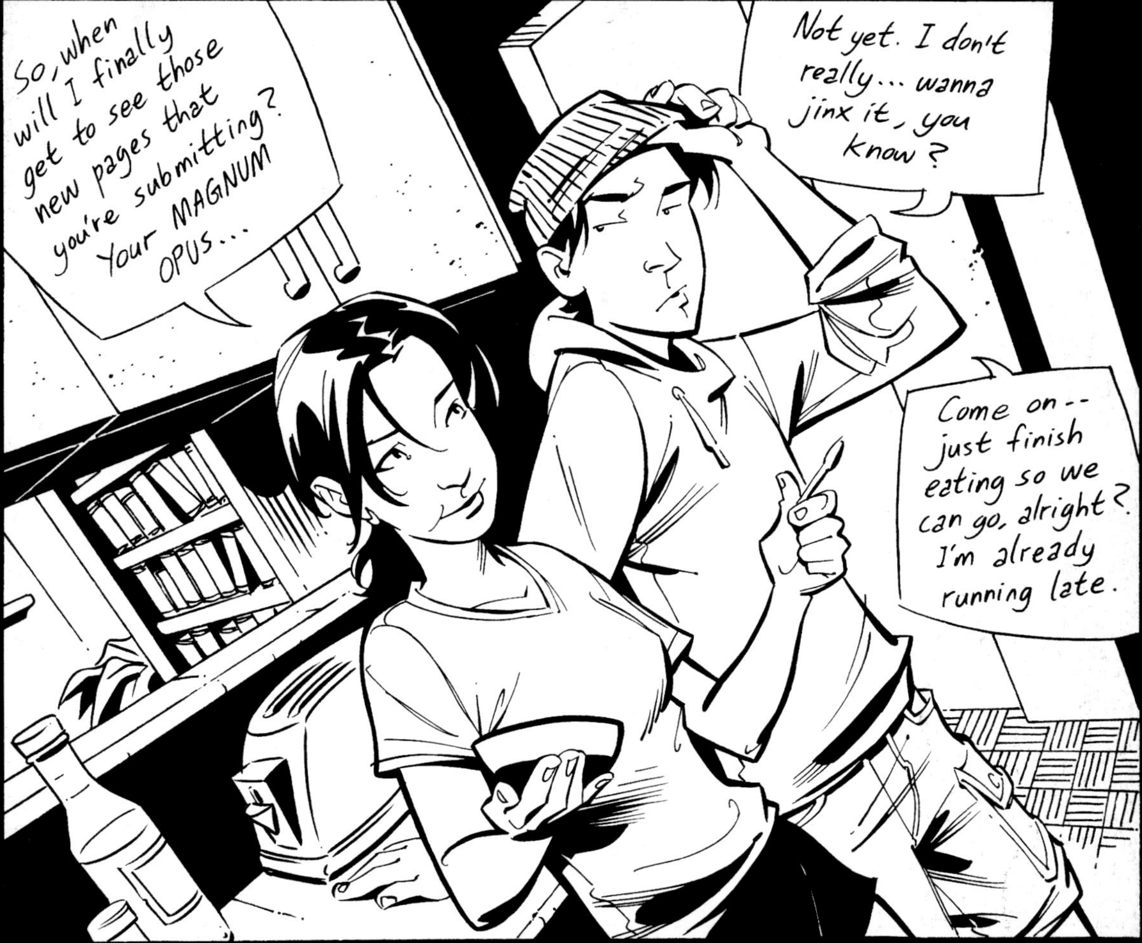

So, when will I finally get to see those new pages that you're submitting? Your MAGNUM OPUS...
Not yet. I don't really... wanna jinx it, you know?
Come on -- just finish eating so we can go, alright? I'm already running late.

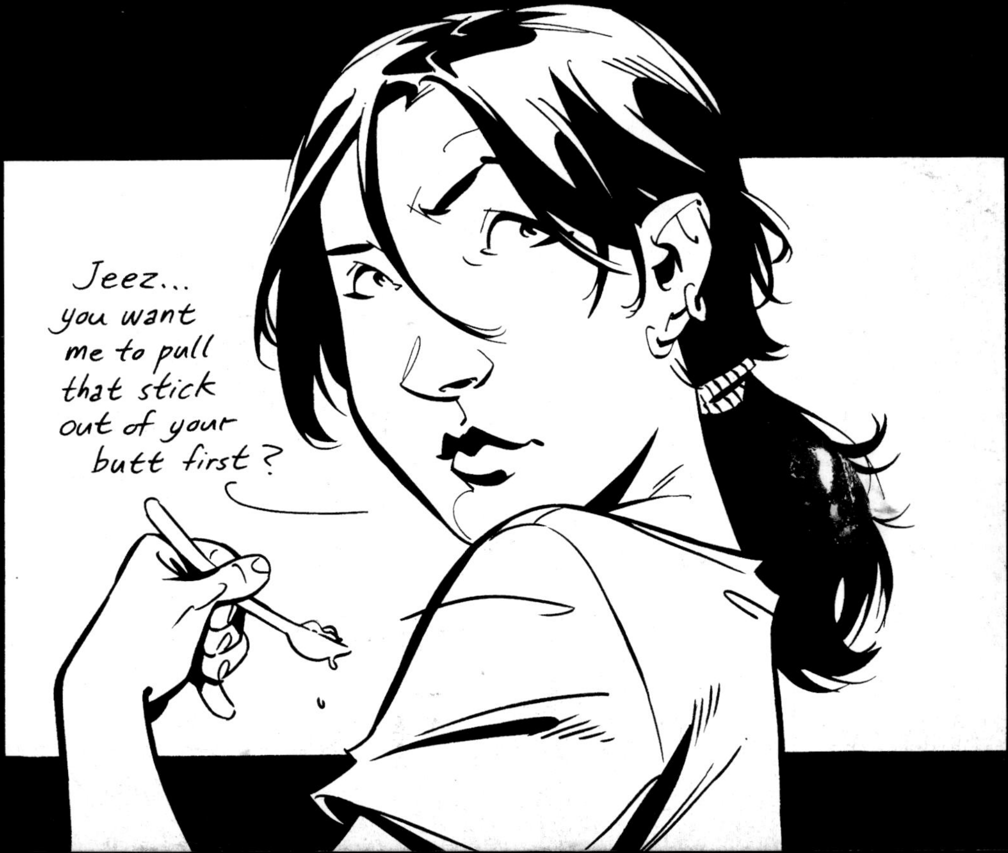

Jeez... you want me to pull that stick out of your butt first?

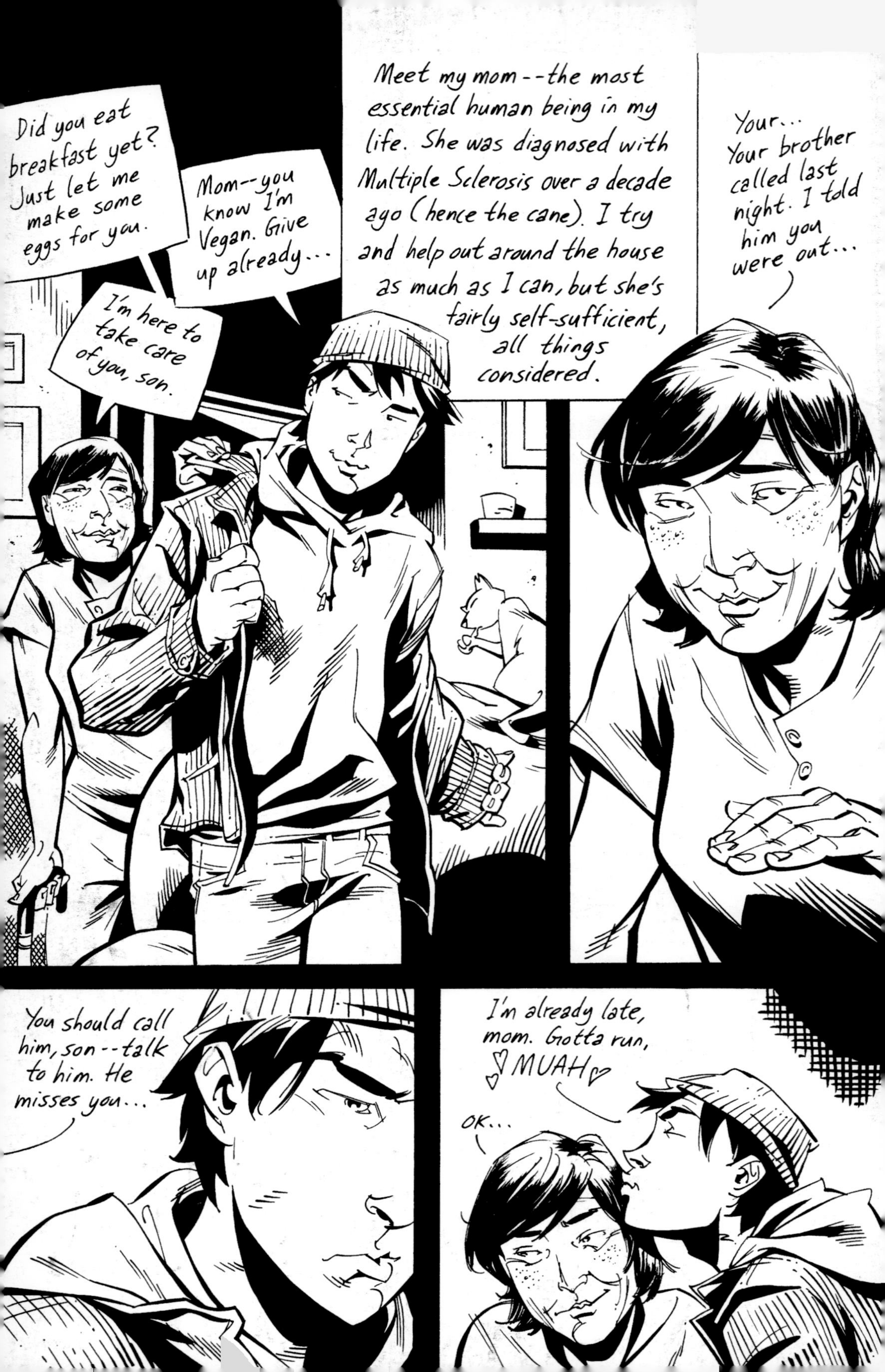
Did you eat breakfast yet? Just let me make some eggs for you.
I'm here to take care of you, son.
Mom--you know I'm Vegan. Give up already...
Meet my mom--the most essential human being in my life. She was diagnosed with Multiple Sclerosis over a decade ago (hence the cane). I try and help out around the house as much as I can, but she's fairly self-sufficient, all things considered.
Your... Your brother called last night. I told him you were out...
You should call him, son--talk to him. He misses you...
I'm already late, mom. Gotta run.
♡MUAH♡
OK...

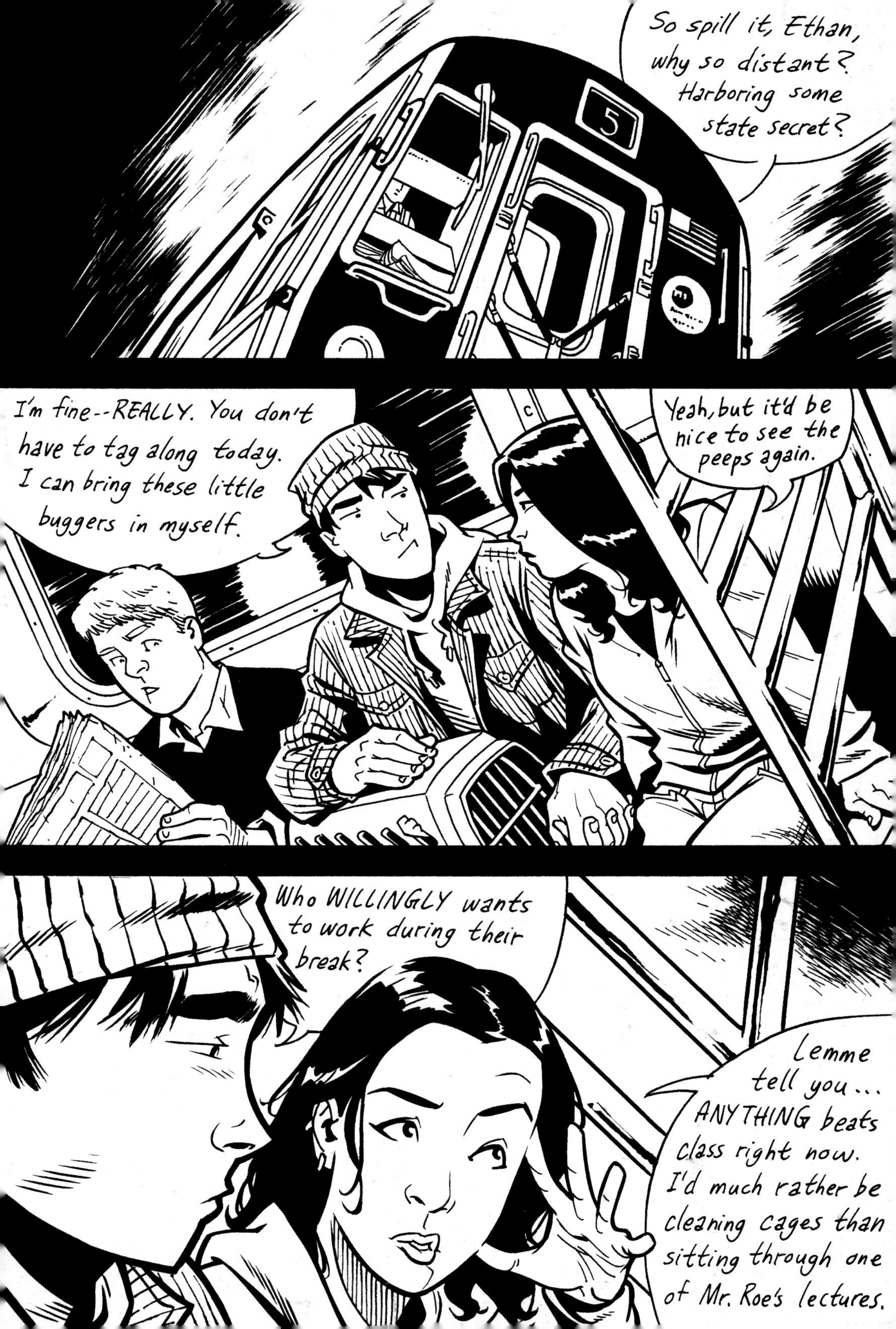
So spill it, Ethan, why so distant? Harboring some state secret?
5
I'm fine--REALLY. You don't have to tag along today. I can bring these little buggers in myself.
Yeah, but it'd be nice to see the peeps again.
Who WILLINGLY wants to work during their break?
Lemme tell you... ANYTHING beats class right now. I'd much rather be cleaning cages than sitting through one of Mr. Roe's lectures.

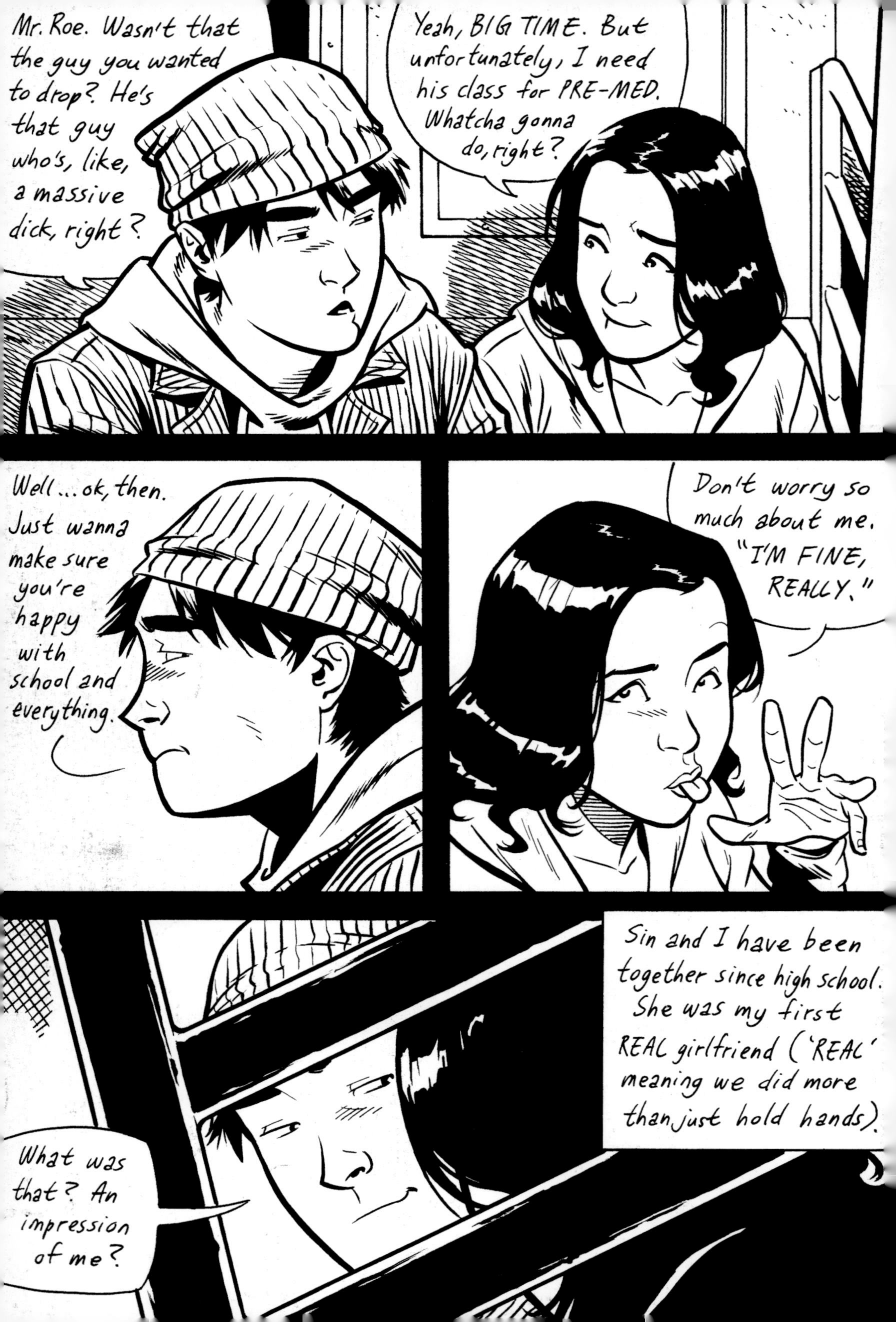
Mr. Roe. Wasn't that the guy you wanted to drop? He's that guy who's, like, a massive dick, right?
Yeah, BIG TIME. But unfortunately, I need his class for PRE-MED. Whatcha gonna do, right?
Well... ok, then. Just wanna make sure you're happy with school and everything.
Don't worry so much about me. "I'M FINE, REALLY."
Sin and I have been together since high school. She was my first REAL girlfriend ('REAL' meaning we did more than just hold hands).
What was that? An impression of me?

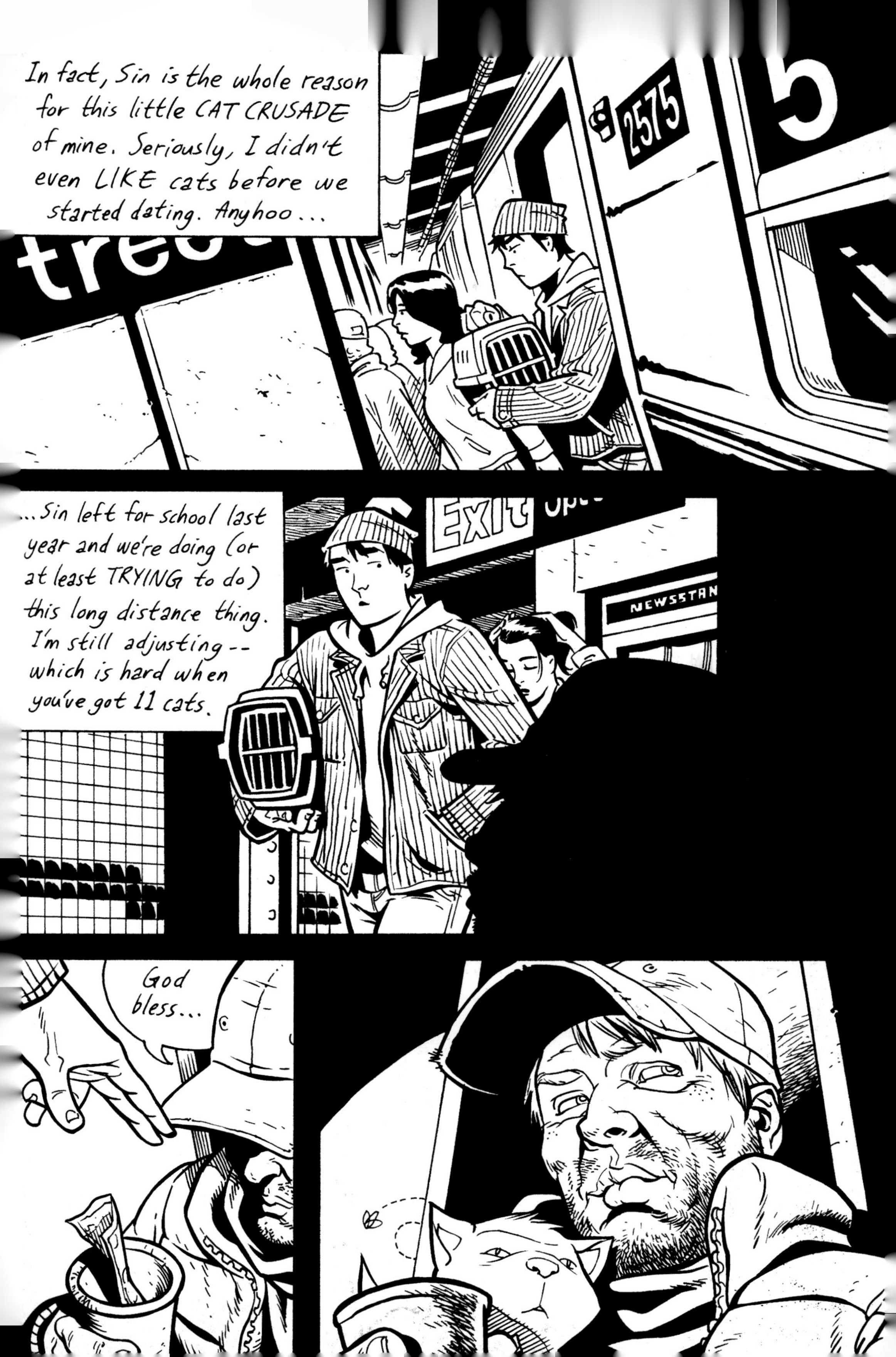
In fact, Sin is the whole reason for this little CAT CRUSADE of mine. Seriously, I didn't even LIKE cats before we started dating. Anyhoo...
2575
...Sin left for school last year and we're doing (or at least TRYING to do) this long distance thing. I'm still adjusting -- which is hard when you've got 11 cats.
EXIT
NEWSSTAN
God bless...

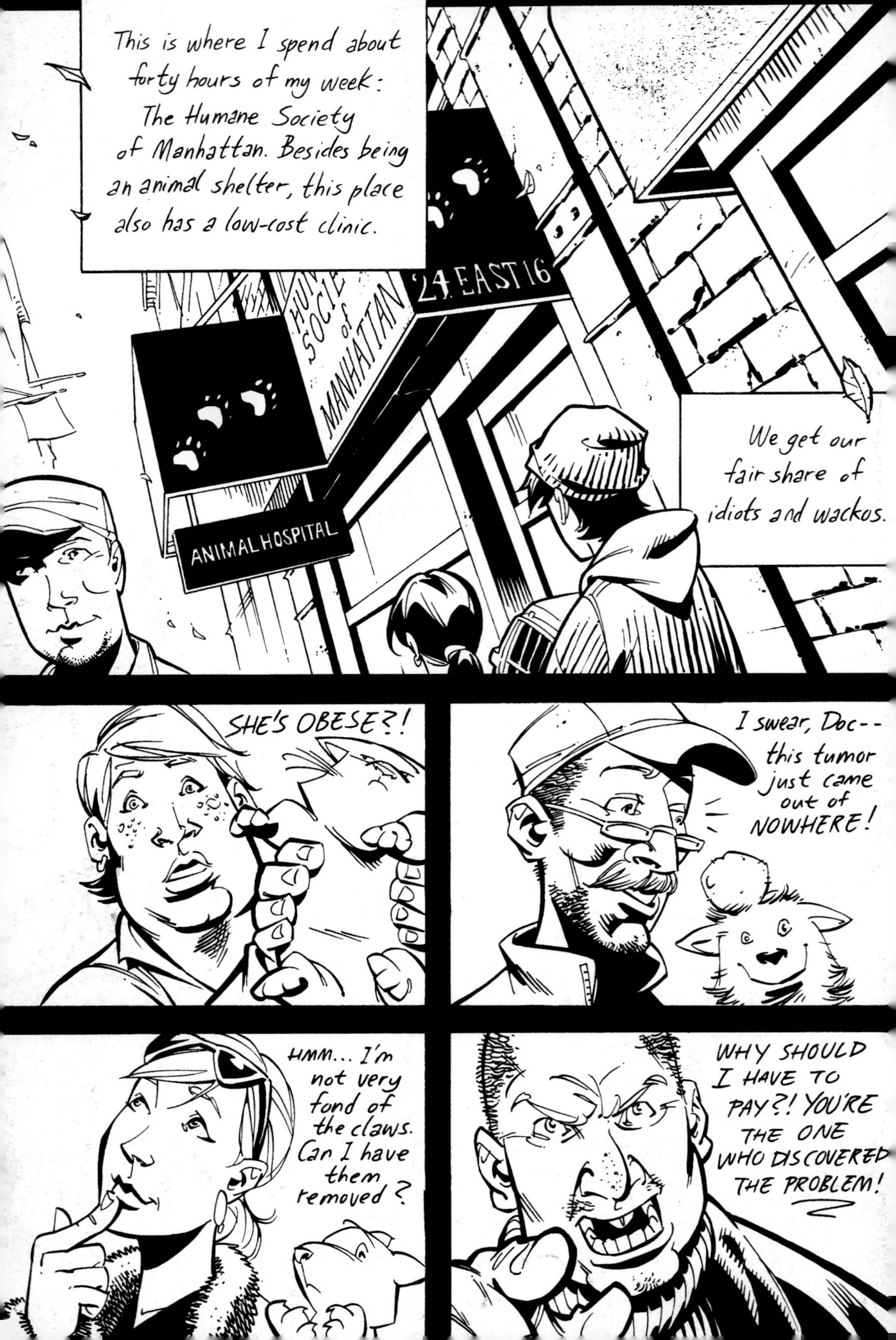

This is where I spend about forty hours of my week: The Humane Society of Manhattan. Besides being an animal shelter, this place also has a low-cost clinic.
24 EAST 16
MANHATTAN
ANIMAL HOSPITAL
We get our fair share of idiots and wackos.
SHE'S OBESE?!
I swear, Doc-- this tumor just came out of NOWHERE!
HMM... I'm not very fond of the claws. Can I have them removed?
WHY SHOULD I HAVE TO PAY?! YOU'RE THE ONE WHO DISCOVERED THE PROBLEM!

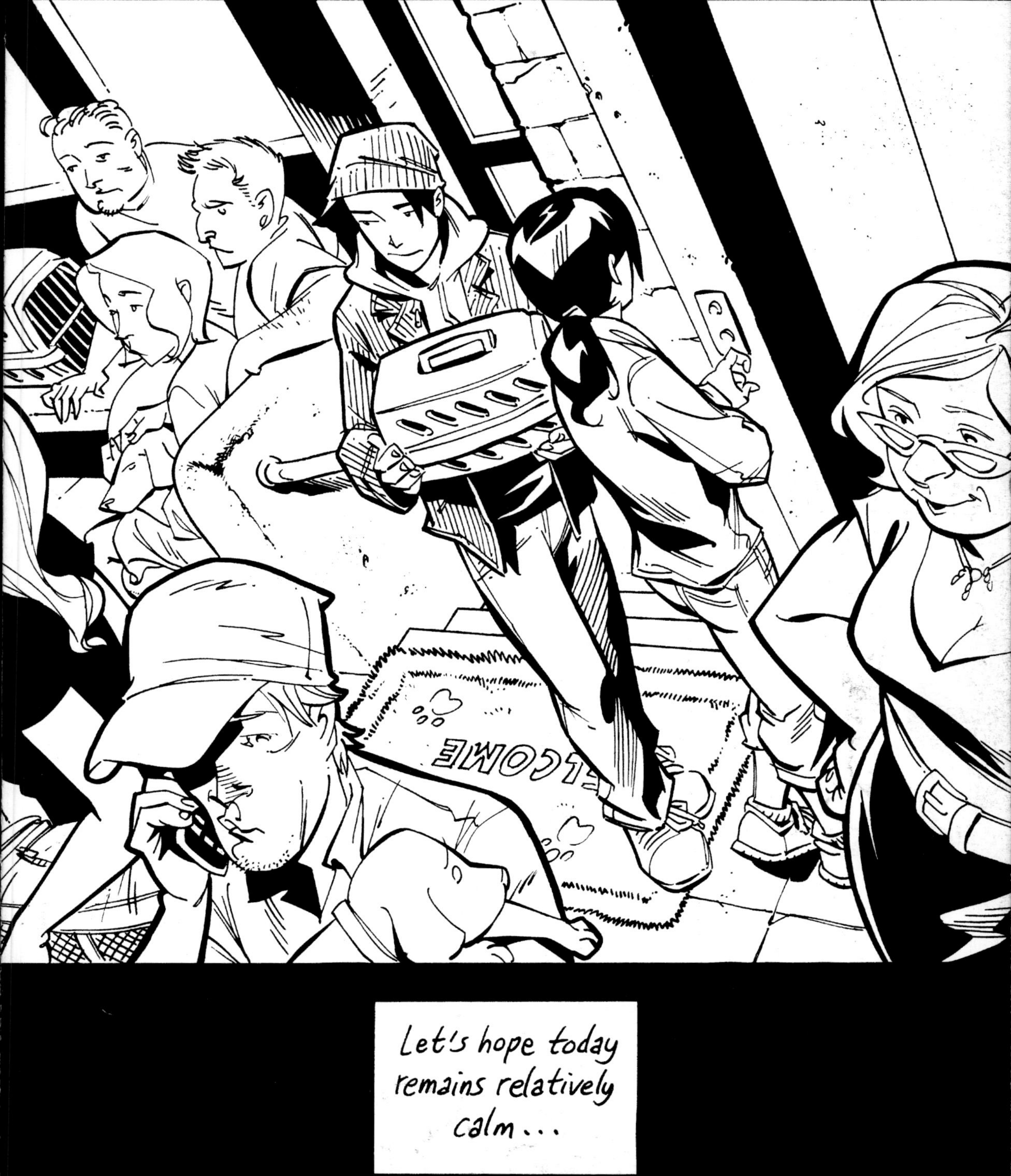
ELCOME
Let's hope today remains relatively calm...

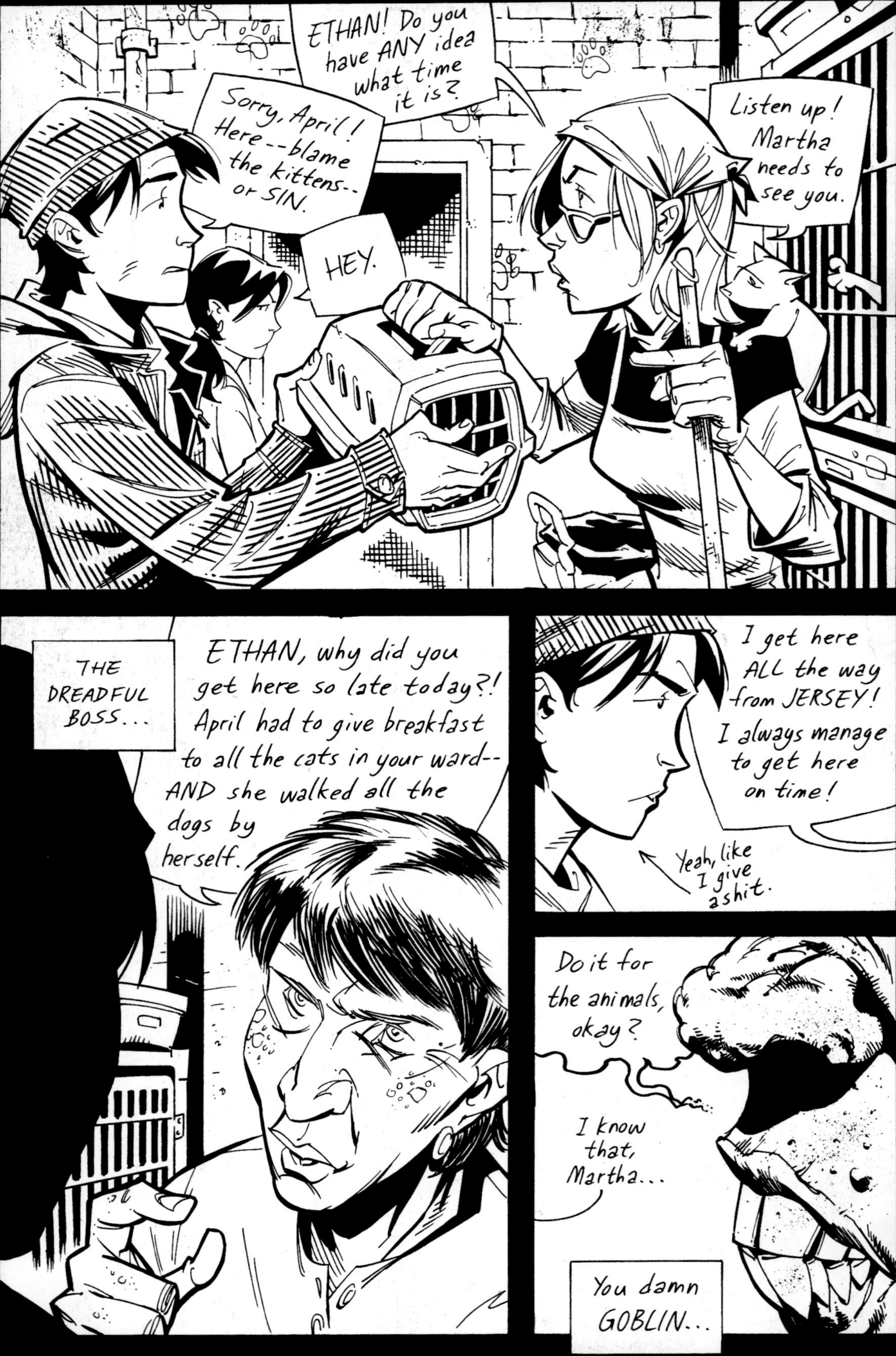
ETHAN! Do you have ANY idea what time it is?
Sorry, April! Here--blame the kittens--or SIN.
HEY.
Listen up! Martha needs to see you.
THE DREADFUL BOSS...
ETHAN, why did you get here so late today?! April had to give breakfast to all the cats in your ward--AND she walked all the dogs by herself.
I get here ALL the way from JERSEY! I always manage to get here on time!
Yeah, like I give a shit.
Do it for the animals, okay?
I know that, Martha...
You damn GOBLIN...

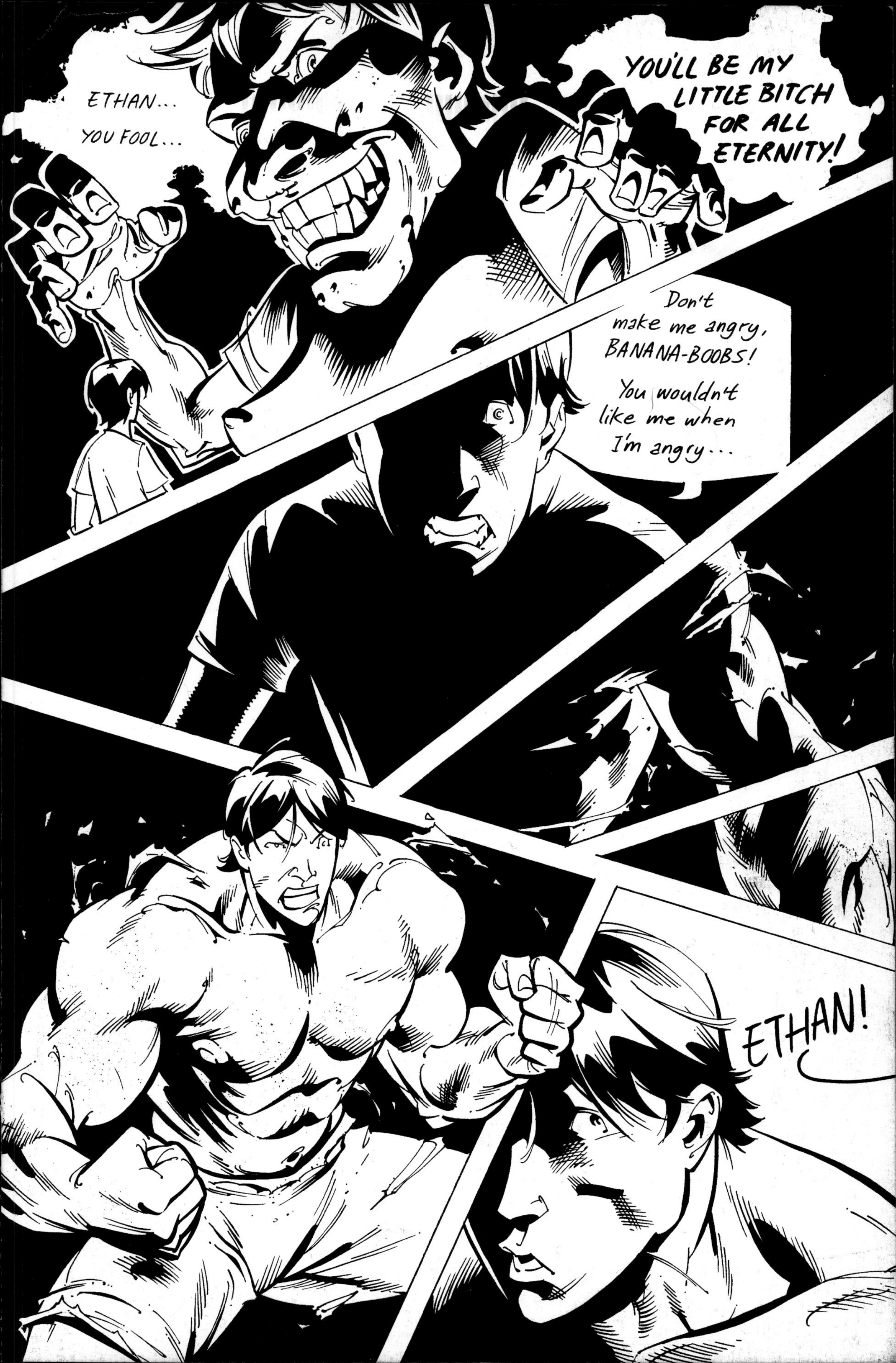
ETHAN...
YOU FOOL...
YOU'LL BE MY LITTLE BITCH FOR ALL ETERNITY!
Don't make me angry, BANANA-BOOBS!
You wouldn't like me when I'm angry...
ETHAN!

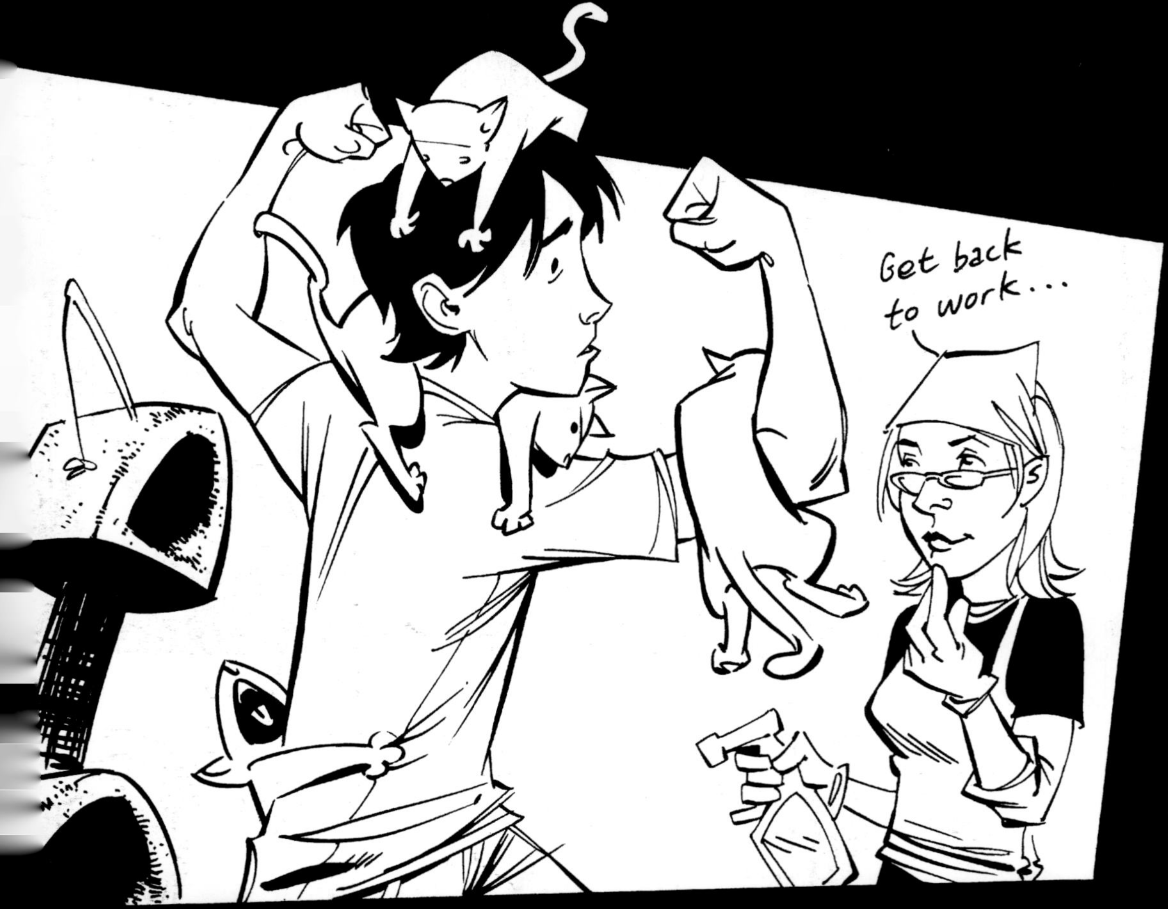
Get back to work...

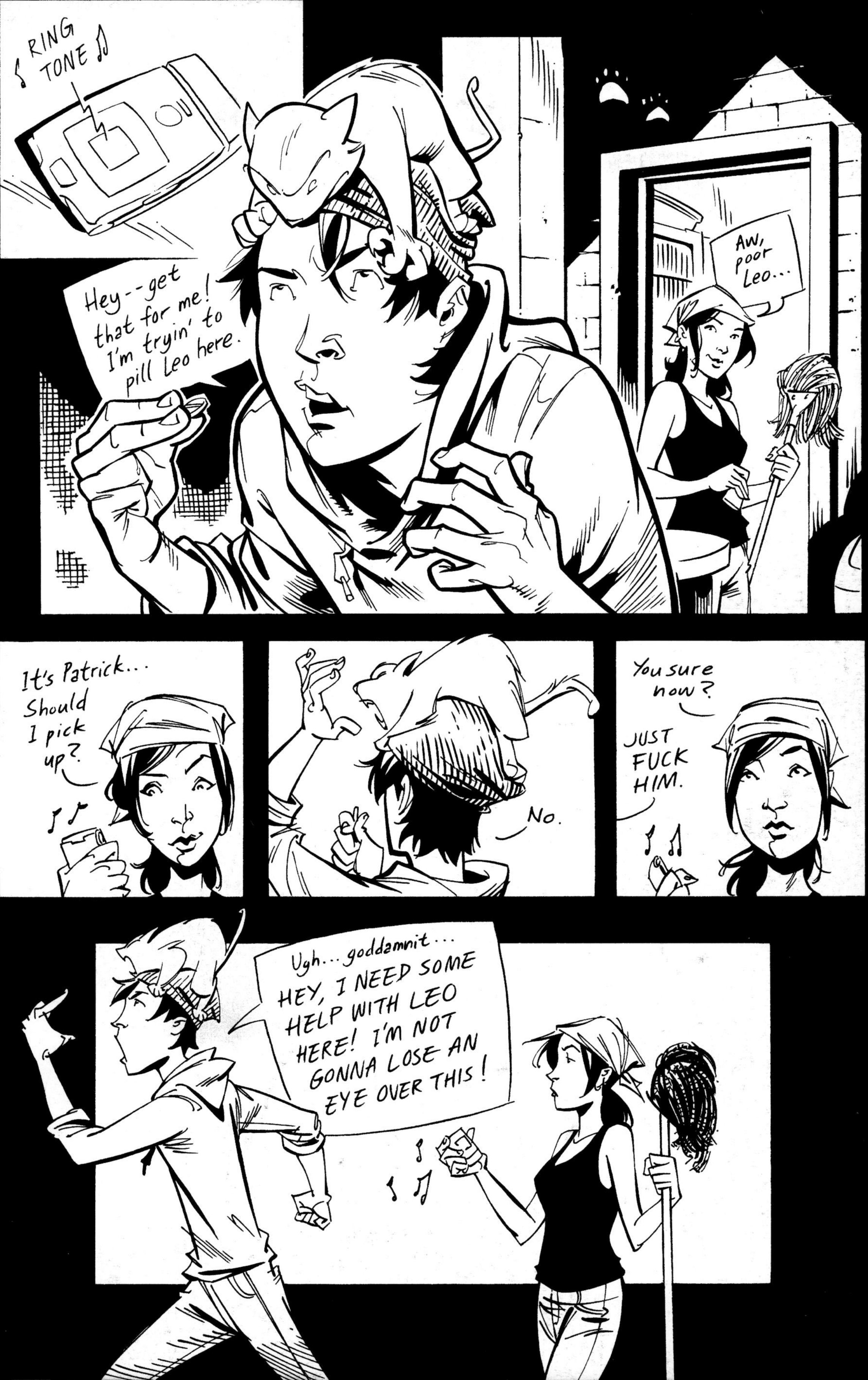
RING TONE
Hey--get that for me! I'm tryin' to pill Leo here.
Aw, poor Leo...
It's Patrick... Should I pick up?
No.
You sure now?
JUST FUCK HIM.
Ugh... goddamnit... HEY, I NEED SOME HELP WITH LEO HERE! I'M NOT GONNA LOSE AN EYE OVER THIS!

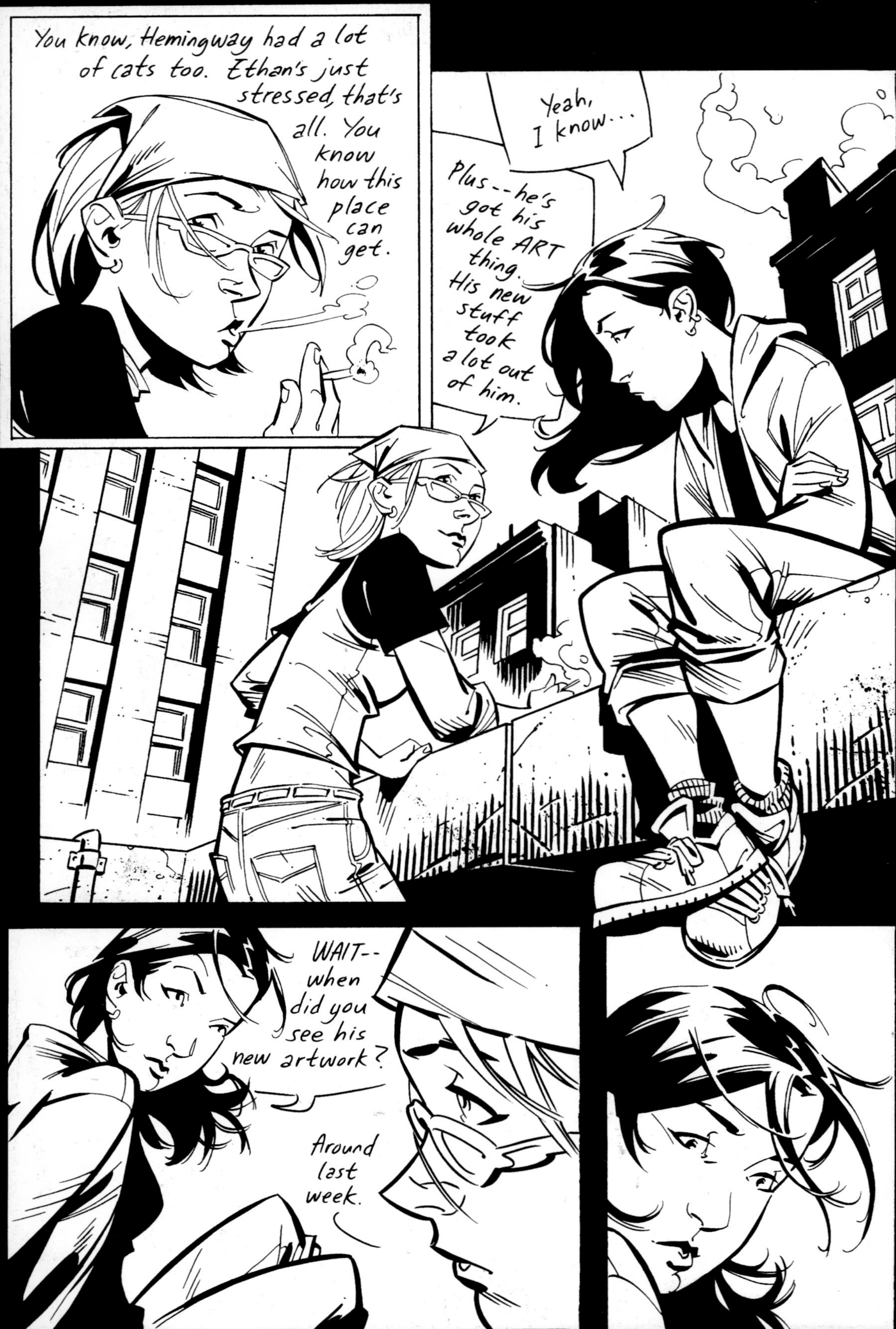
You know, Hemingway had a lot of cats too. Ethan's just stressed, that's all. You know how this place can get.
Yeah, I know...
Plus--he's got his whole ART thing. His new stuff took a lot out of him.
WAIT--when did you see his new artwork?
Around last week.

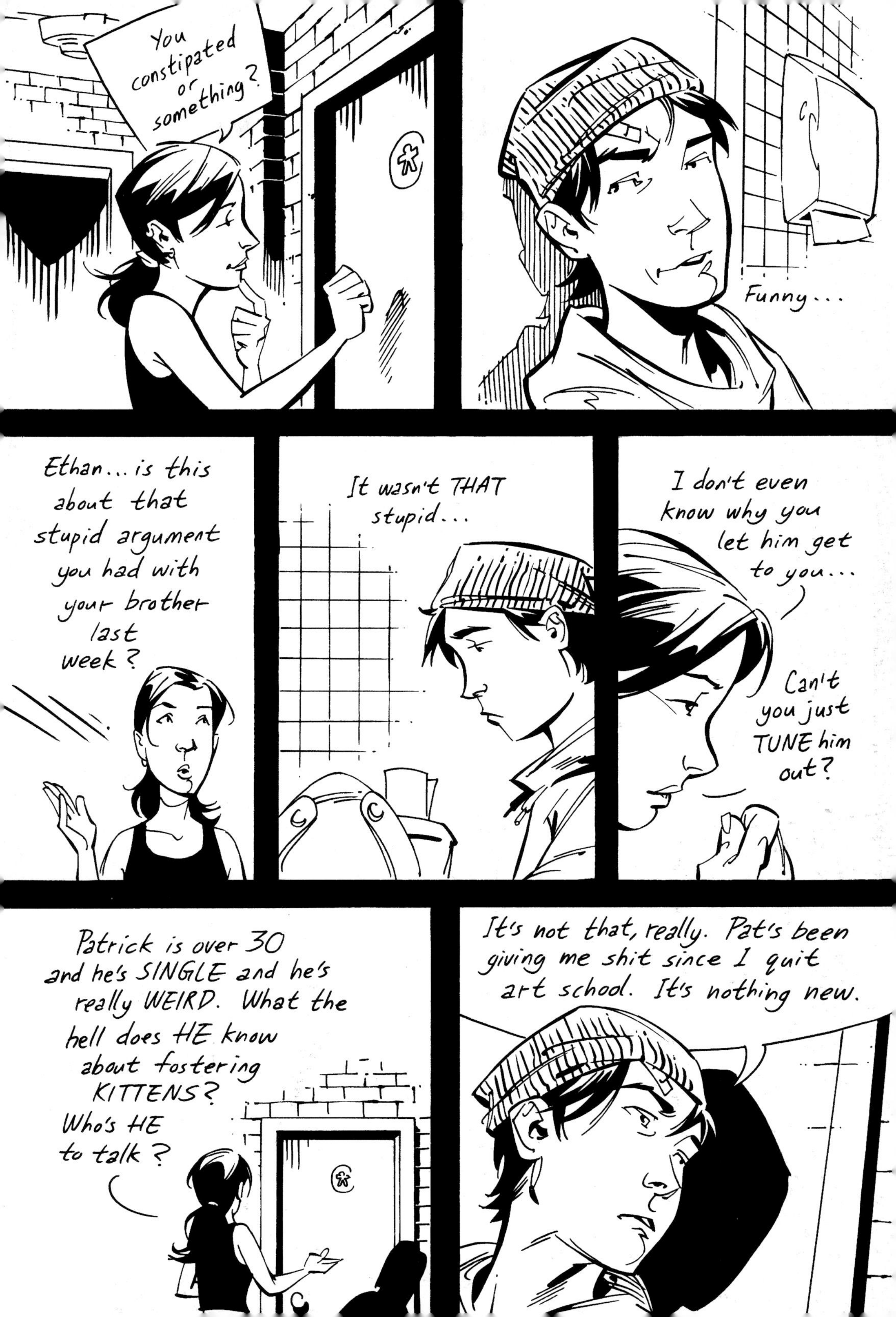
You constipated or something?
Funny...
Ethan... is this about that stupid argument you had with your brother last week?
It wasn't THAT stupid...
I don't even know why you let him get to you...
Can't you just TUNE him out?
Patrick is over 30 and he's SINGLE and he's really WEIRD. What the hell does HE know about fostering KITTENS? Who's HE to talk?
It's not that, really. Pat's been giving me shit since I quit art school. It's nothing new.

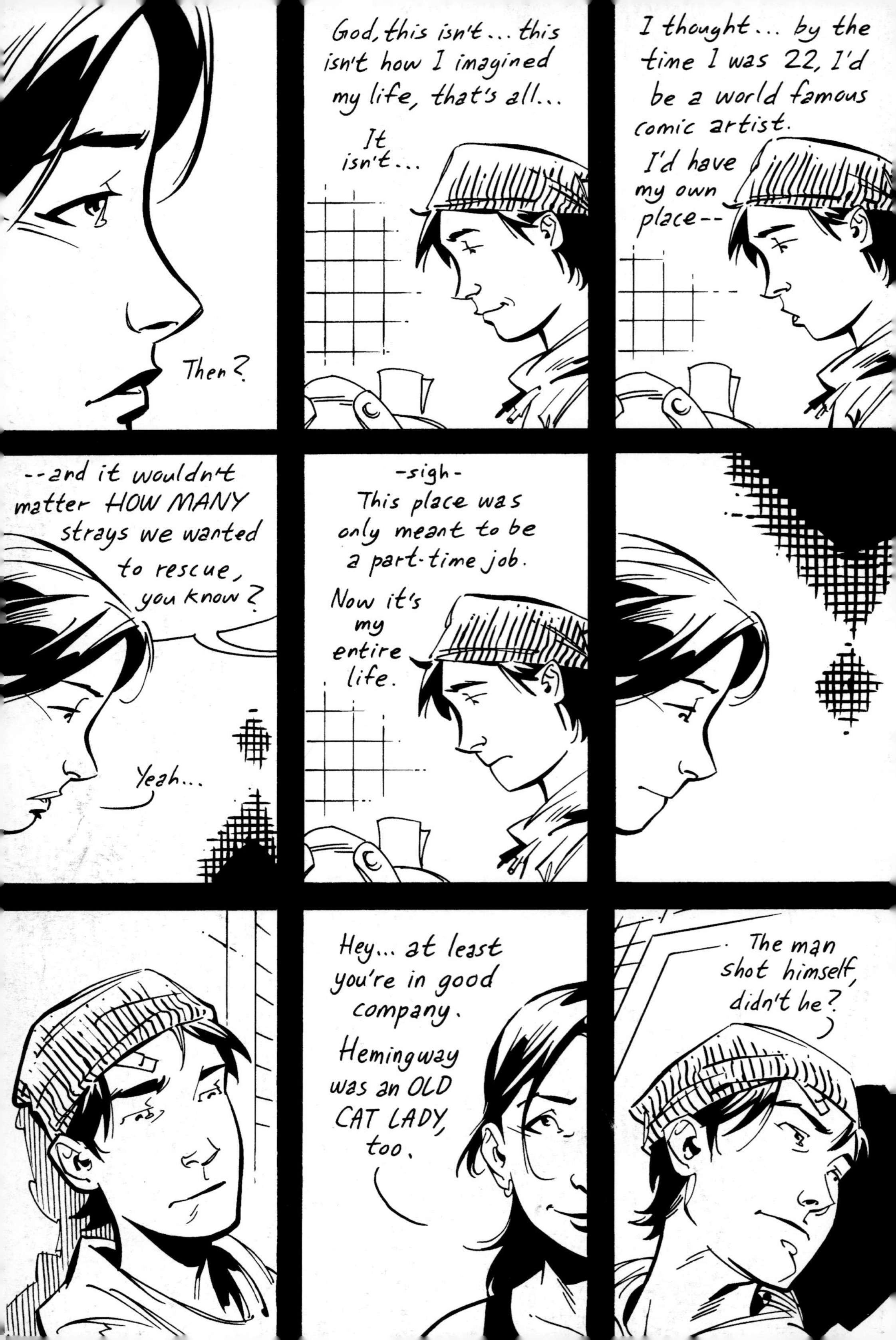
Then?
God, this isn't... this isn't how I imagined my life, that's all...
It isn't...
I thought... by the time I was 22, I'd be a world famous comic artist.
I'd have my own place--
--and it wouldn't matter HOW MANY strays we wanted to rescue, you know?
Yeah...
-sigh-
This place was only meant to be a part-time job.
Now it's my entire life.
Hey... at least you're in good company.
Hemingway was an OLD CAT LADY, too.
The man shot himself, didn't he?

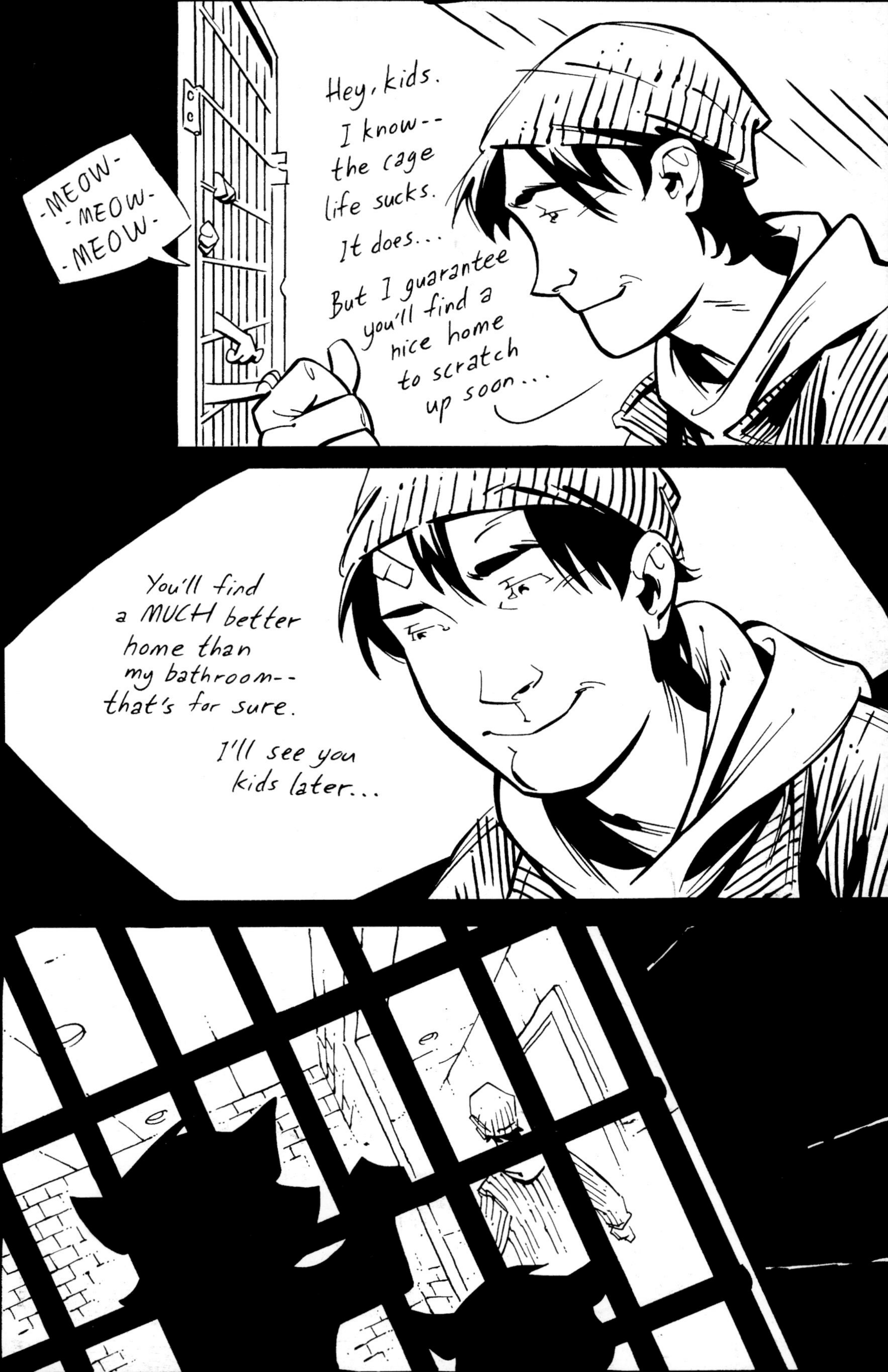

Hey, kids.
I know--
the cage
life sucks.
It does...
But I guarantee
you'll find a
nice home
to scratch
up soon...
-MEOW-
-MEOW-
-MEOW-
You'll find
a MUCH better
home than
my bathroom--
that's for sure.
I'll see you
kids later...

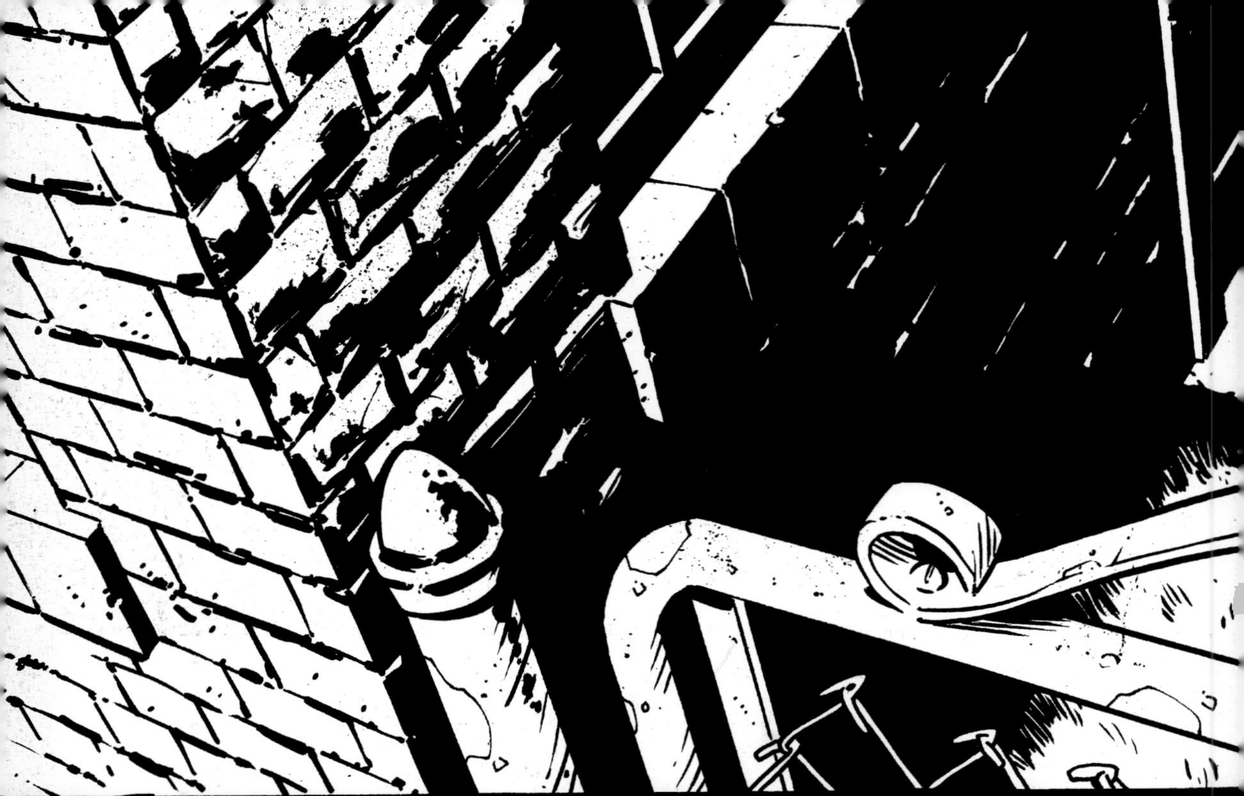

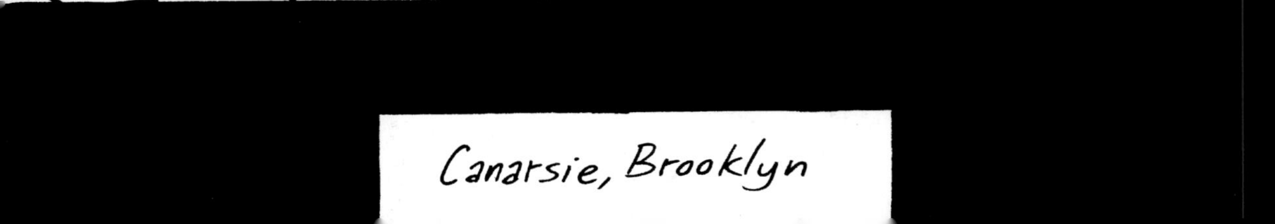
Canarsie, Brooklyn

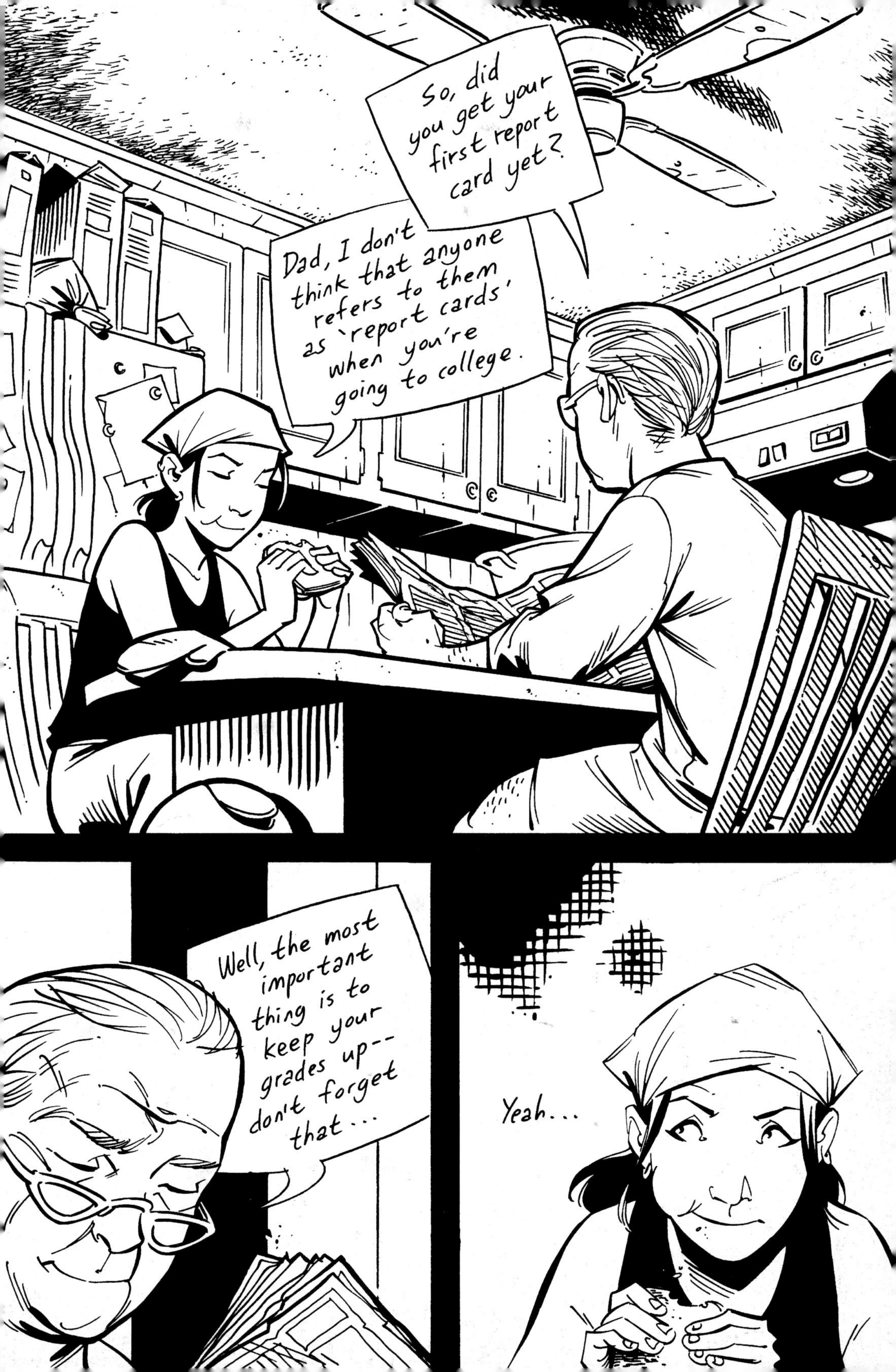
So, did you get your first report card yet?
Dad, I don't think that anyone refers to them as 'report cards' when you're going to college.
Well, the most important thing is to keep your grades up-- don't forget that...
Yeah...

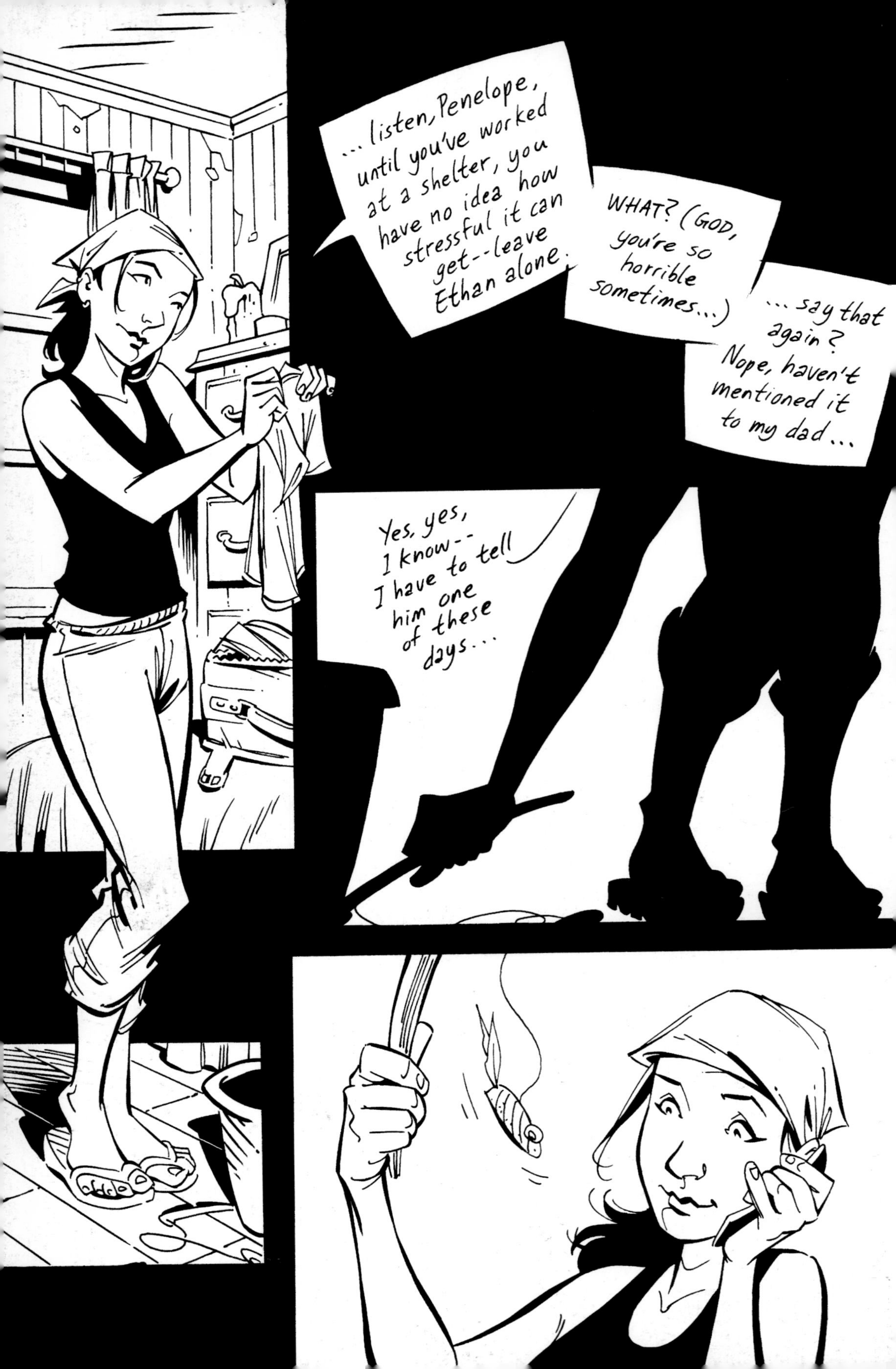
...listen, Penelope, until you've worked at a shelter, you have no idea how stressful it can get--leave Ethan alone.
WHAT? (GOD, you're so horrible sometimes...)
...say that again? Nope, haven't mentioned it to my dad...
Yes, yes, I know-- I have to tell him one of these days...

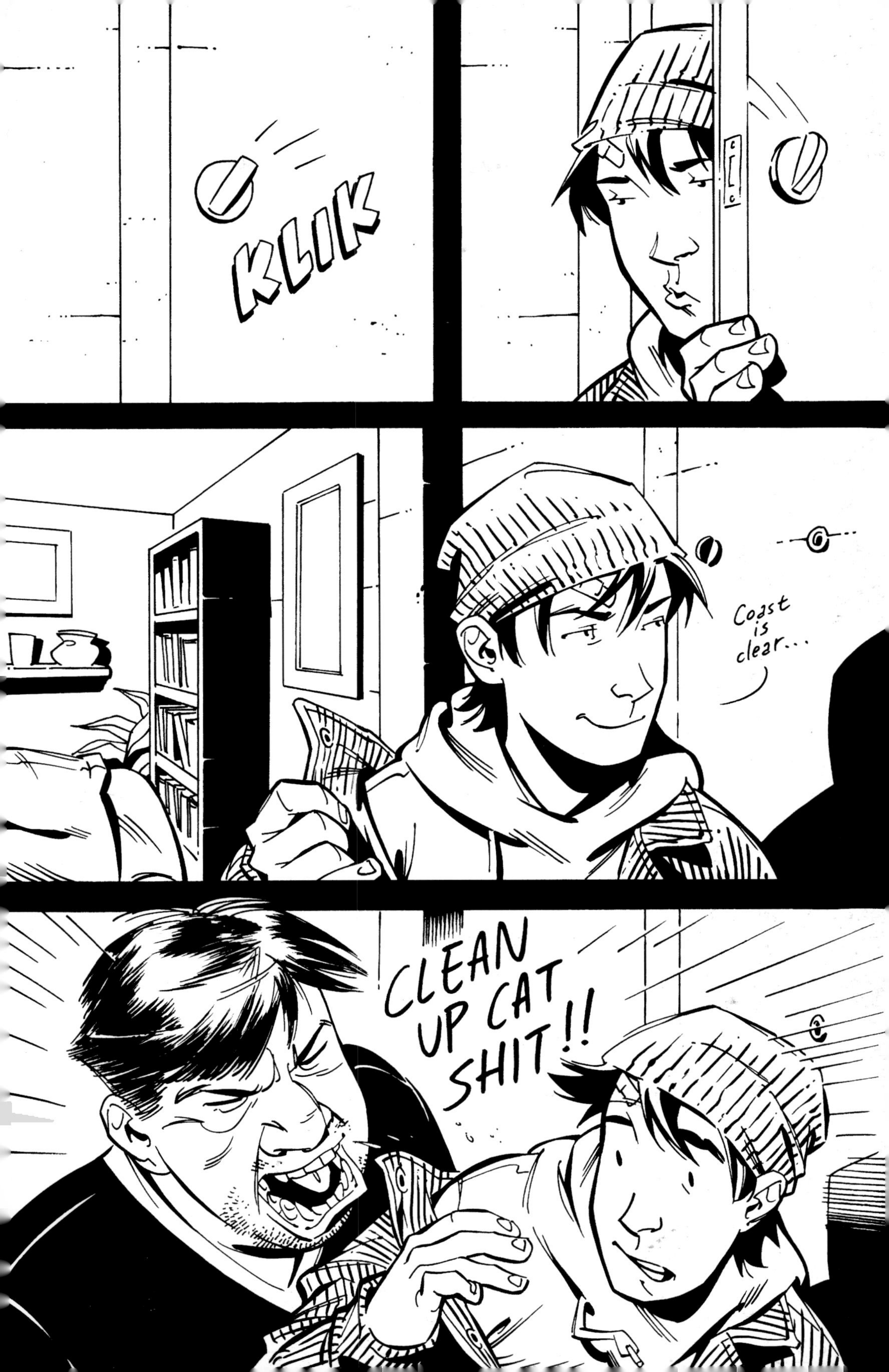
KLIK
Coast is clear...
CLEAN UP CAT SHIT!!

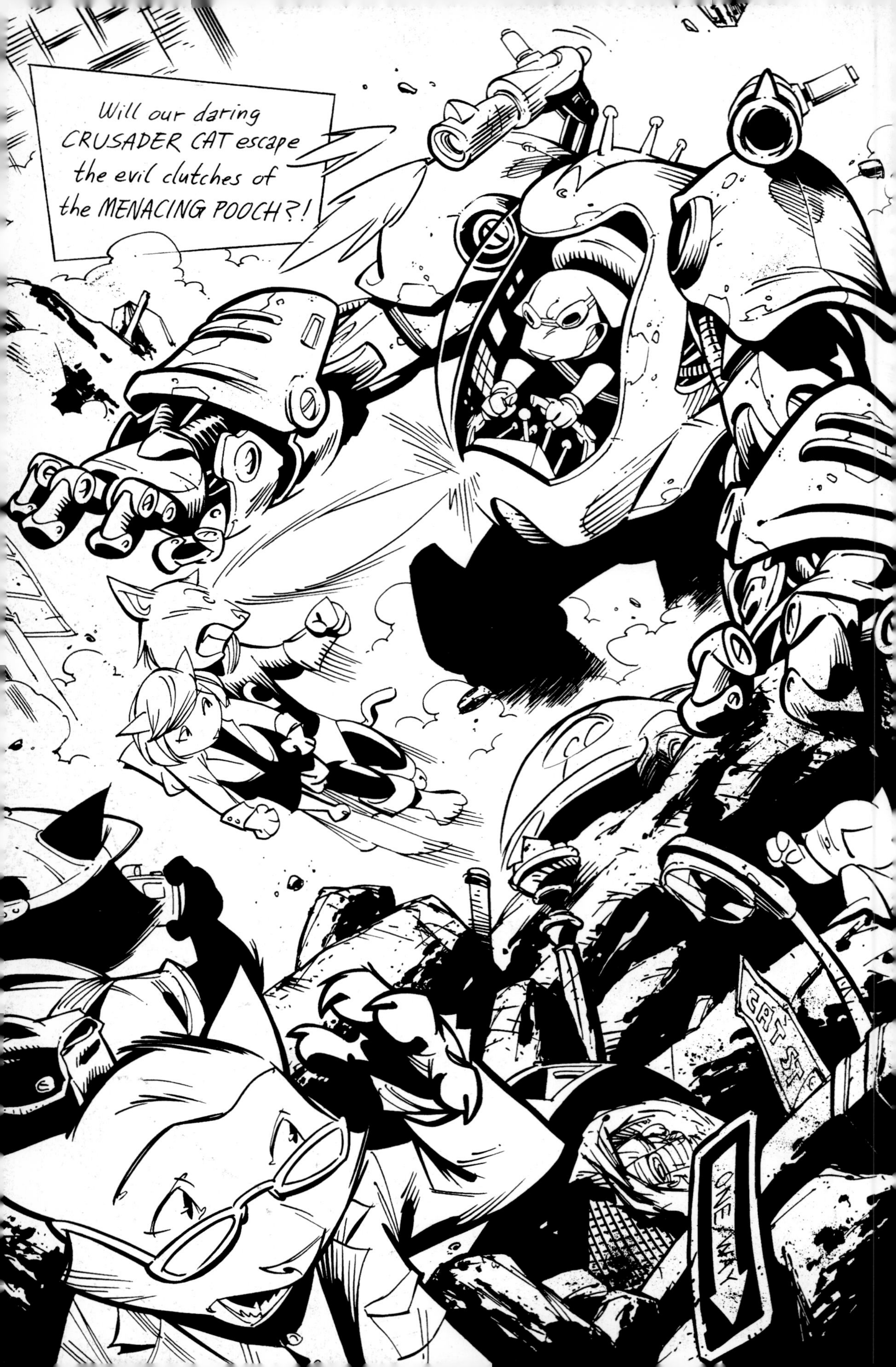
Will our daring CRUSADER CAT escape the evil clutches of the MENACING POOCH?!
CAT ST
ONE WAY

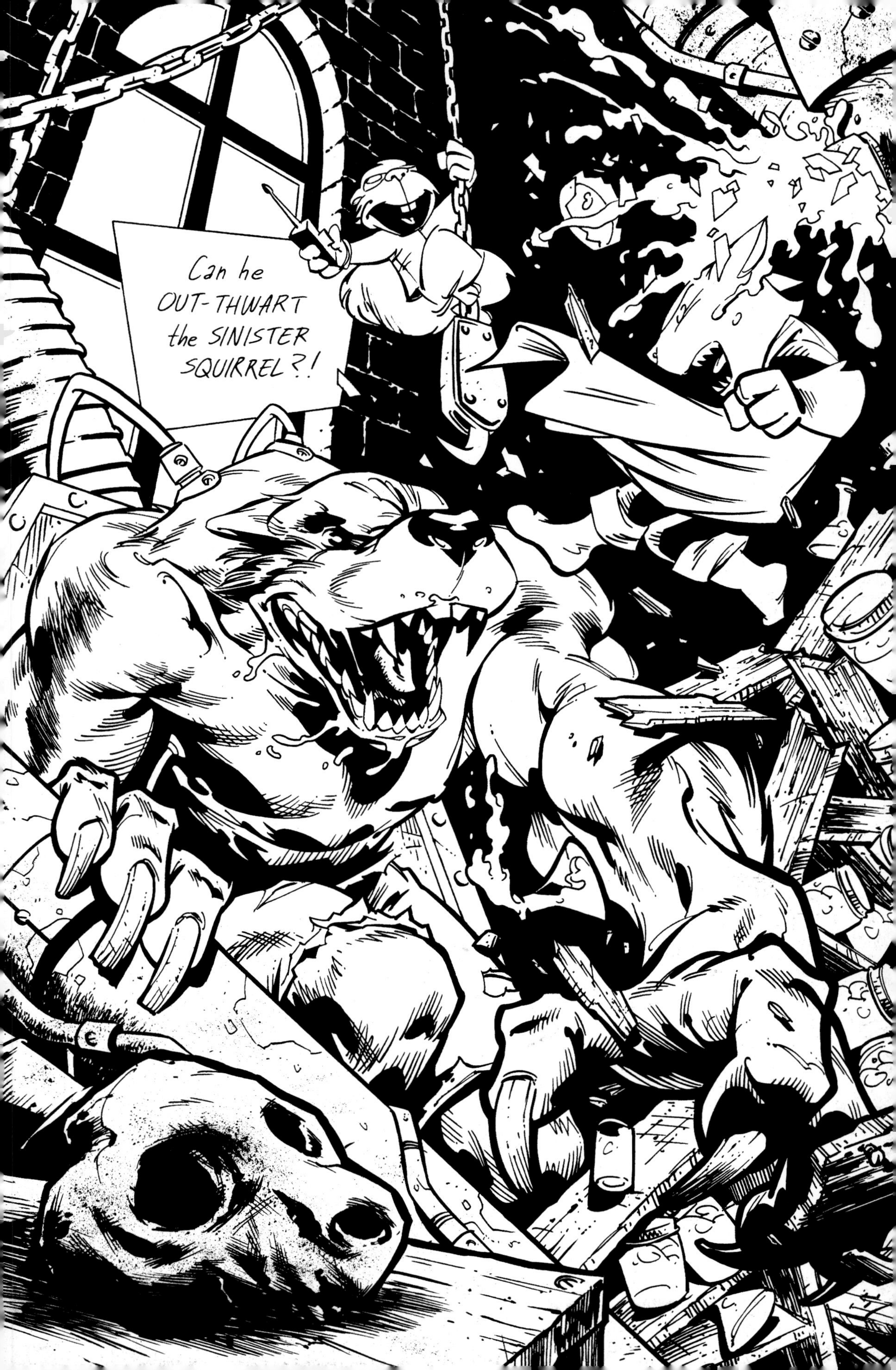
Can he OUT-THWART the SINISTER SQUIRREL?!

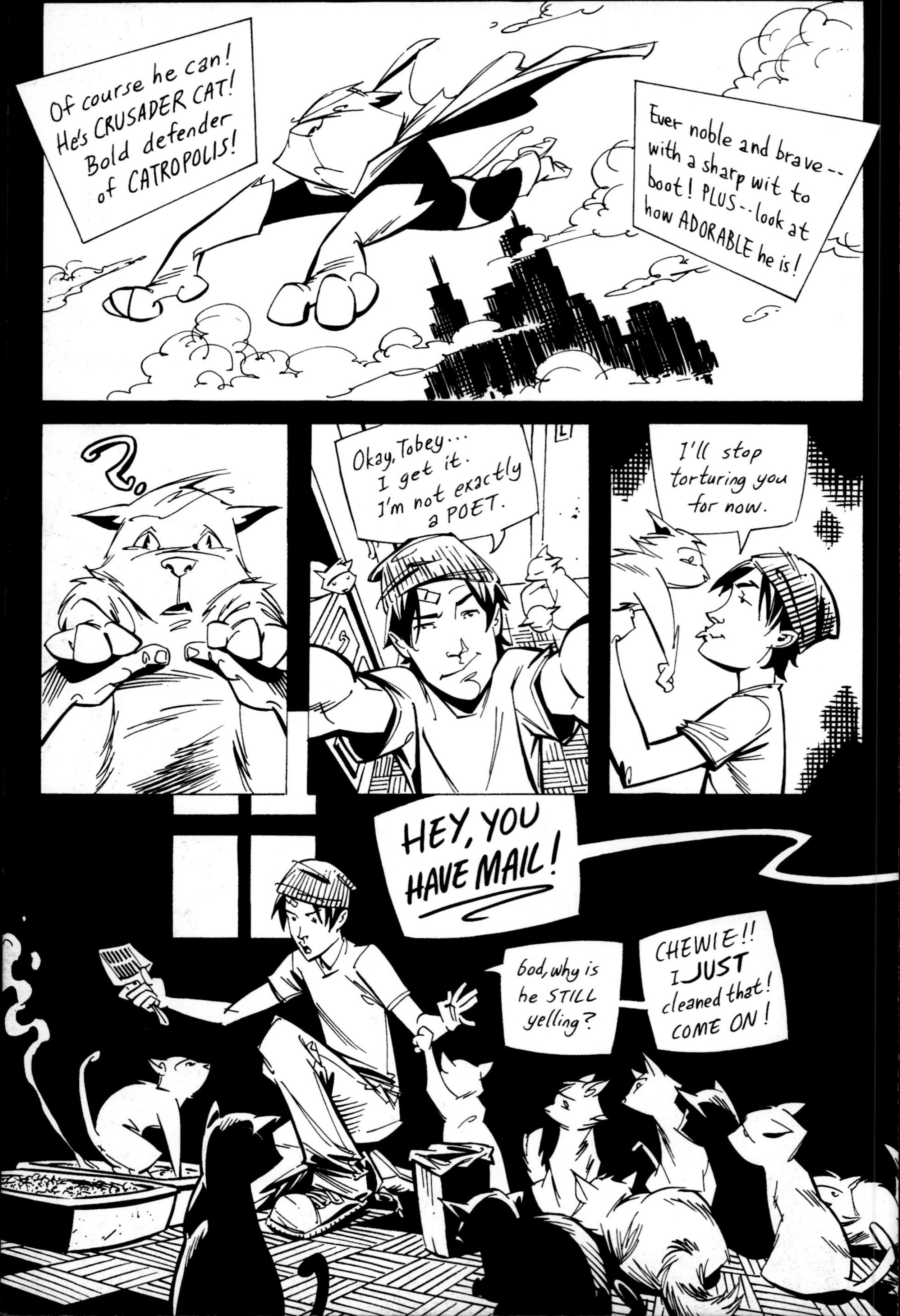

Of course he can! He's CRUSADER CAT! Bold defender of CATROPOLIS!
Ever noble and brave -- with a sharp wit to boot! PLUS -- look at how ADORABLE he is!
Okay, Tobey... I get it. I'm not exactly a POET.
I'll stop torturing you for now.
HEY, YOU HAVE MAIL!
God, why is he STILL yelling?
CHEWIE!! I JUST cleaned that! COME ON!

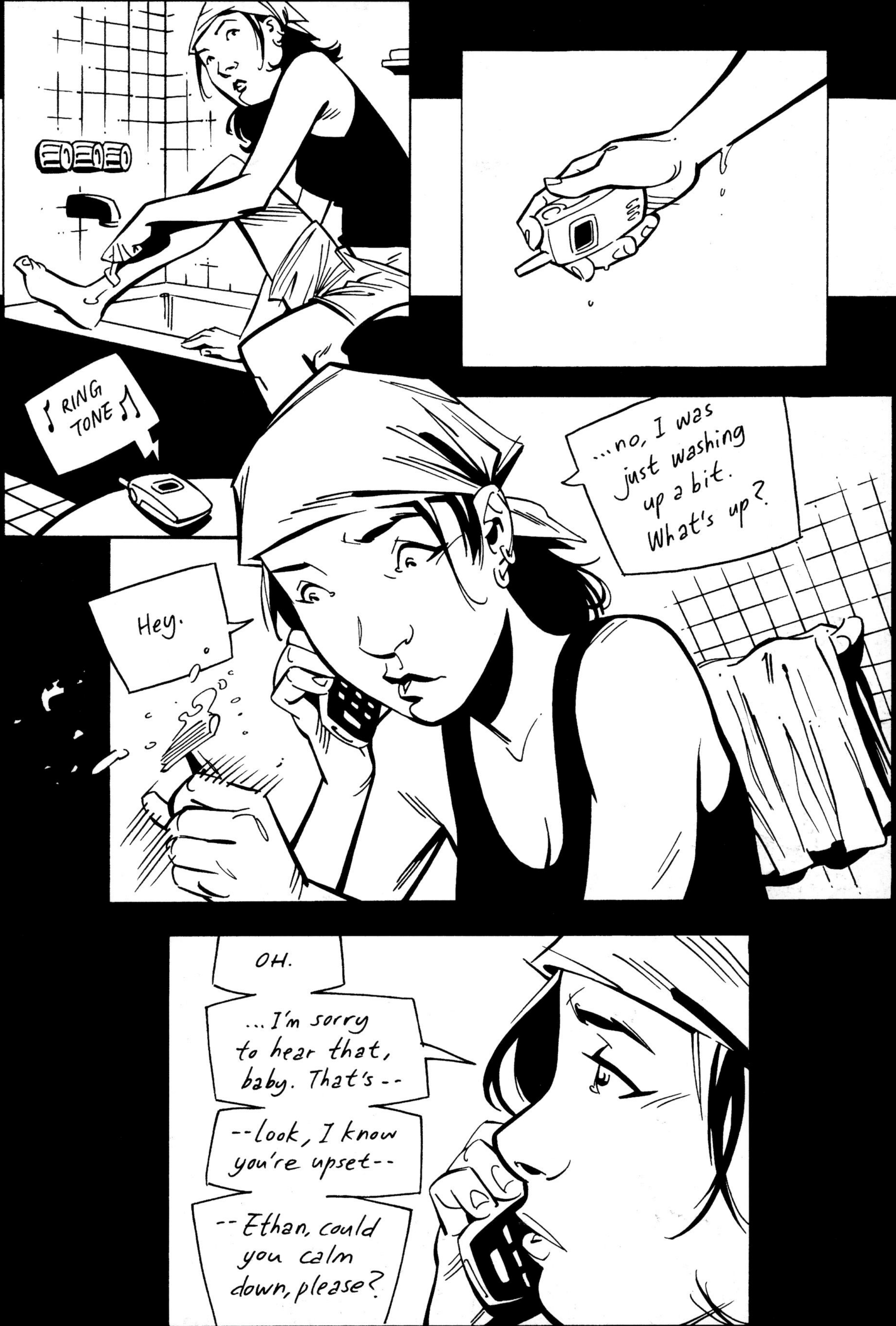
RING TONE
Hey.
...no, I was just washing up a bit. What's up?
OH.
...I'm sorry to hear that, baby. That's --
--look, I know you're upset--
--Ethan, could you calm down, please?

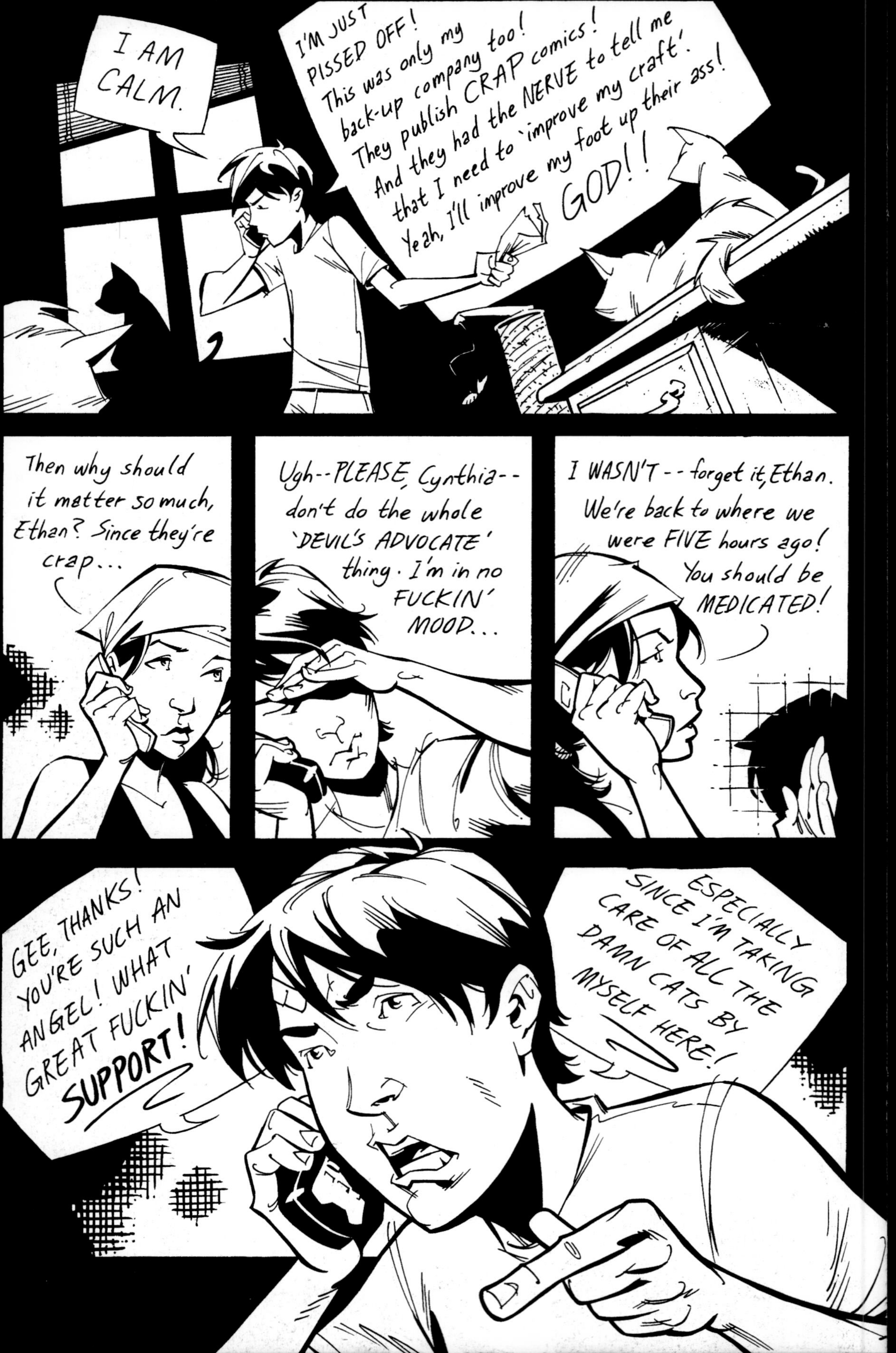
I AM CALM.
I'M JUST PISSED OFF! This was only my back-up company too! They publish CRAP comics! And they had the NERVE to tell me that I need to 'improve my craft'. Yeah, I'll improve my foot up their ass! GOD!!
Then why should it matter so much, Ethan? Since they're crap...
Ugh--PLEASE, Cynthia--don't do the whole 'DEVIL'S ADVOCATE' thing. I'm in no FUCKIN' MOOD...
I WASN'T--forget it, Ethan. We're back to where we were FIVE hours ago! You should be MEDICATED!
GEE, THANKS! YOU'RE SUCH AN ANGEL! WHAT GREAT FUCKIN' SUPPORT!
ESPECIALLY SINCE I'M TAKING CARE OF ALL THE DAMN CATS BY MYSELF HERE!

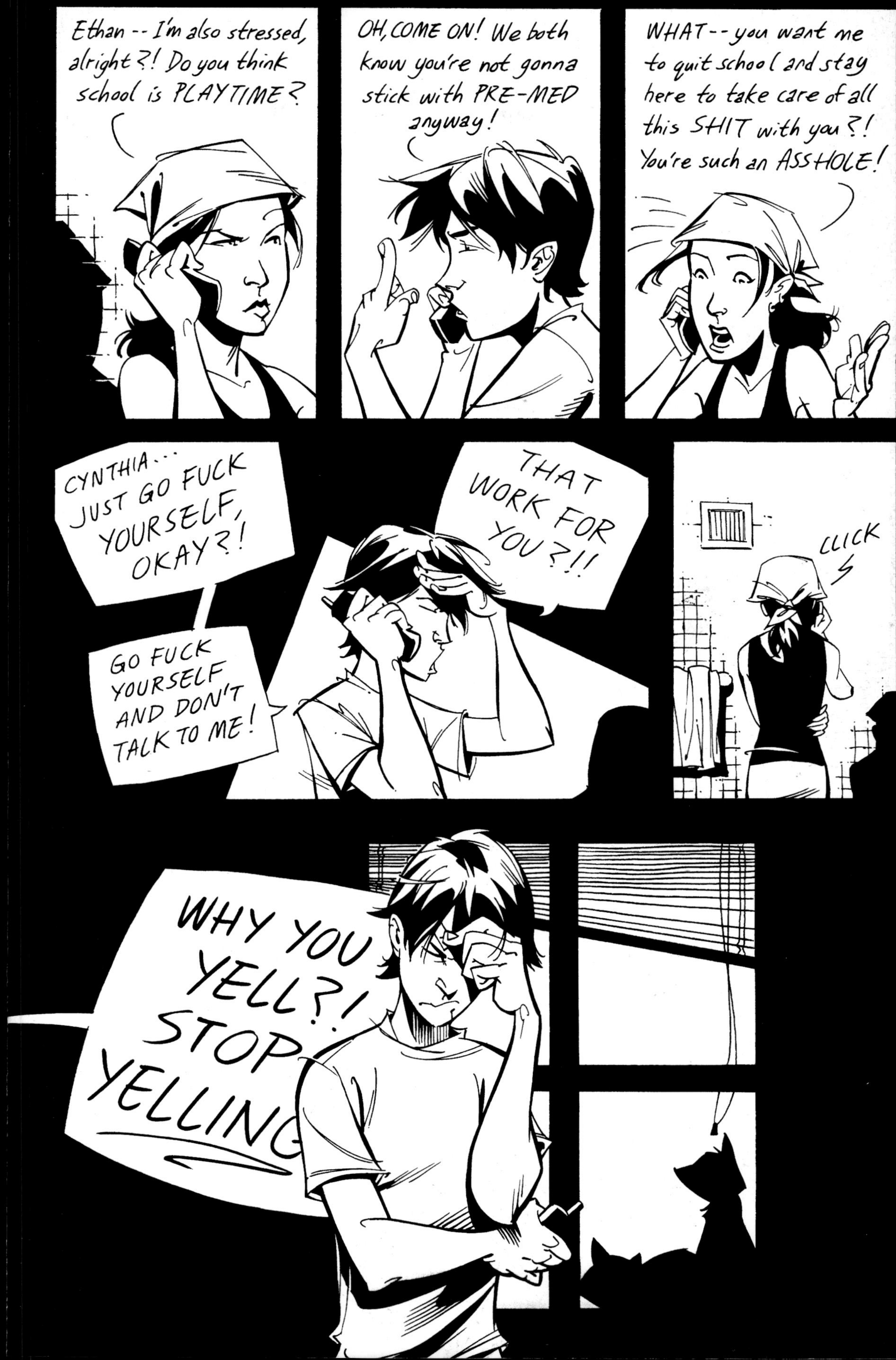
Ethan -- I'm also stressed, alright?! Do you think school is PLAYTIME?
OH, COME ON! We both know you're not gonna stick with PRE-MED anyway!
WHAT -- you want me to quit school and stay here to take care of all this SHIT with you?! You're such an ASSHOLE!
CYNTHIA... JUST GO FUCK YOURSELF, OKAY?!
THAT WORK FOR YOU?!!
GO FUCK YOURSELF AND DON'T TALK TO ME!
CLICK
WHY YOU YELL?! STOP YELLING

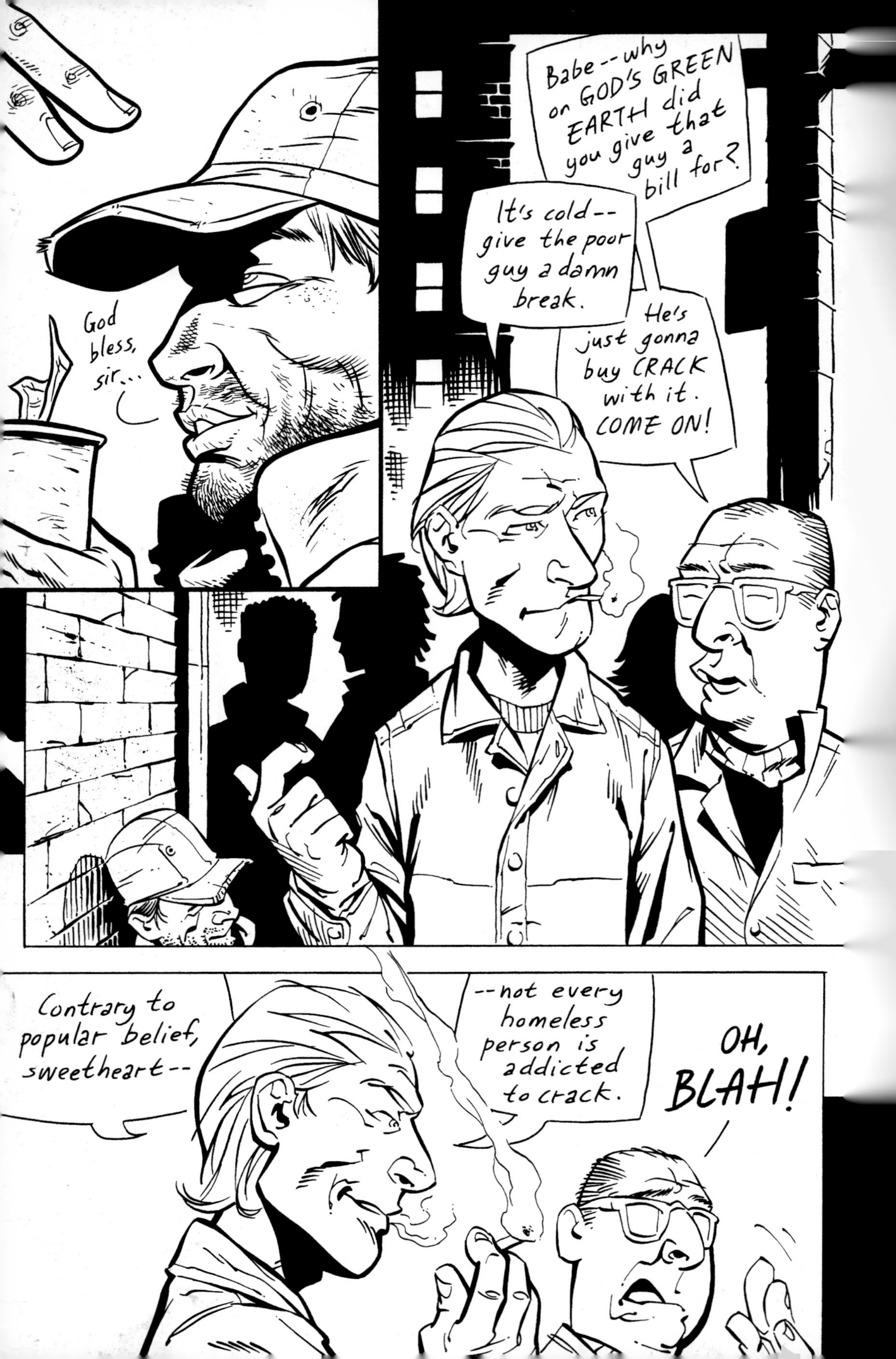
God bless, sir...
Babe--why on GOD'S GREEN EARTH did you give that guy a bill for?
It's cold--give the poor guy a damn break.
He's just gonna buy CRACK with it. COME ON!
Contrary to popular belief, sweetheart--
--not every homeless person is addicted to crack.
OH, BLAH!

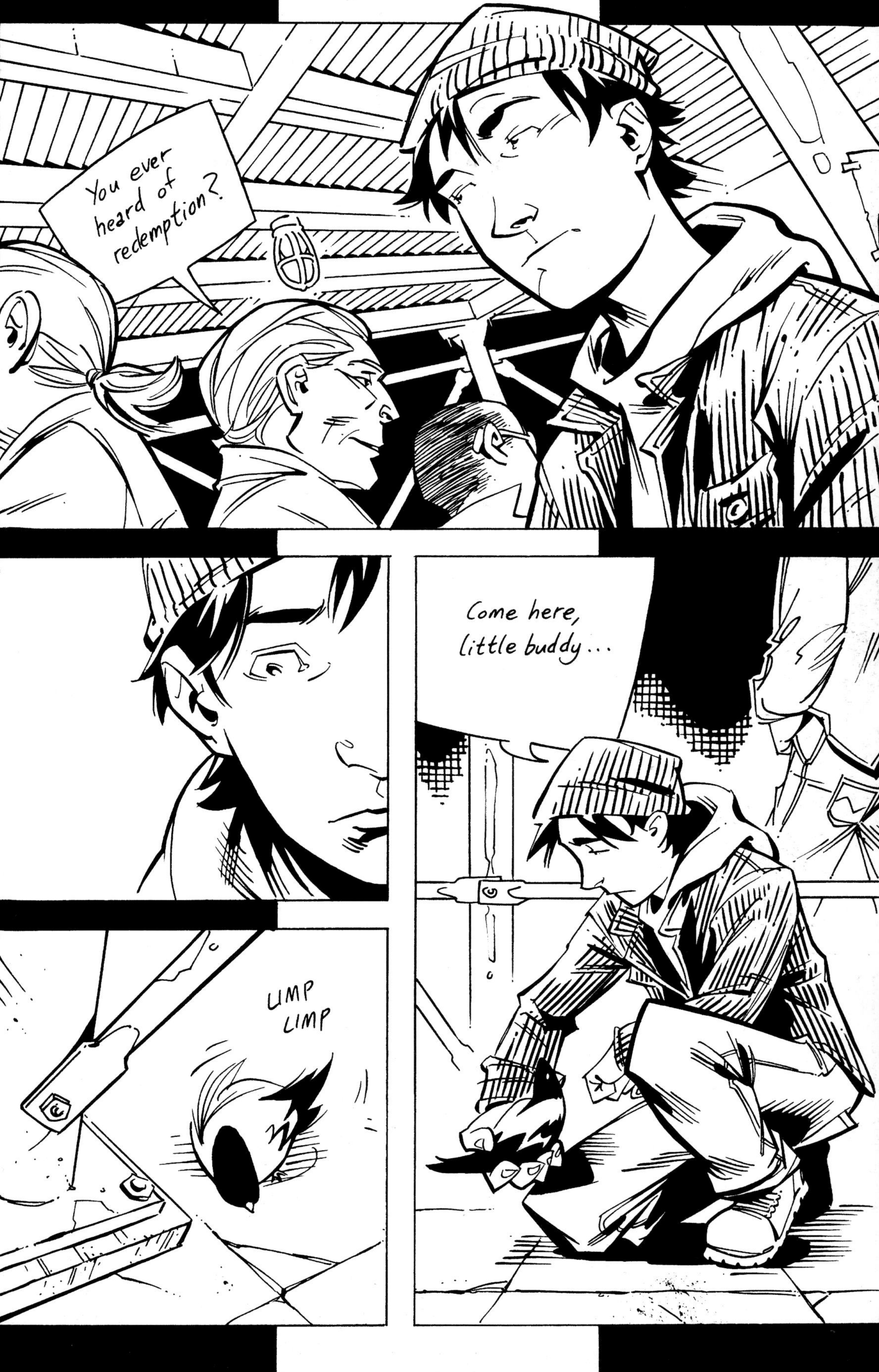
You ever heard of redemption?
Come here, little buddy...
LIMP
LIMP

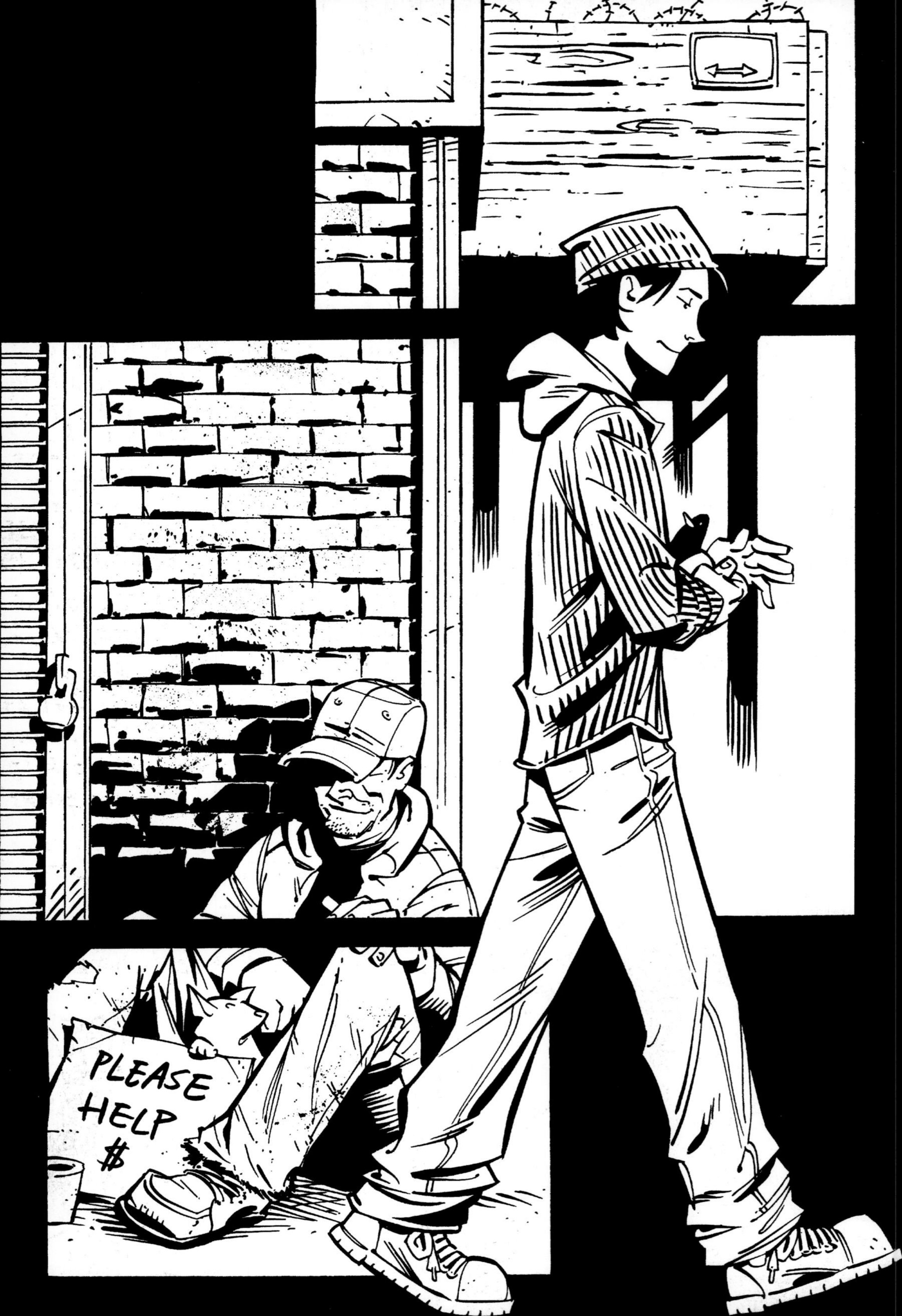
PLEASE
HELP
$

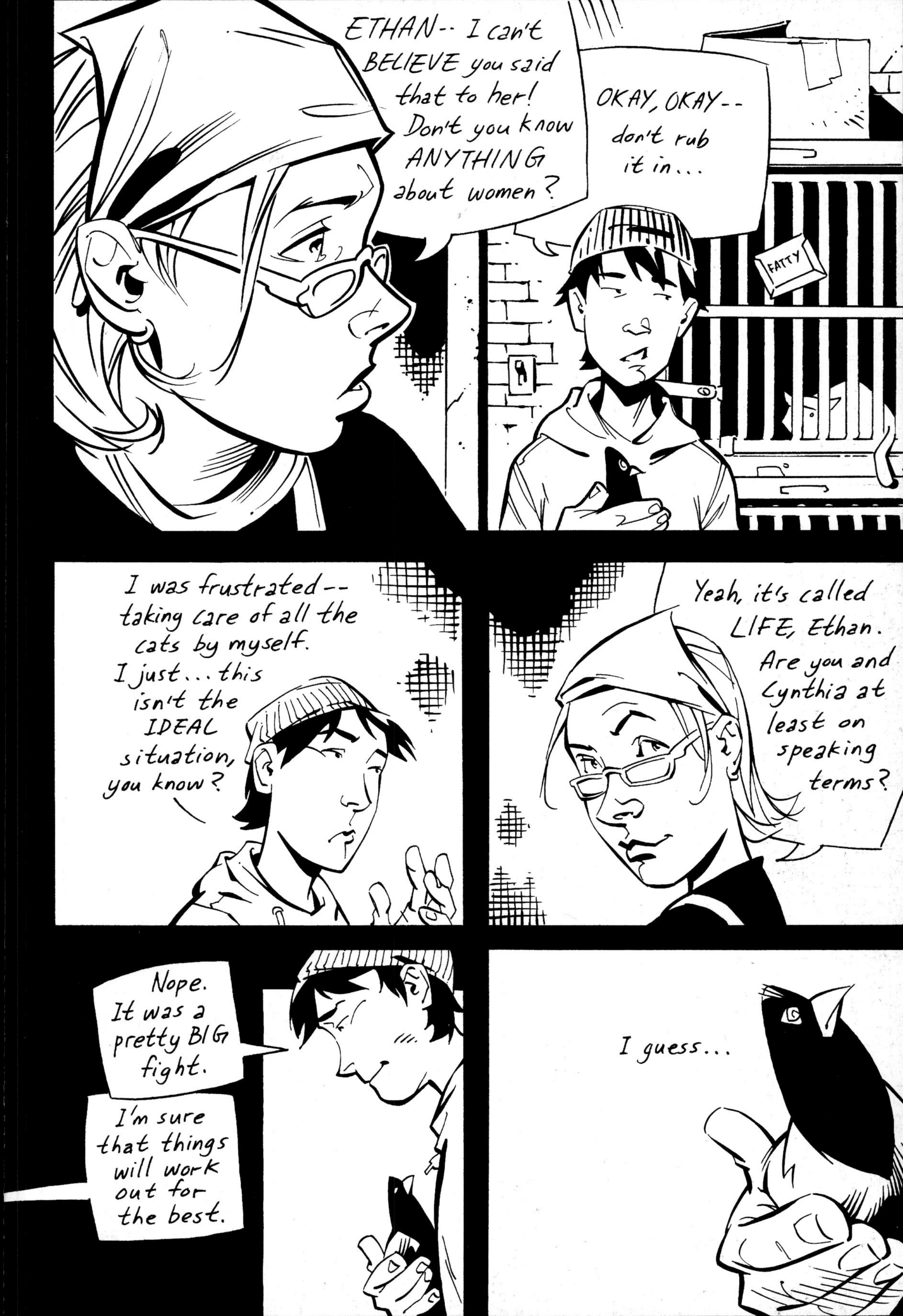

ETHAN-- I can't BELIEVE you said that to her! Don't you know ANYTHING about women?
OKAY, OKAY-- don't rub it in...
FATTY
I was frustrated-- taking care of all the cats by myself. I just... this isn't the IDEAL situation, you know?
Yeah, it's called LIFE, Ethan. Are you and Cynthia at least on speaking terms?
Nope. It was a pretty BIG fight.
I'm sure that things will work out for the best.
I guess...

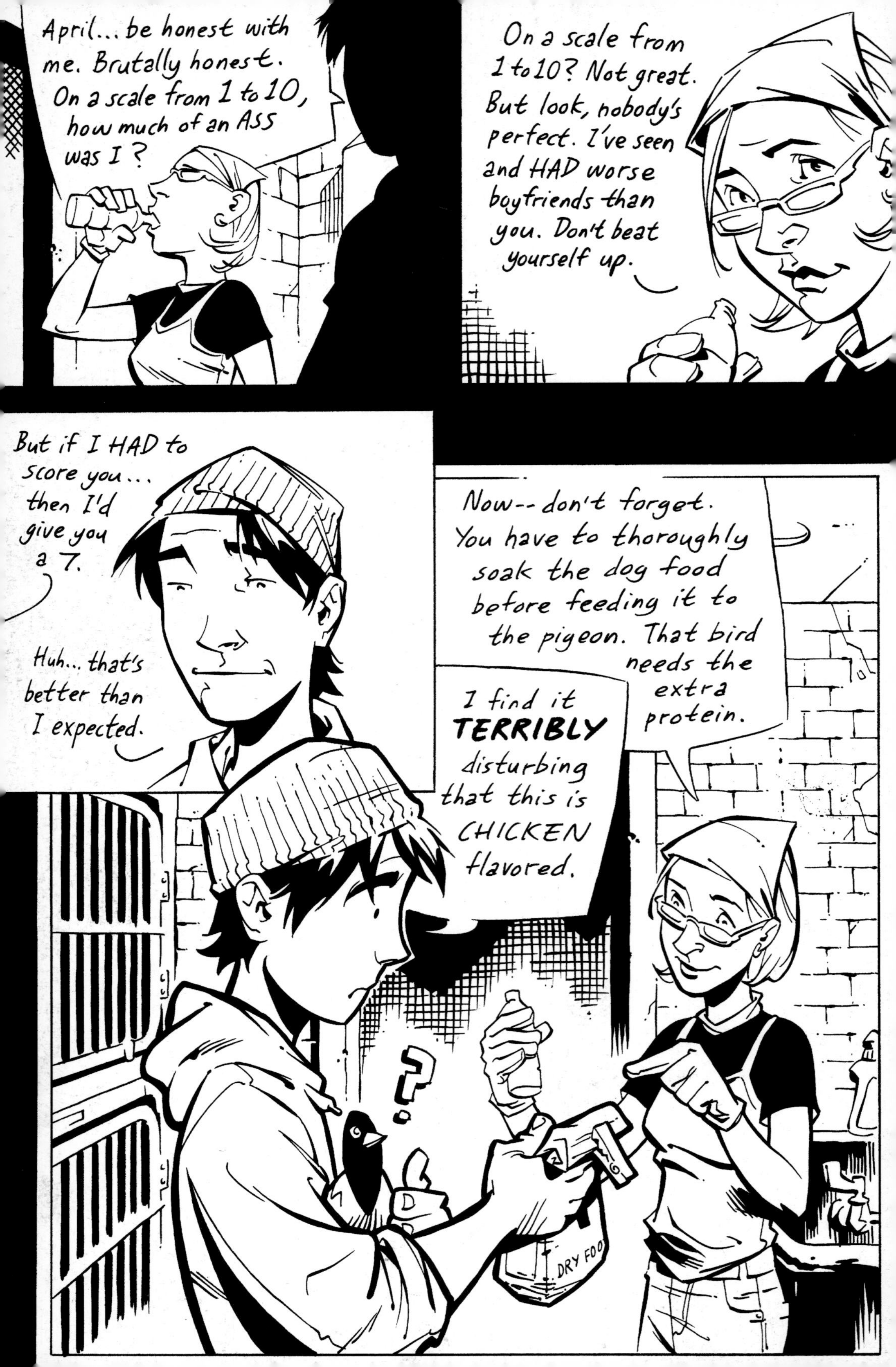
April... be honest with me. Brutally honest. On a scale from 1 to 10, how much of an ASS was I?
On a scale from 1 to 10? Not great. But look, nobody's perfect. I've seen and HAD worse boyfriends than you. Don't beat yourself up.
But if I HAD to score you... then I'd give you a 7.
Huh... that's better than I expected.
Now-- don't forget. You have to thoroughly soak the dog food before feeding it to the pigeon. That bird needs the extra protein.
I find it **TERRIBLY** disturbing that this is CHICKEN flavored.
?
DRY FOO

ADDICTED TO SIN

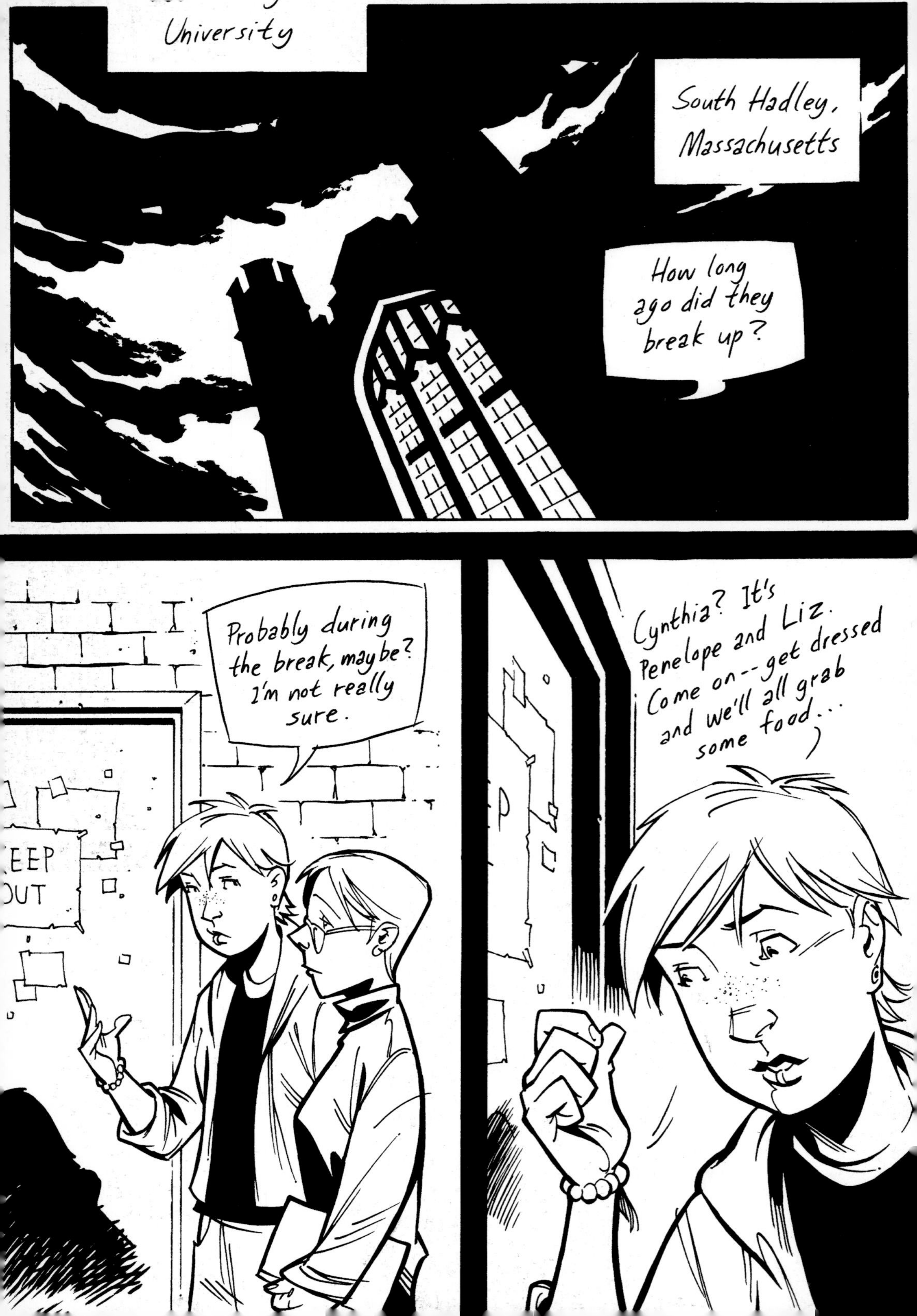
University
South Hadley, Massachusetts
How long ago did they break up?
Probably during the break, maybe? I'm not really sure.
Cynthia? It's Penelope and Liz. Come on--get dressed and we'll all grab some food...

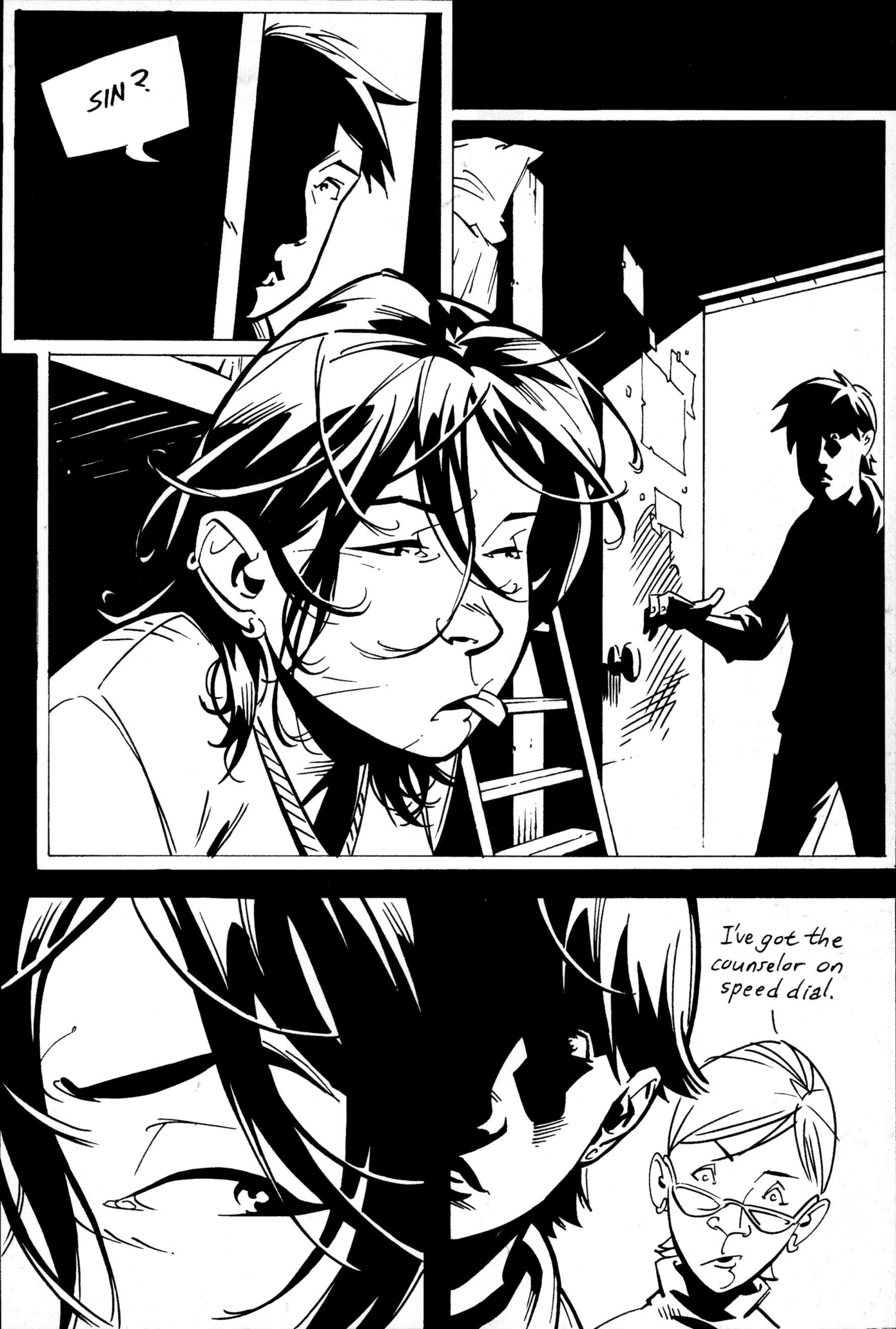
SIN?
I've got the counselor on speed dial.

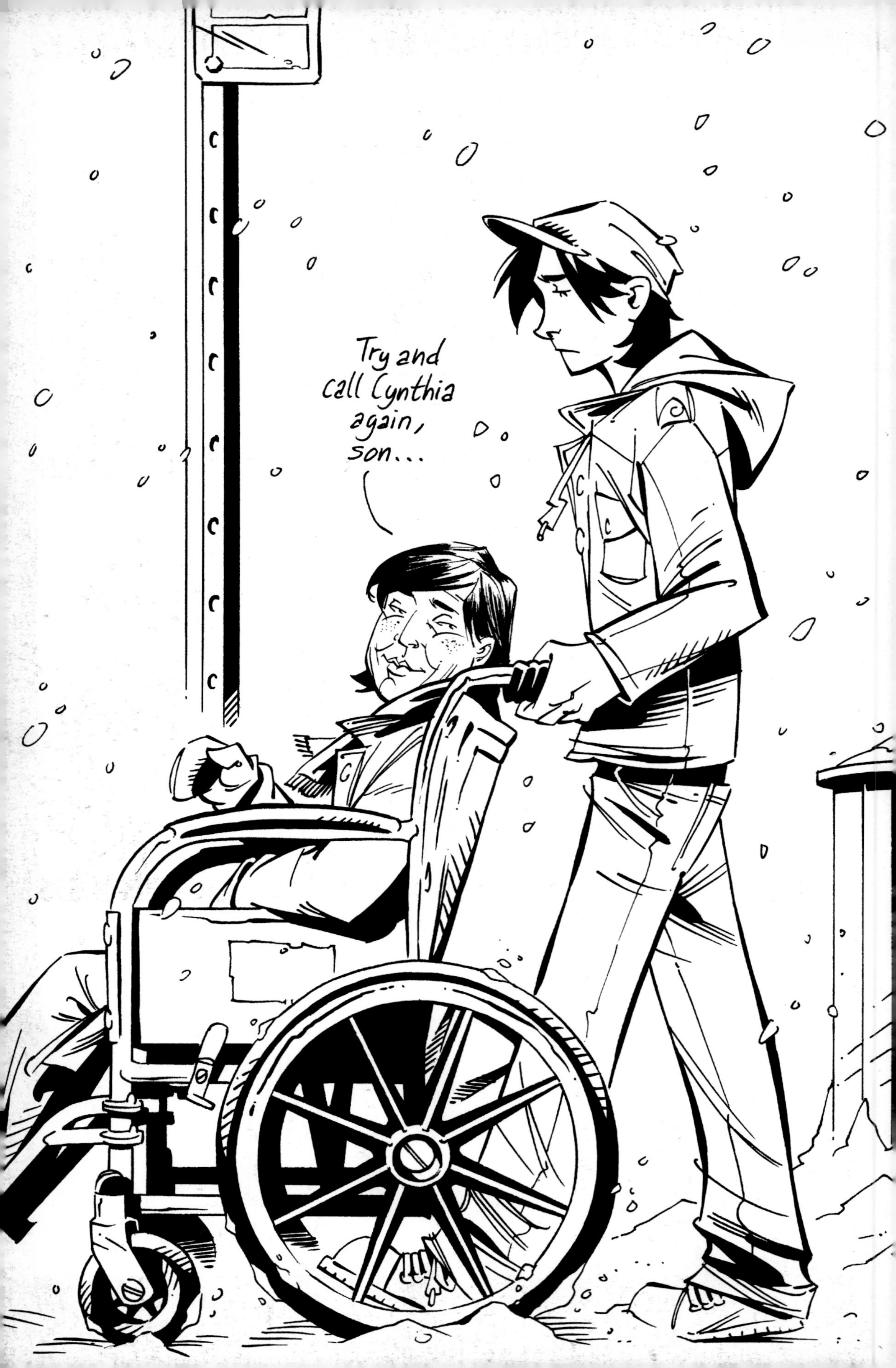
Try and call Cynthia again, son...

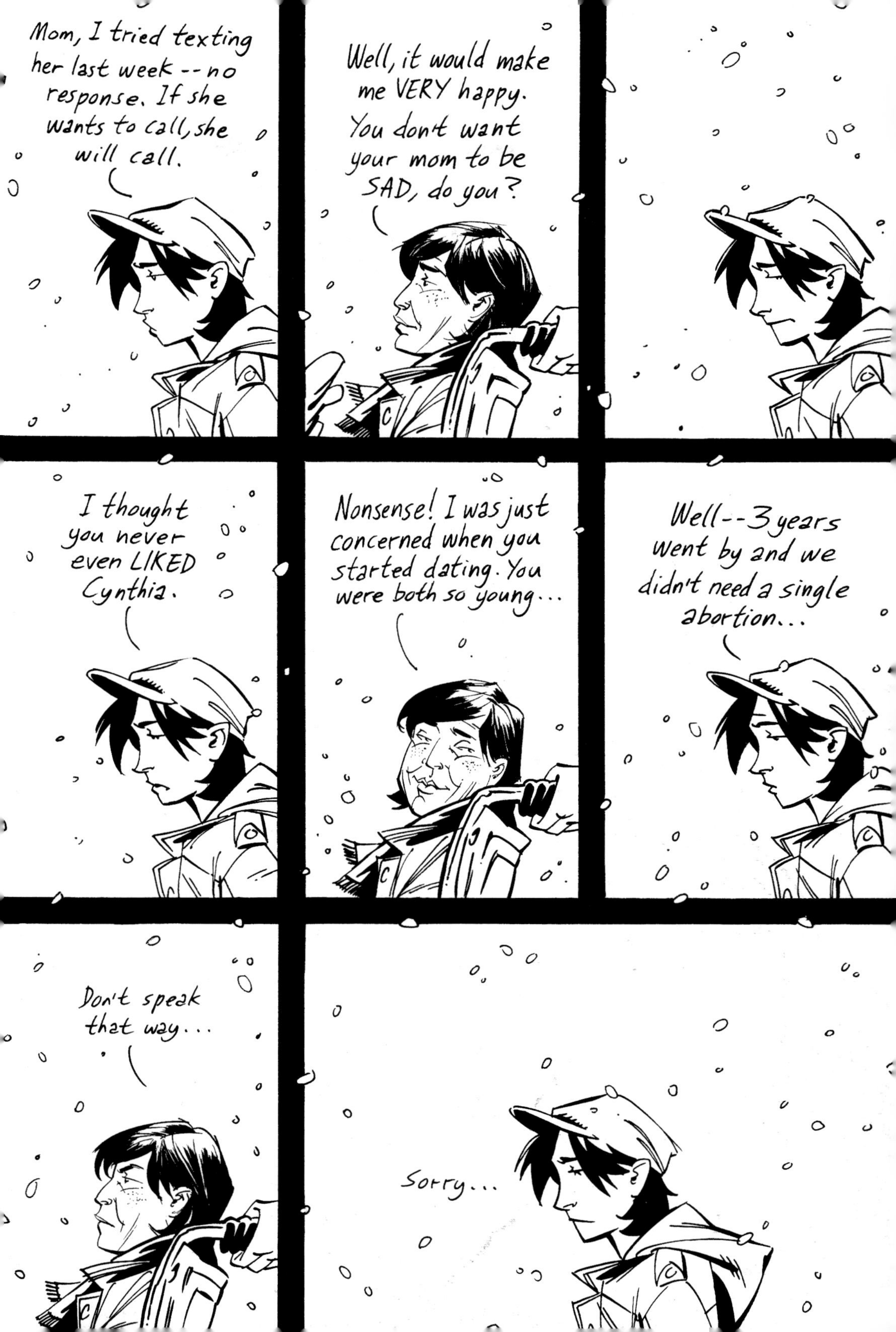
Mom, I tried texting her last week -- no response. If she wants to call, she will call.
Well, it would make me VERY happy. You don't want your mom to be SAD, do you?
I thought you never even LIKED Cynthia.
Nonsense! I was just concerned when you started dating. You were both so young...
Well--3 years went by and we didn't need a single abortion...
Don't speak that way...
Sorry...

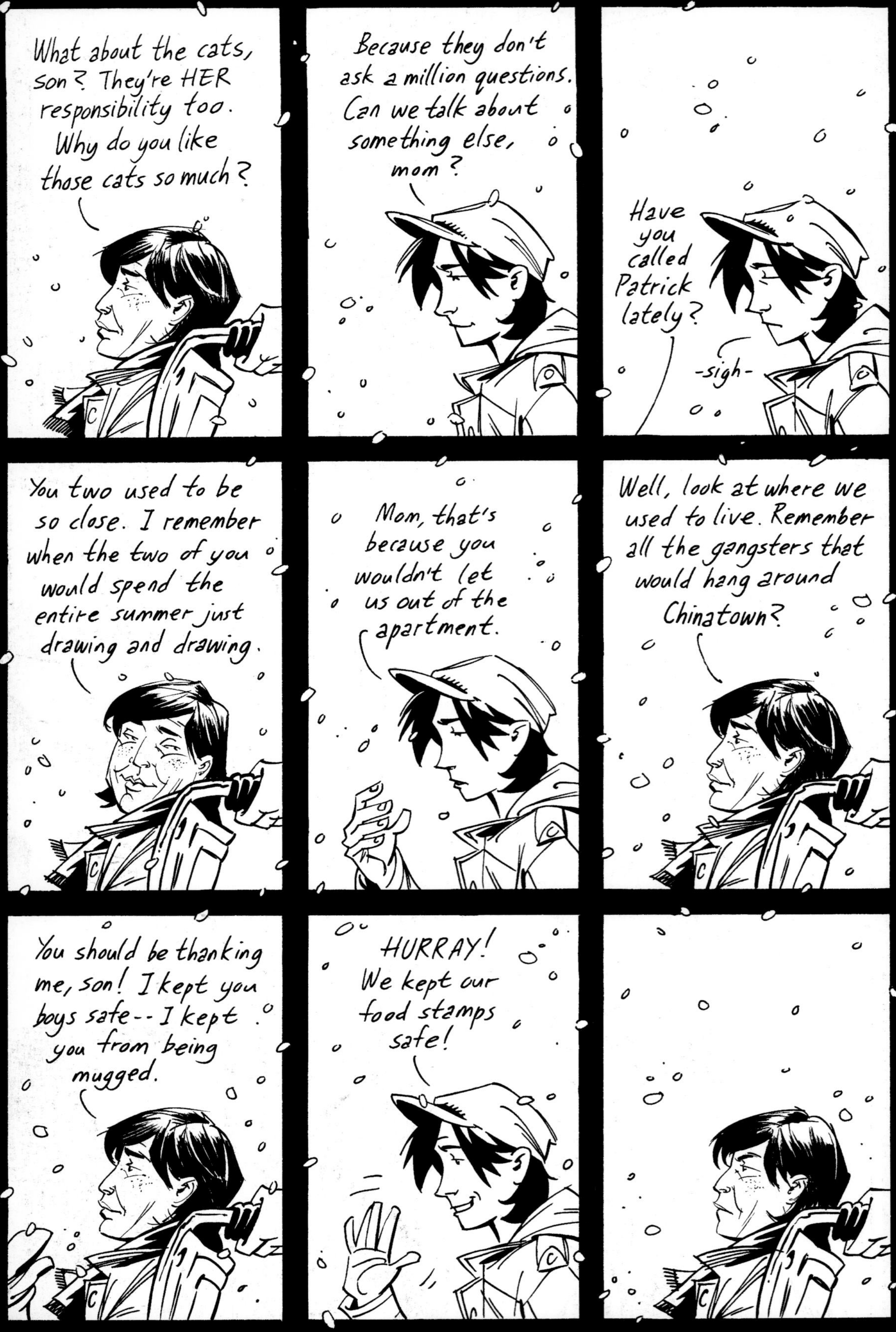
What about the cats, son? They're HER responsibility too. Why do you like those cats so much?
Because they don't ask a million questions. Can we talk about something else, mom?
Have you called Patrick lately?
-sigh-
You two used to be so close. I remember when the two of you would spend the entire summer just drawing and drawing.
Mom, that's because you wouldn't let us out of the apartment.
Well, look at where we used to live. Remember all the gangsters that would hang around Chinatown?
You should be thanking me, son! I kept you boys safe-- I kept you from being mugged.
HURRAY! We kept our food stamps safe!

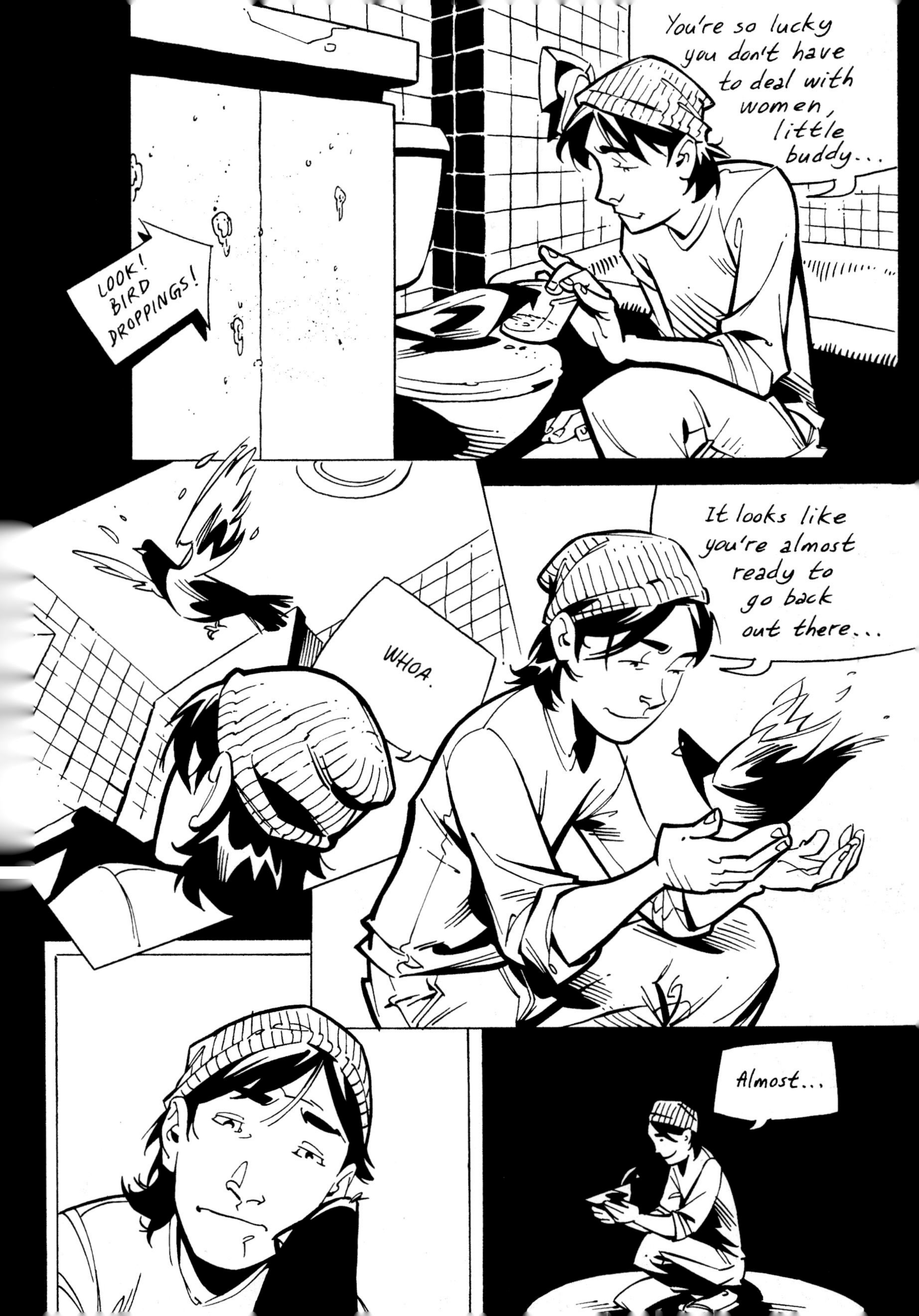
You're so lucky you don't have to deal with women, little buddy...
LOOK! BIRD DROPPINGS!
It looks like you're almost ready to go back out there...
WHOA.
Almost...

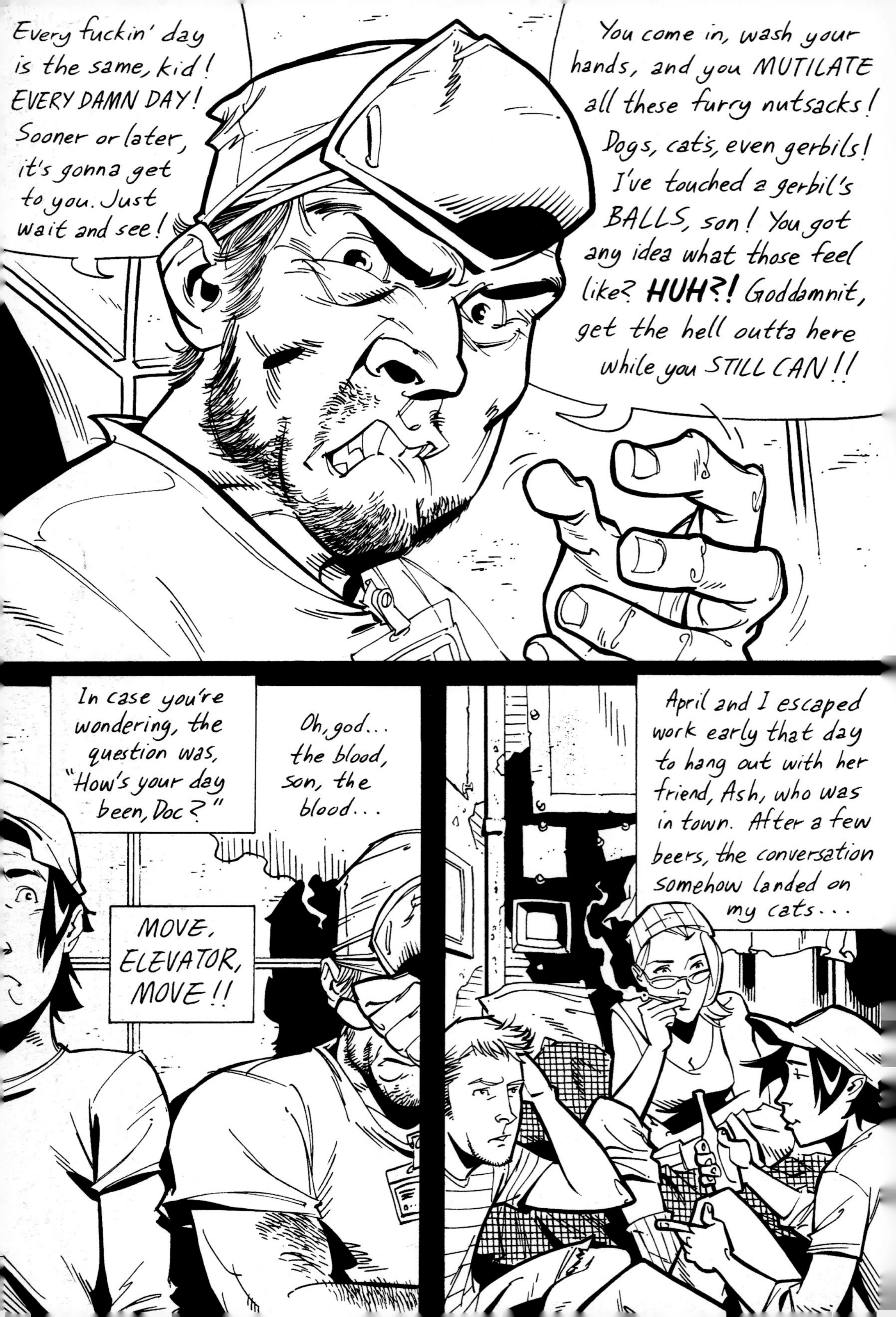
Every fuckin' day is the same, kid! EVERY DAMN DAY! Sooner or later, it's gonna get to you. Just wait and see!
You come in, wash your hands, and you MUTILATE all these furry nutsacks! Dogs, cats, even gerbils! I've touched a gerbil's BALLS, son! You got any idea what those feel like? HUH?! Goddamnit, get the hell outta here while you STILL CAN!!
In case you're wondering, the question was, "How's your day been, Doc?"
Oh, god... the blood, son, the blood...
MOVE. ELEVATOR, MOVE!!
April and I escaped work early that day to hang out with her friend, Ash, who was in town. After a few beers, the conversation somehow landed on my cats...

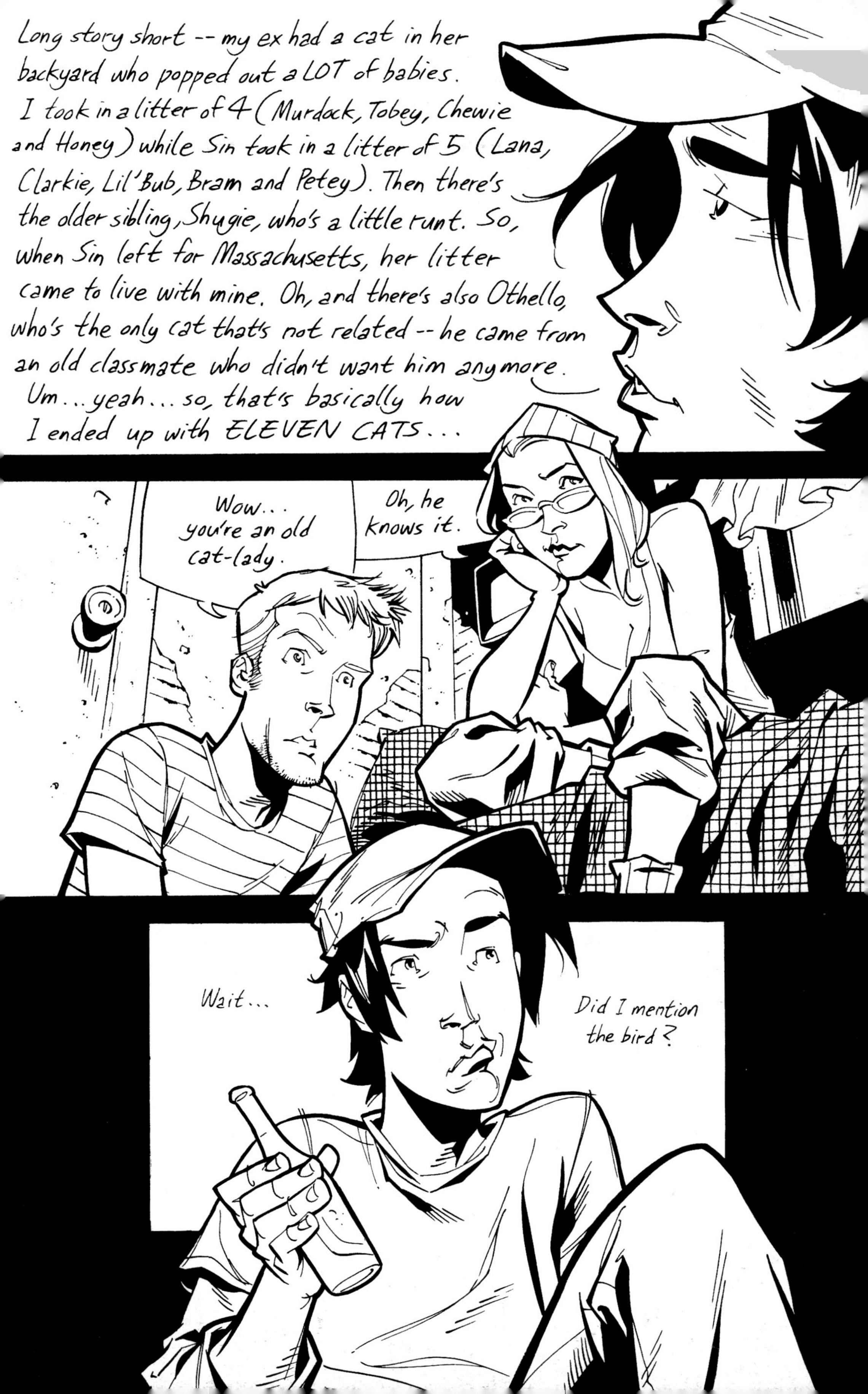
Long story short -- my ex had a cat in her backyard who popped out a LOT of babies. I took in a litter of 4 (Murdack, Tobey, Chewie and Honey) while Sin took in a litter of 5 (Lana, Clarkie, Lil'Bub, Bram and Petey). Then there's the older sibling, Shugie, who's a little runt. So, when Sin left for Massachusetts, her litter came to live with mine. Oh, and there's also Othello, who's the only cat that's not related -- he came from an old classmate who didn't want him anymore.
Um... yeah... so, that's basically how I ended up with ELEVEN CATS...
Wow... you're an old cat-lady.
Oh, he knows it.
Wait...
Did I mention the bird?

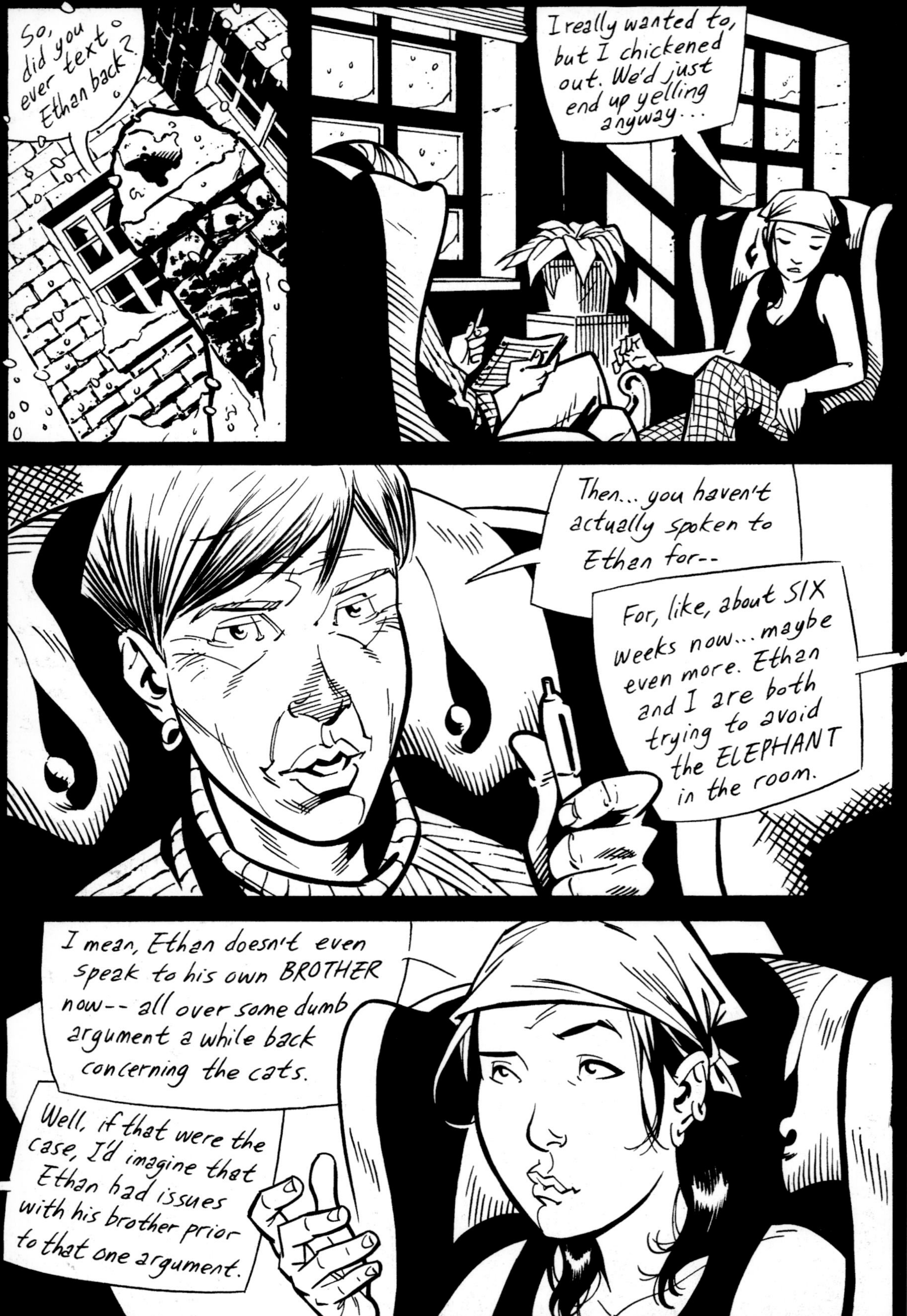
So, did you ever text Ethan back?
I really wanted to, but I chickened out. We'd just end up yelling anyway...
Then... you haven't actually spoken to Ethan for--
For, like, about SIX weeks now... maybe even more. Ethan and I are both trying to avoid the ELEPHANT in the room.
I mean, Ethan doesn't even speak to his own BROTHER now-- all over some dumb argument a while back concerning the cats.
Well, if that were the case, I'd imagine that Ethan had issues with his brother prior to that one argument.

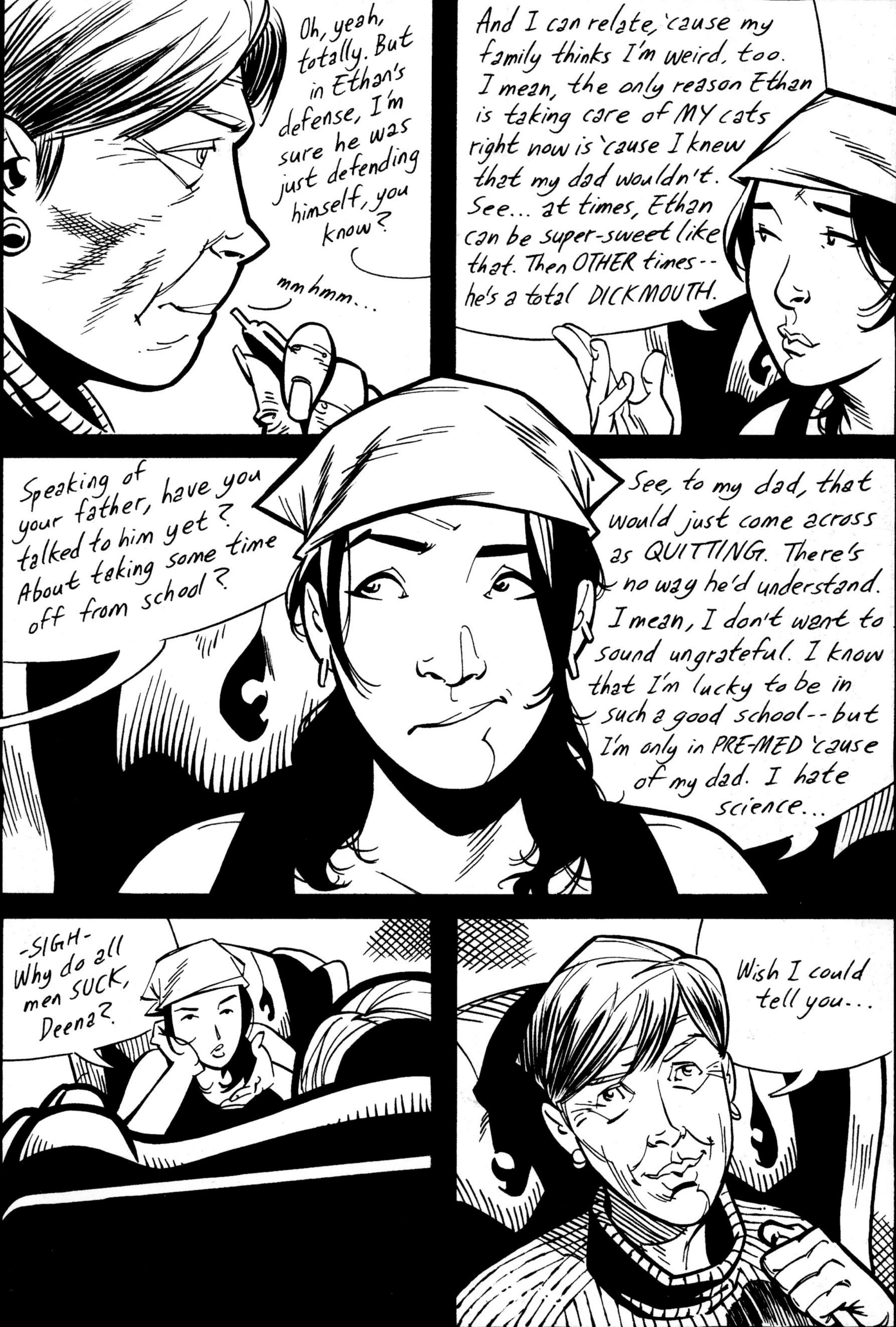
Oh, yeah, totally. But in Ethan's defense, I'm sure he was just defending himself, you know?
mmhmm...
And I can relate, 'cause my family thinks I'm weird, too. I mean, the only reason Ethan is taking care of MY cats right now is 'cause I knew that my dad wouldn't. See... at times, Ethan can be super-sweet like that. Then OTHER times-- he's a total DICKMOUTH.
Speaking of your father, have you talked to him yet? About taking some time off from school?
See, to my dad, that would just come across as QUITTING. There's no way he'd understand. I mean, I don't want to sound ungrateful. I know that I'm lucky to be in such a good school--but I'm only in PRE-MED 'cause of my dad. I hate science...
-SIGH- Why do all men SUCK, Deena?
Wish I could tell you...

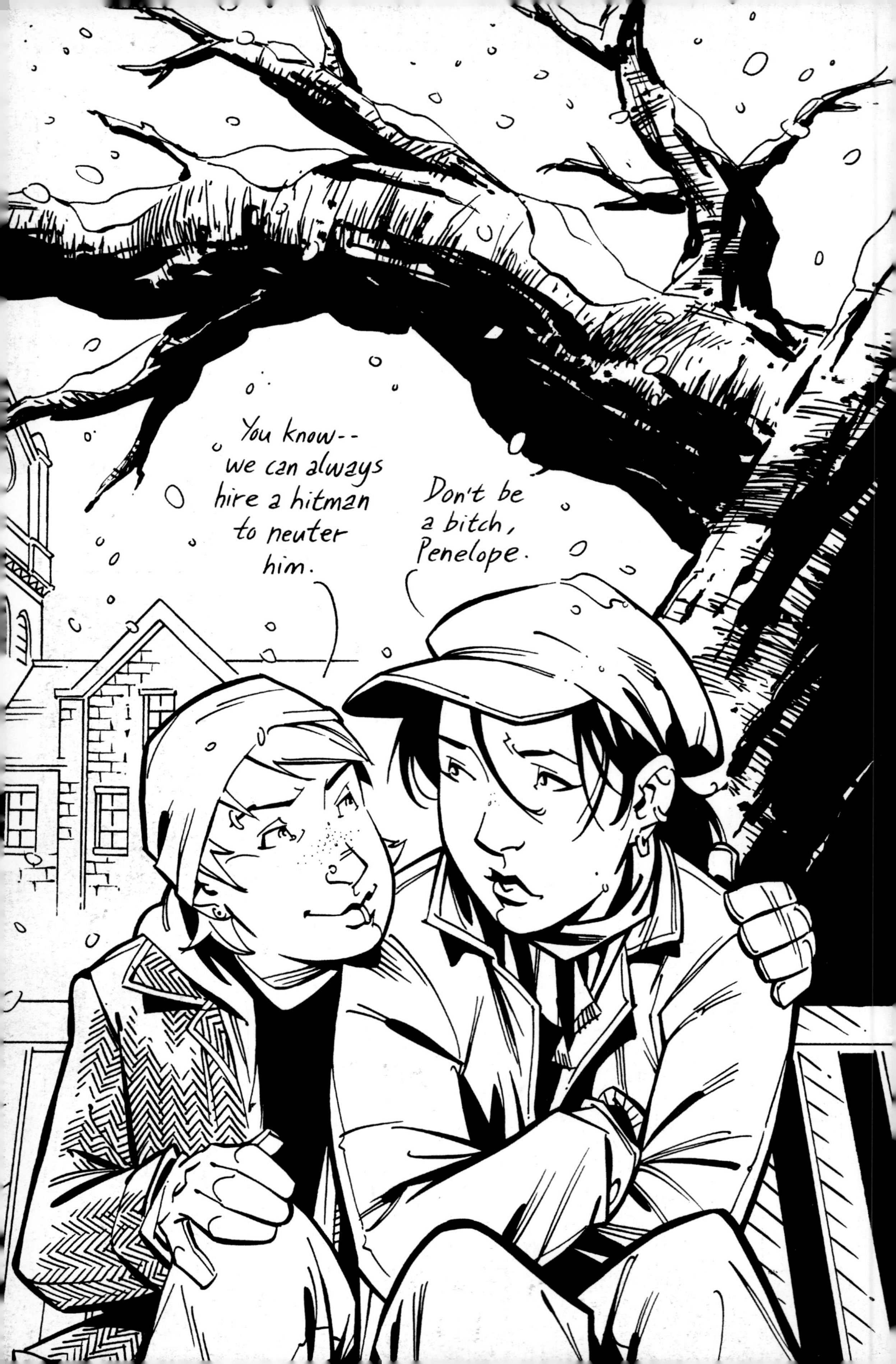
You know-- we can always hire a hitman to neuter him.
Don't be a bitch, Penelope.

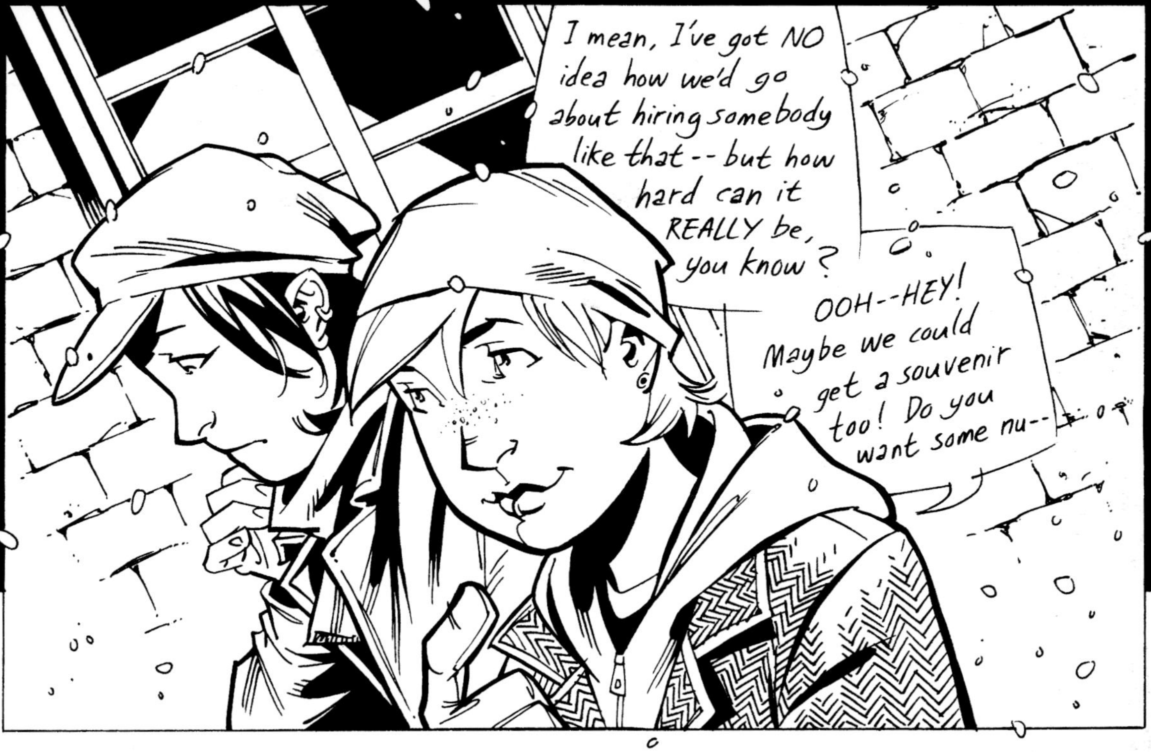
I mean, I've got NO idea how we'd go about hiring somebody like that -- but how hard can it REALLY be, you know?
OOH--HEY! Maybe we could get a souvenir too! Do you want some nu--

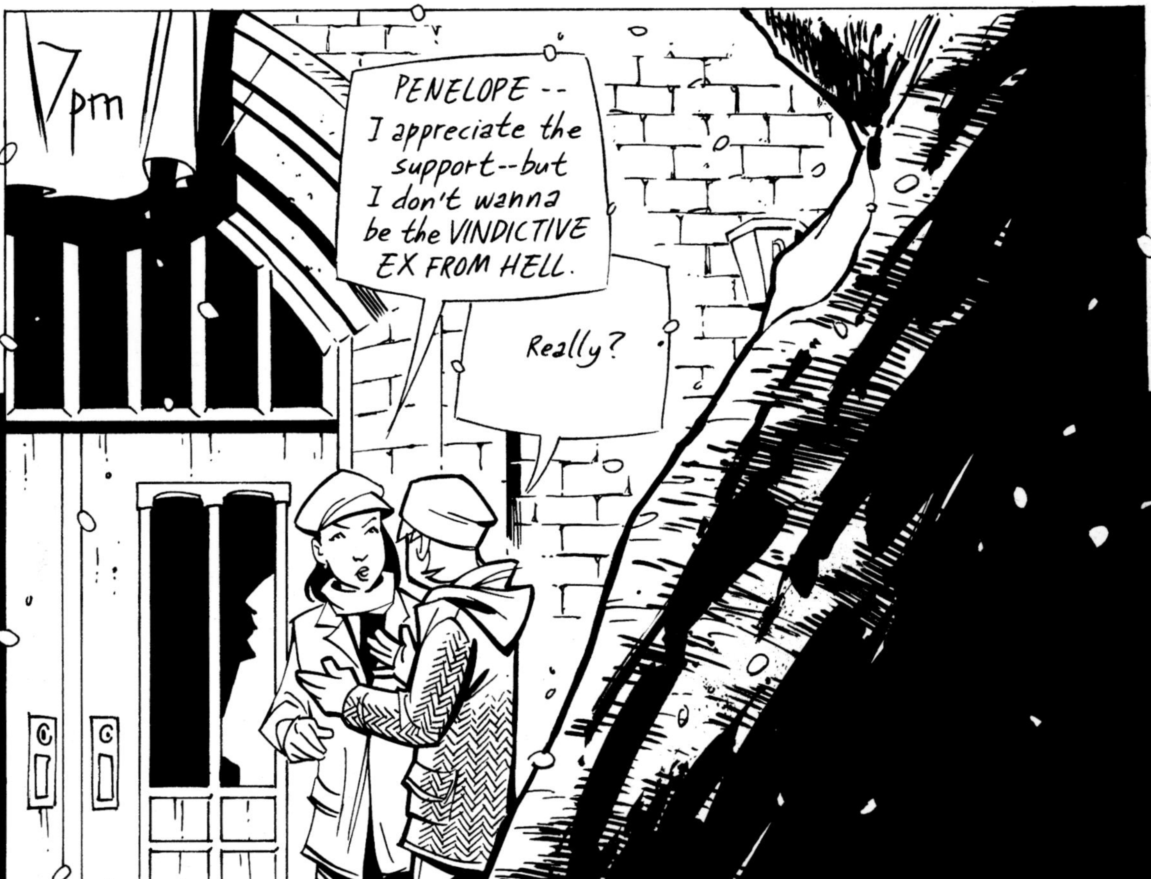
7pm
PENELOPE -- I appreciate the support--but I don't wanna be the VINDICTIVE EX FROM HELL.
Really?

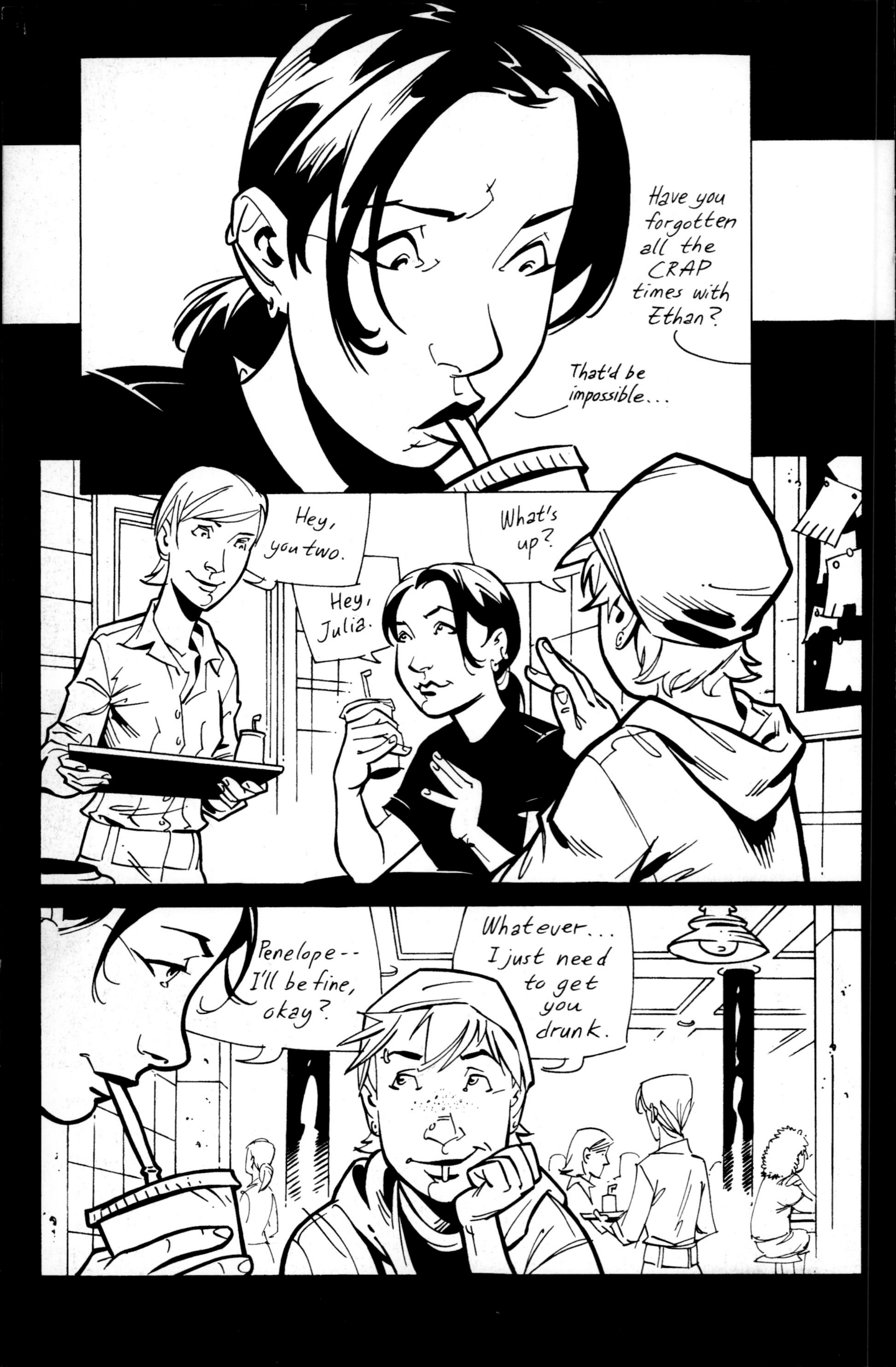
Have you forgotten all the CRAP times with Ethan?
That'd be impossible...
Hey, you two.
What's up?
Hey, Julia.
Penelope-- I'll be fine, okay?
Whatever... I just need to get you drunk.

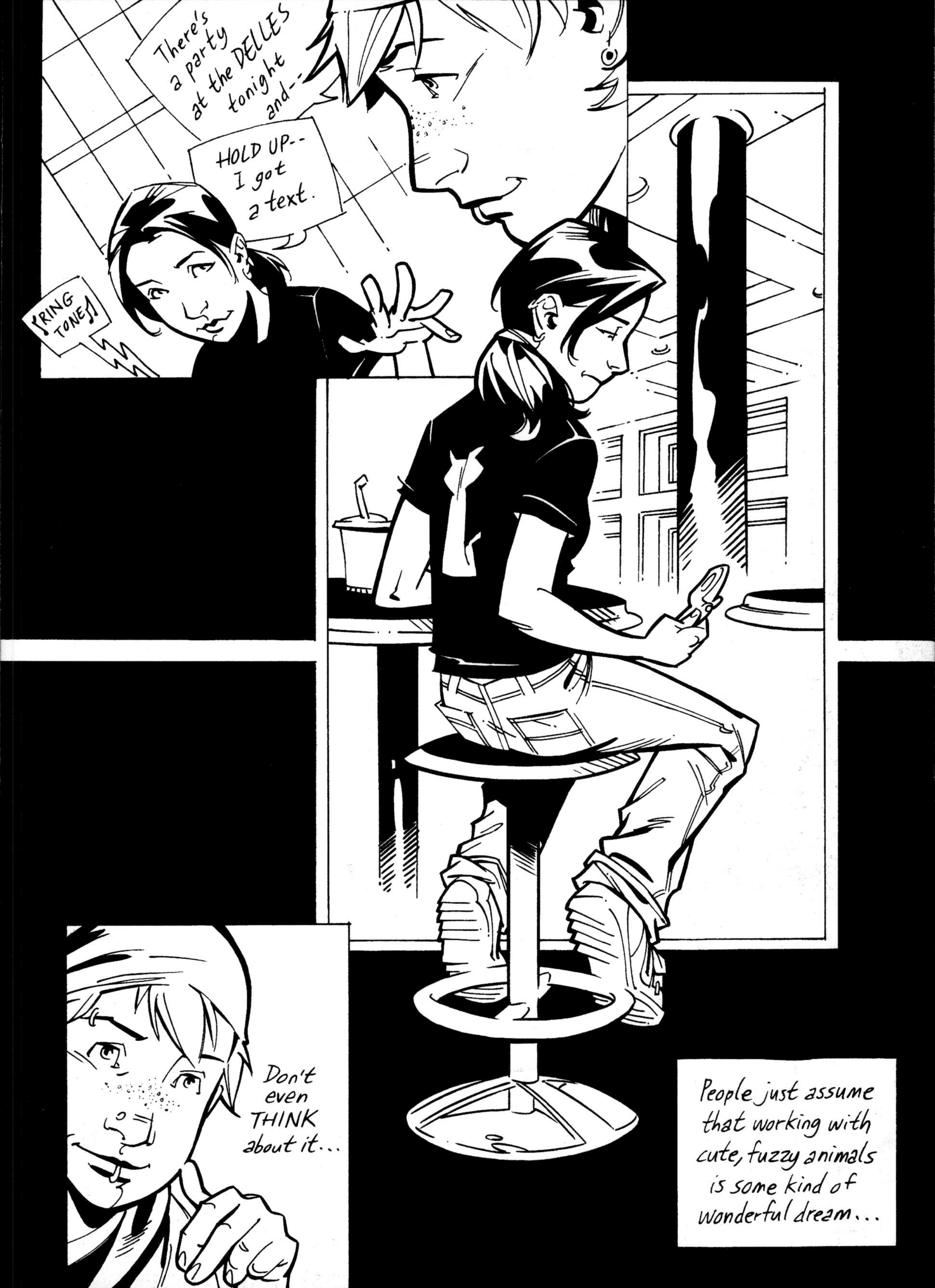
There's a party at the DELLES tonight and--
HOLD UP-- I got a text.
♪RING TONE♪
Don't even THINK about it...
People just assume that working with cute, fuzzy animals is some kind of wonderful dream...

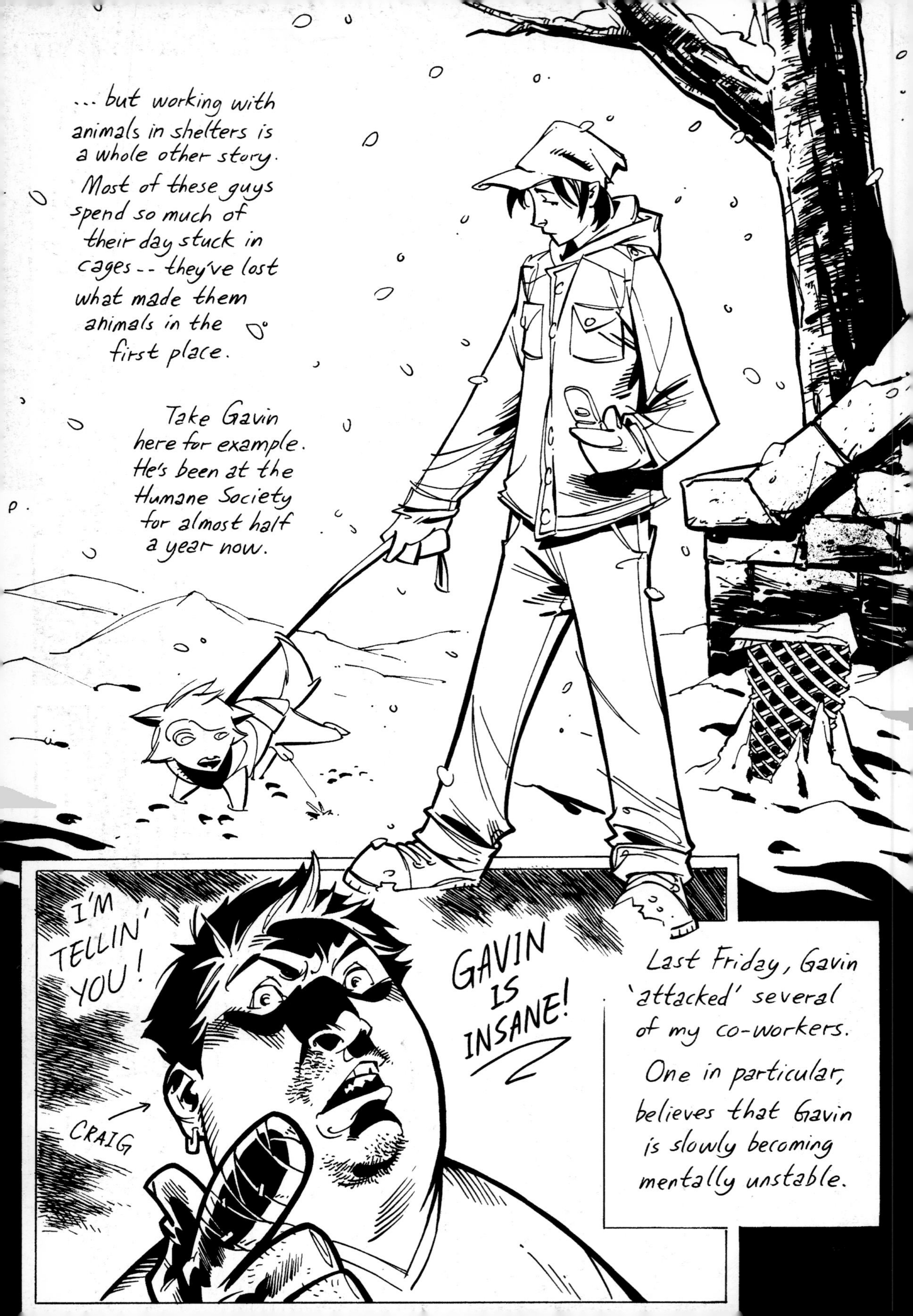
... but working with animals in shelters is a whole other story. Most of these guys spend so much of their day stuck in cages -- they've lost what made them animals in the first place.
Take Gavin here for example. He's been at the Humane Society for almost half a year now.
I'M TELLIN' YOU!
GAVIN IS INSANE!
CRAIG
Last Friday, Gavin 'attacked' several of my co-workers.
One in particular, believes that Gavin is slowly becoming mentally unstable.

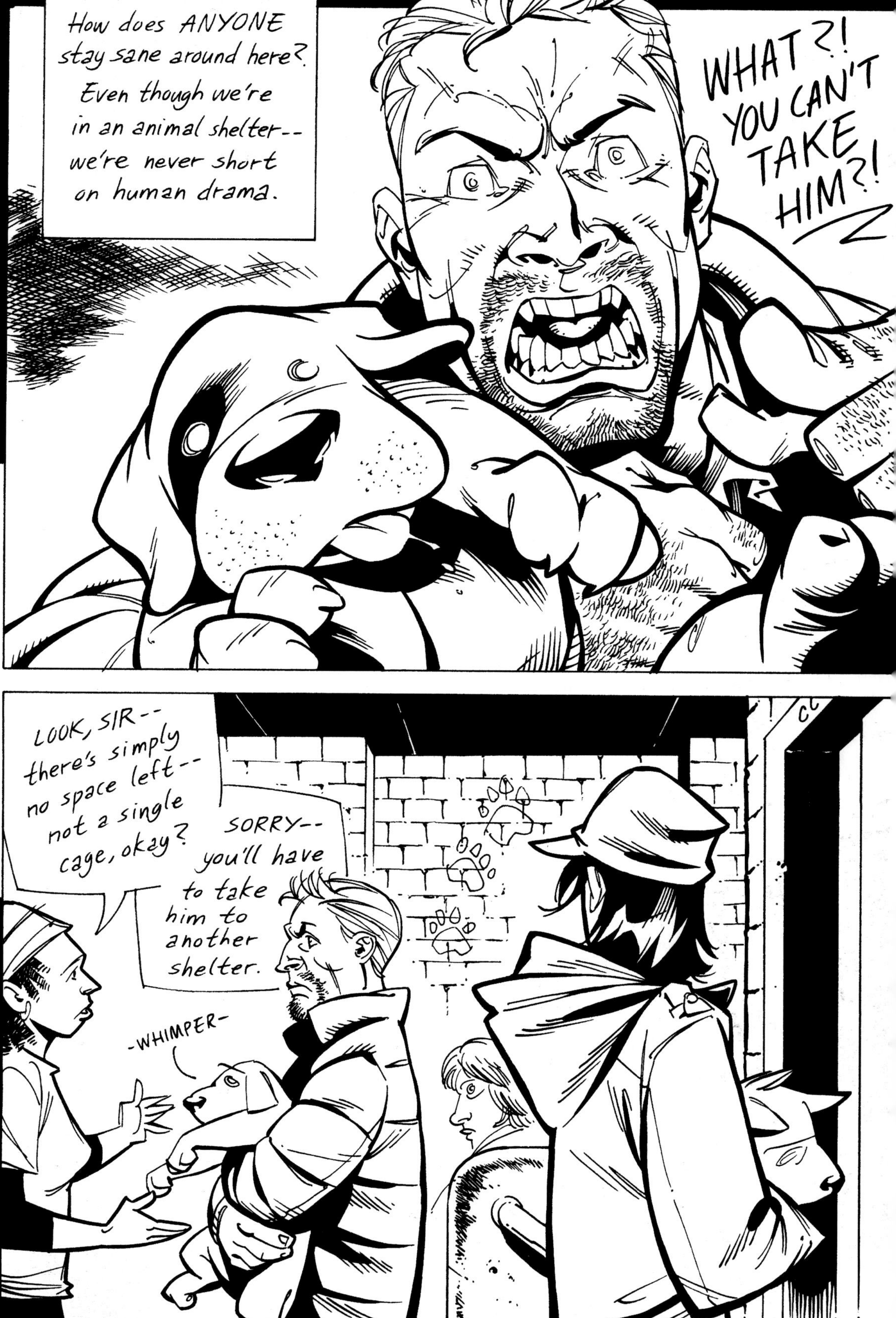
How does ANYONE stay sane around here? Even though we're in an animal shelter-- we're never short on human drama.
WHAT?! YOU CAN'T TAKE HIM?!
LOOK, SIR-- there's simply no space left-- not a single cage, okay?
SORRY-- you'll have to take him to another shelter.
-WHIMPER-

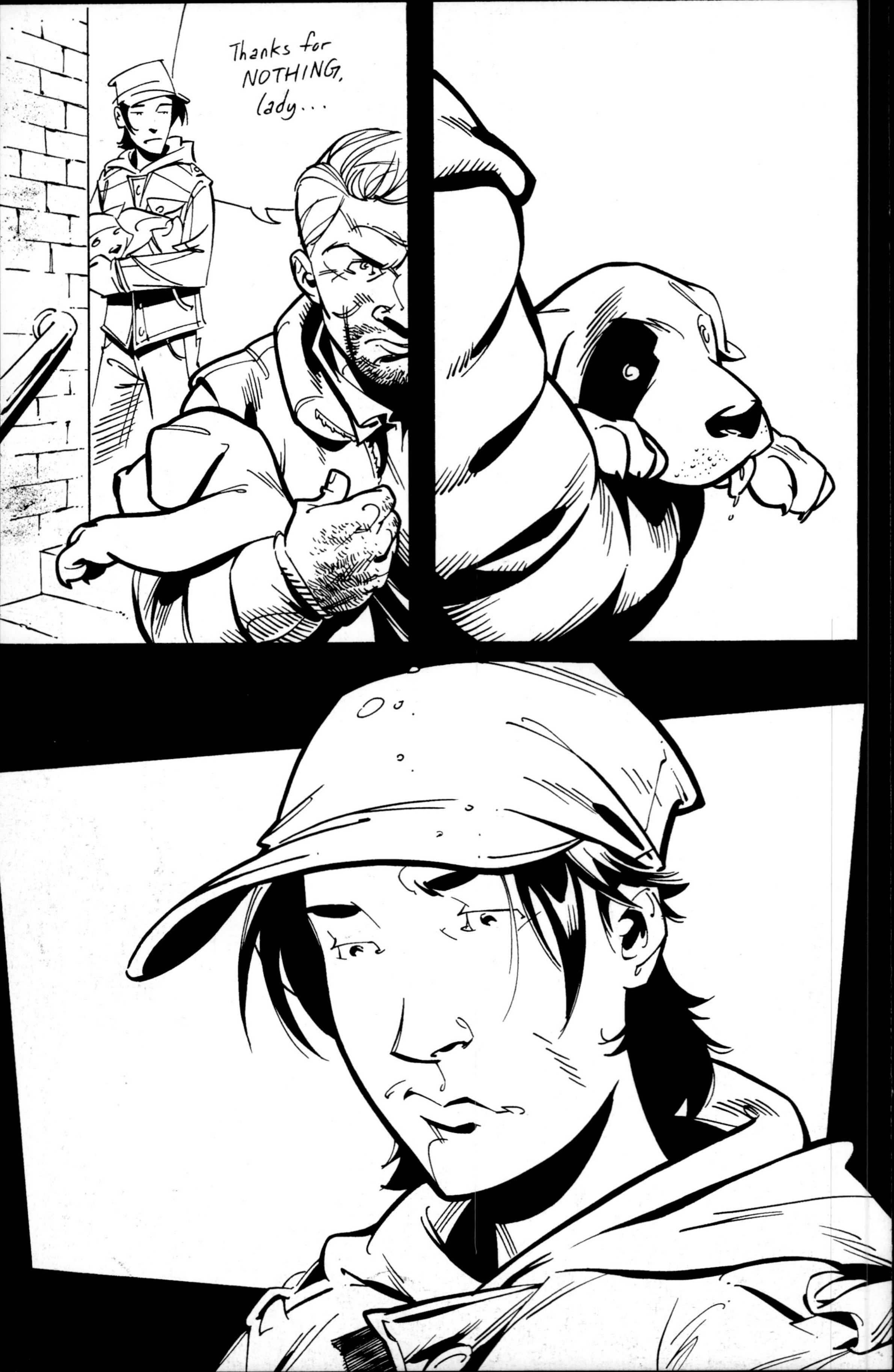
Thanks for NOTHING, lady...

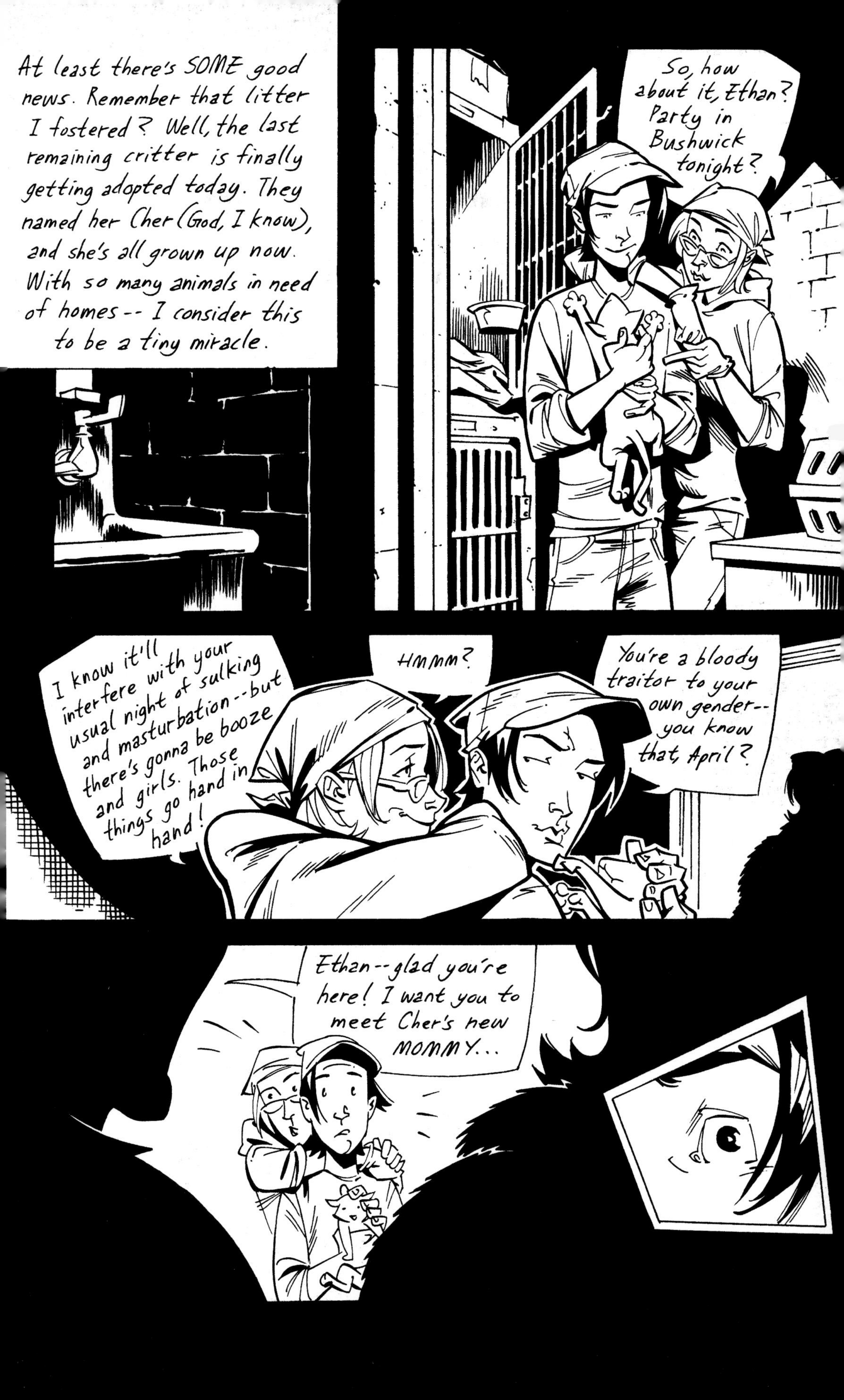
At least there's SOME good news. Remember that litter I fostered? Well, the last remaining critter is finally getting adopted today. They named her Cher (God, I know), and she's all grown up now. With so many animals in need of homes -- I consider this to be a tiny miracle.
So, how about it, Ethan? Party in Bushwick tonight?
I know it'll interfere with your usual night of sulking and masturbation--but there's gonna be booze and girls. Those things go hand in hand!
HMMM?
You're a bloody traitor to your own gender-- you know that, April?
Ethan--glad you're here! I want you to meet Cher's new MOMMY...

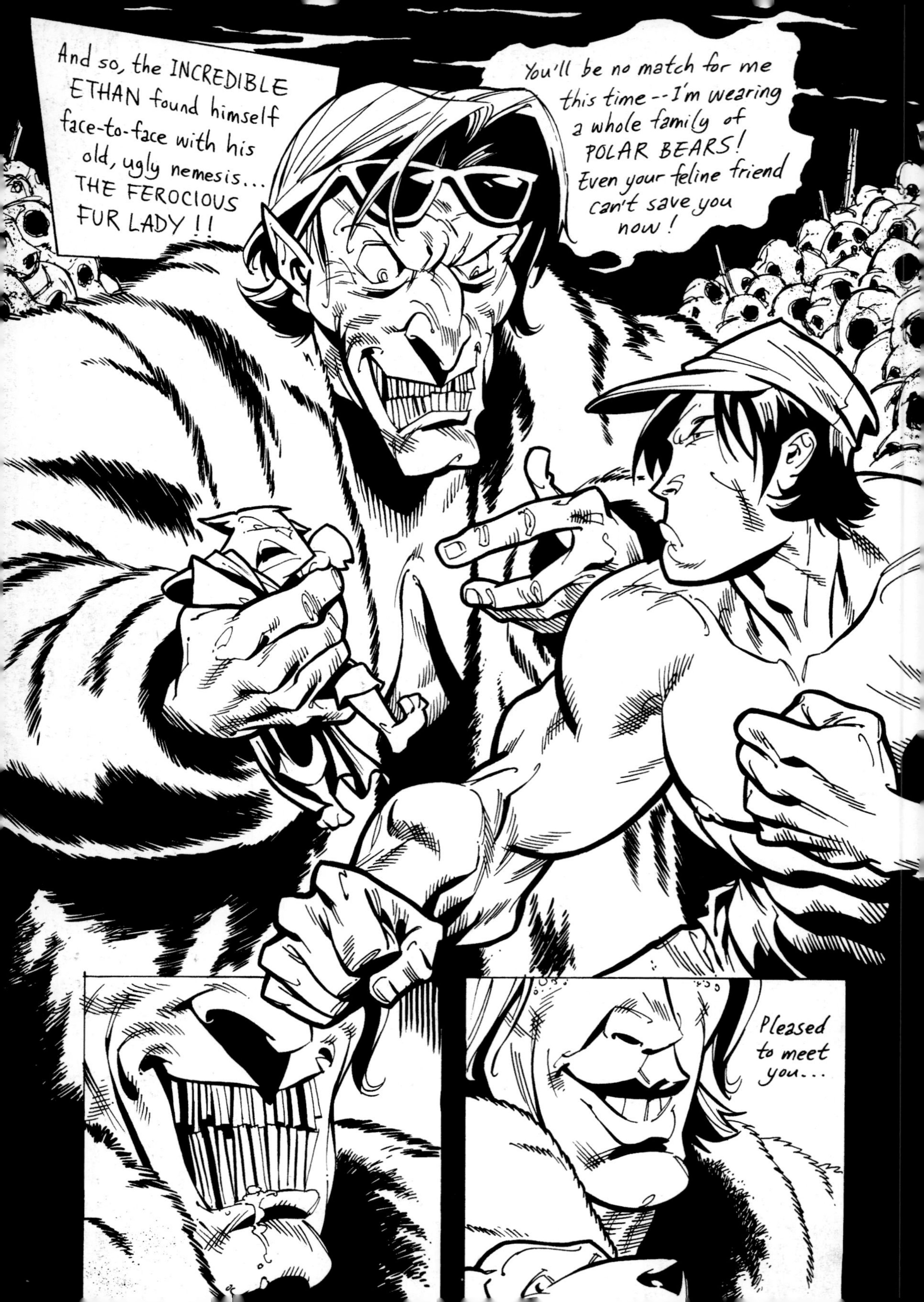
And so, the INCREDIBLE ETHAN found himself face-to-face with his old, ugly nemesis... THE FEROCIOUS FUR LADY!!
You'll be no match for me this time--I'm wearing a whole family of POLAR BEARS! Even your feline friend can't save you now!
Pleased to meet you...

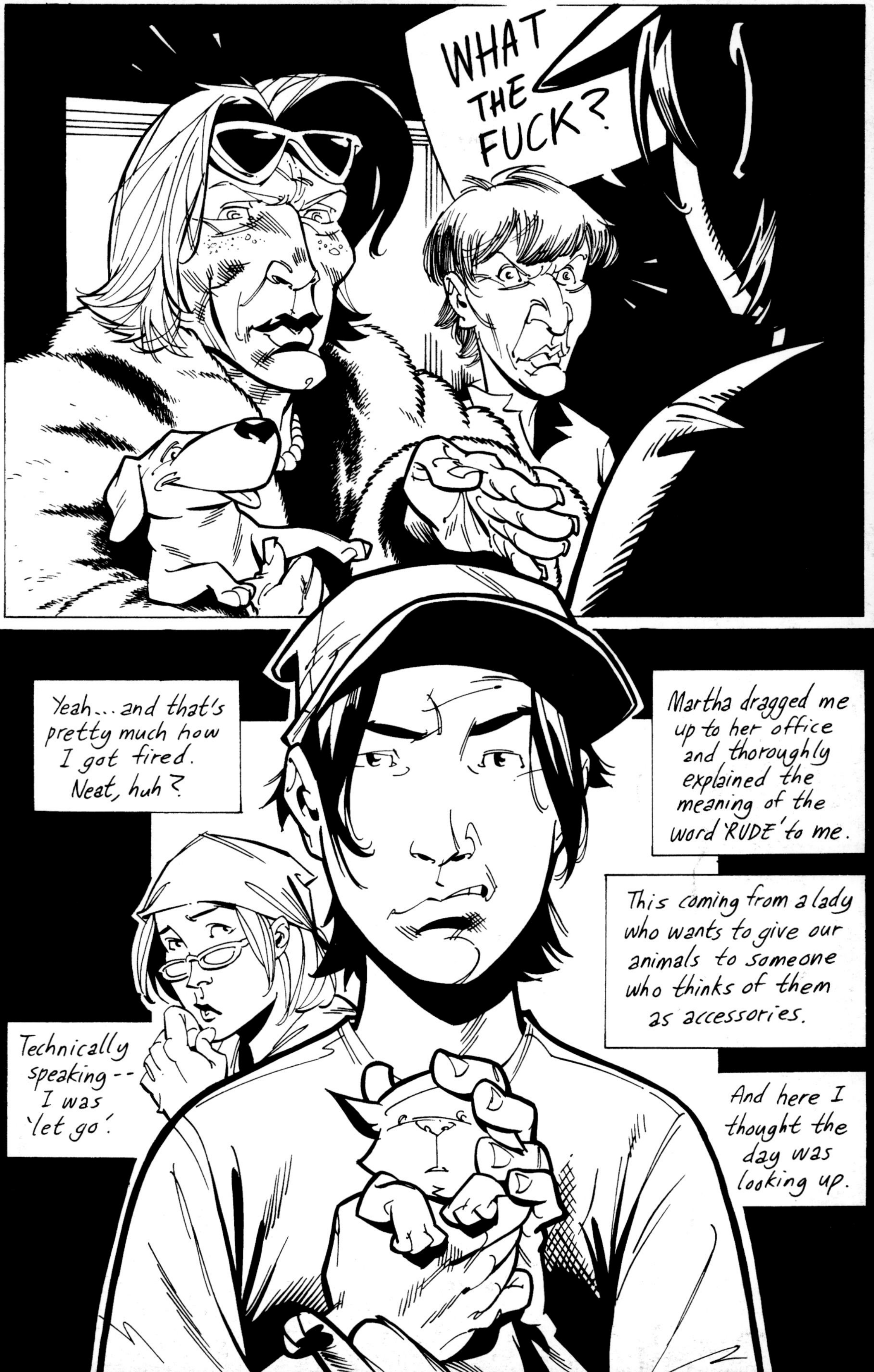

WHAT THE FUCK?
Yeah... and that's pretty much how I got fired. Neat, huh?
Martha dragged me up to her office and thoroughly explained the meaning of the word 'RUDE' to me.
This coming from a lady who wants to give our animals to someone who thinks of them as accessories.
Technically speaking -- I was 'let go'.
And here I thought the day was looking up.

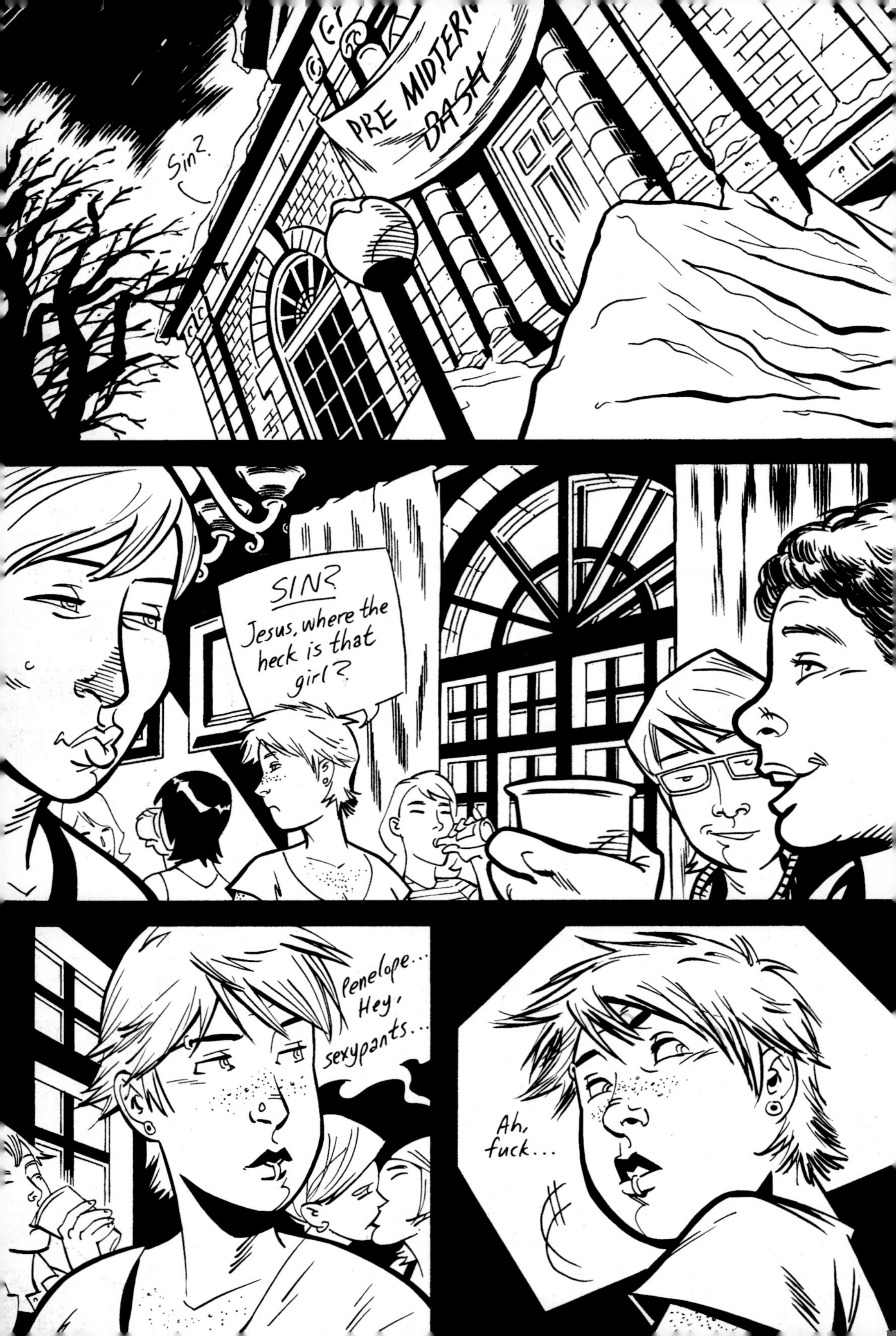
PRE MIDTERM BASH
Sin?
SIN?
Jesus, where the heck is that girl?
Penelope... Hey, sexypants...
Ah, fuck...

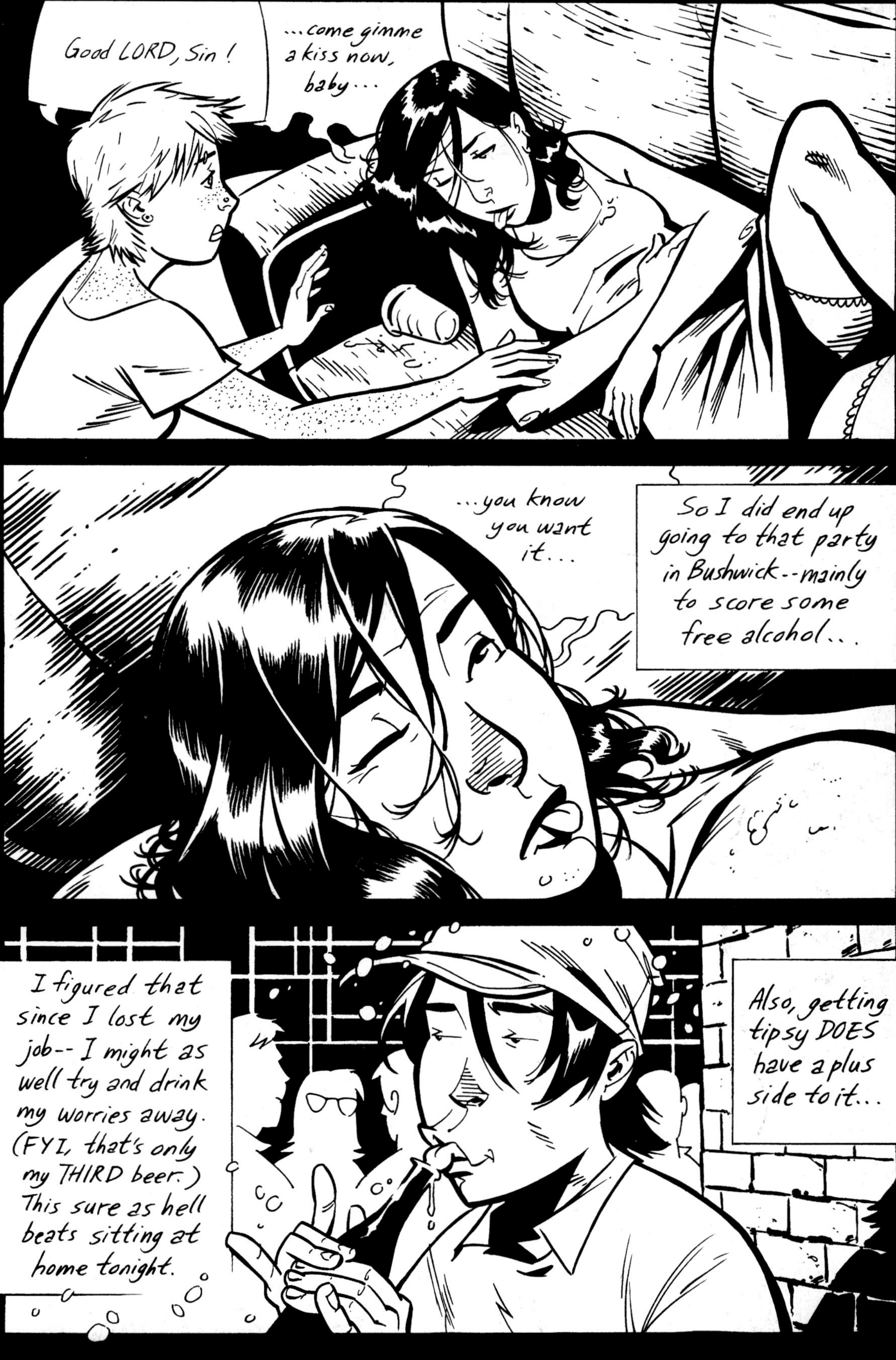
Good LORD, Sin!
...come gimme a kiss now, baby...
...you know you want it...
So I did end up going to that party in Bushwick--mainly to score some free alcohol...
I figured that since I lost my job-- I might as well try and drink my worries away. (FYI, that's only my THIRD beer.) This sure as hell beats sitting at home tonight.
Also, getting tipsy DOES have a plus side to it...

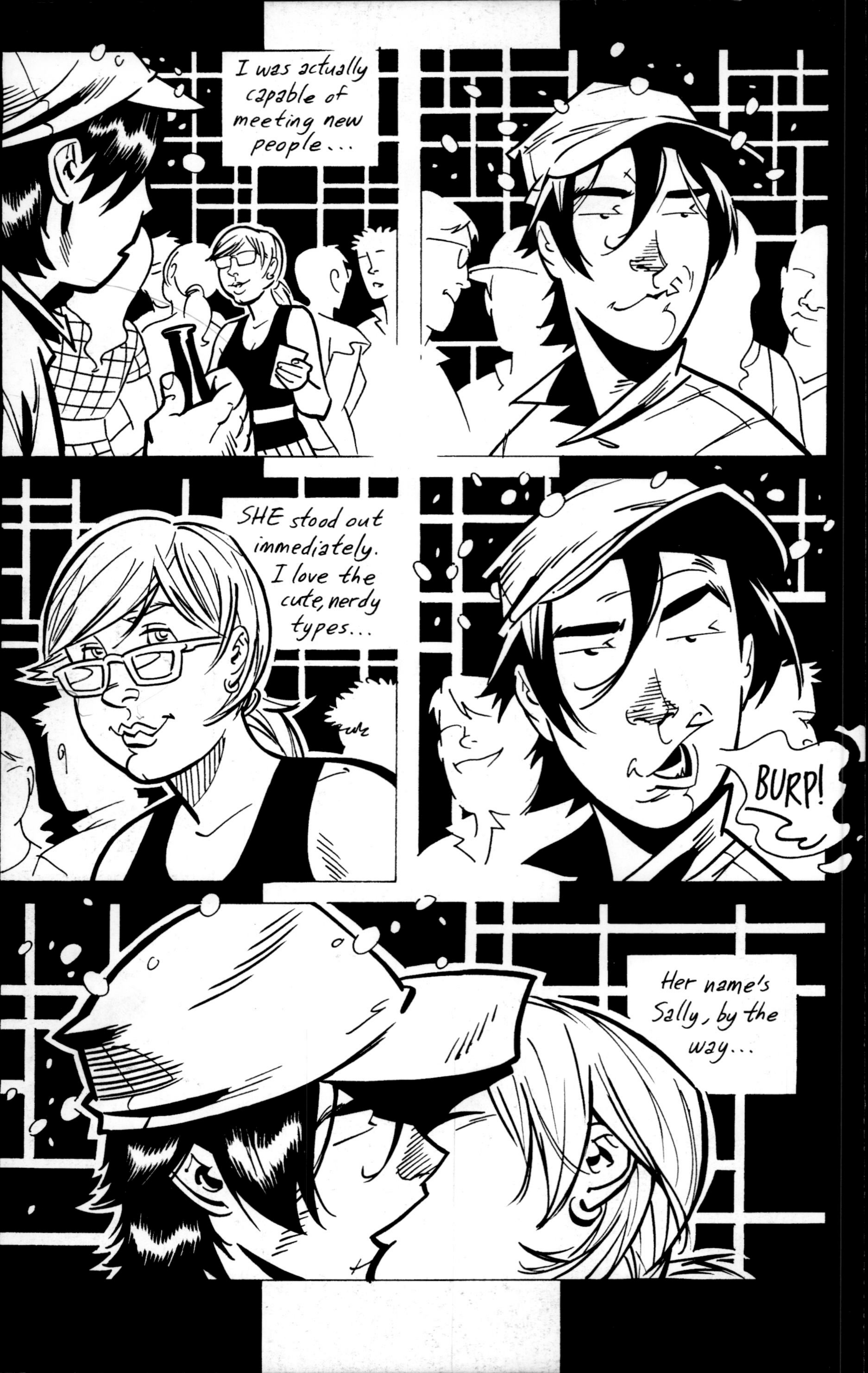
I was actually capable of meeting new people...
SHE stood out immediately. I love the cute, nerdy types...
BURP!
Her name's Sally, by the way...

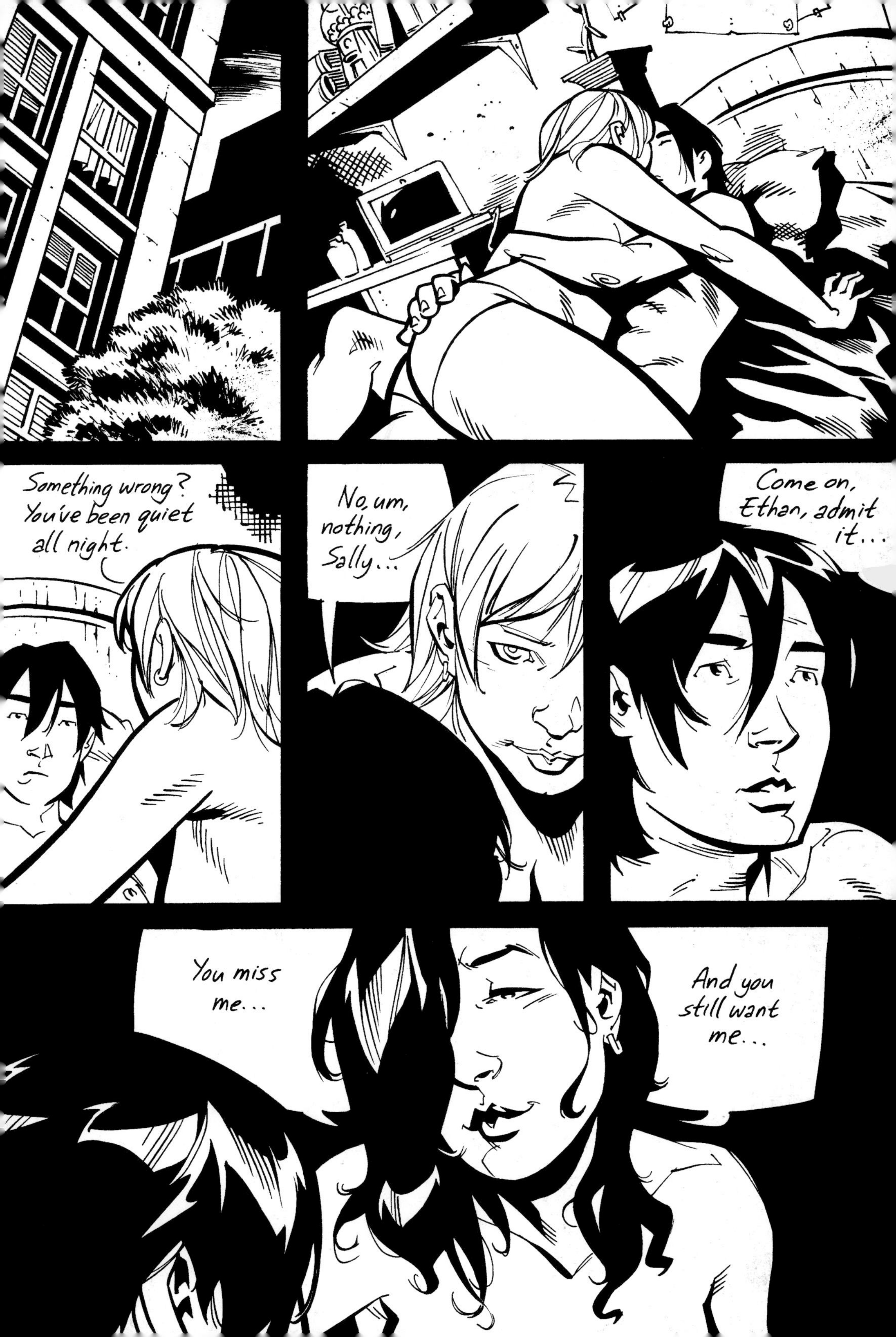
Something wrong? You've been quiet all night.
No, um, nothing, Sally...
Come on, Ethan, admit it...
You miss me...
And you still want me...

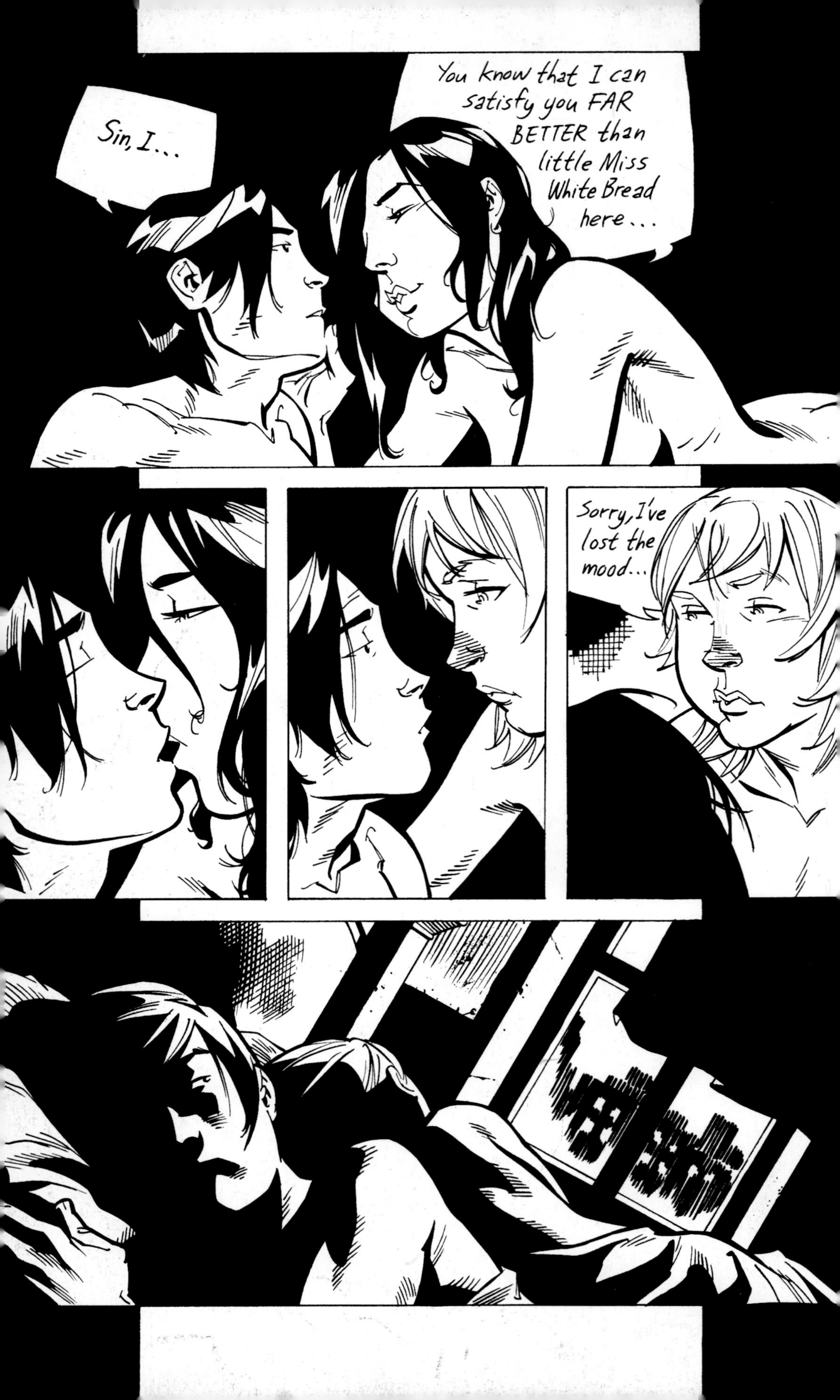

Sin, I...
You know that I can satisfy you FAR BETTER than little Miss White Bread here...
Sorry, I've lost the mood...

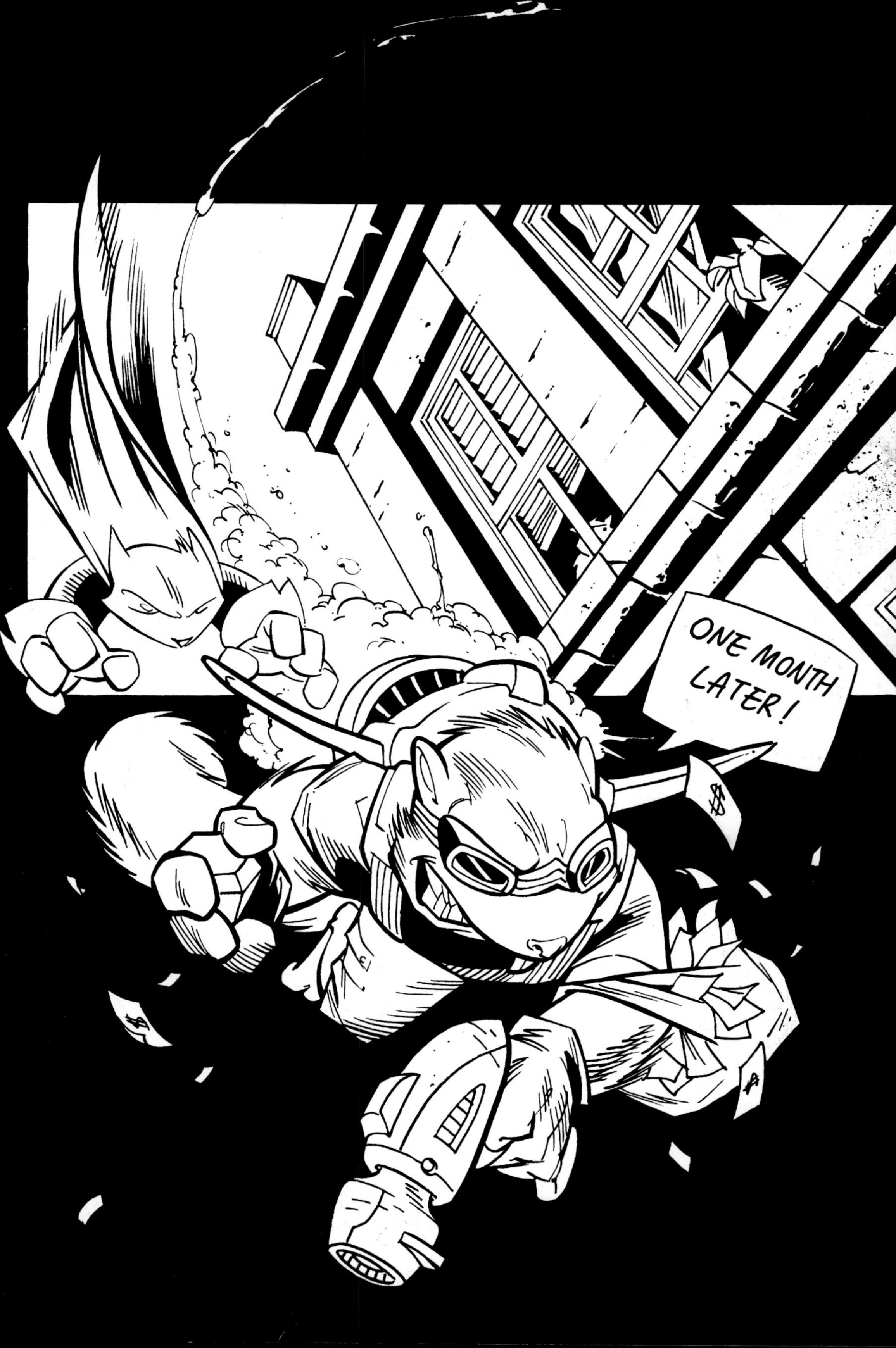
ONE MONTH LATER!

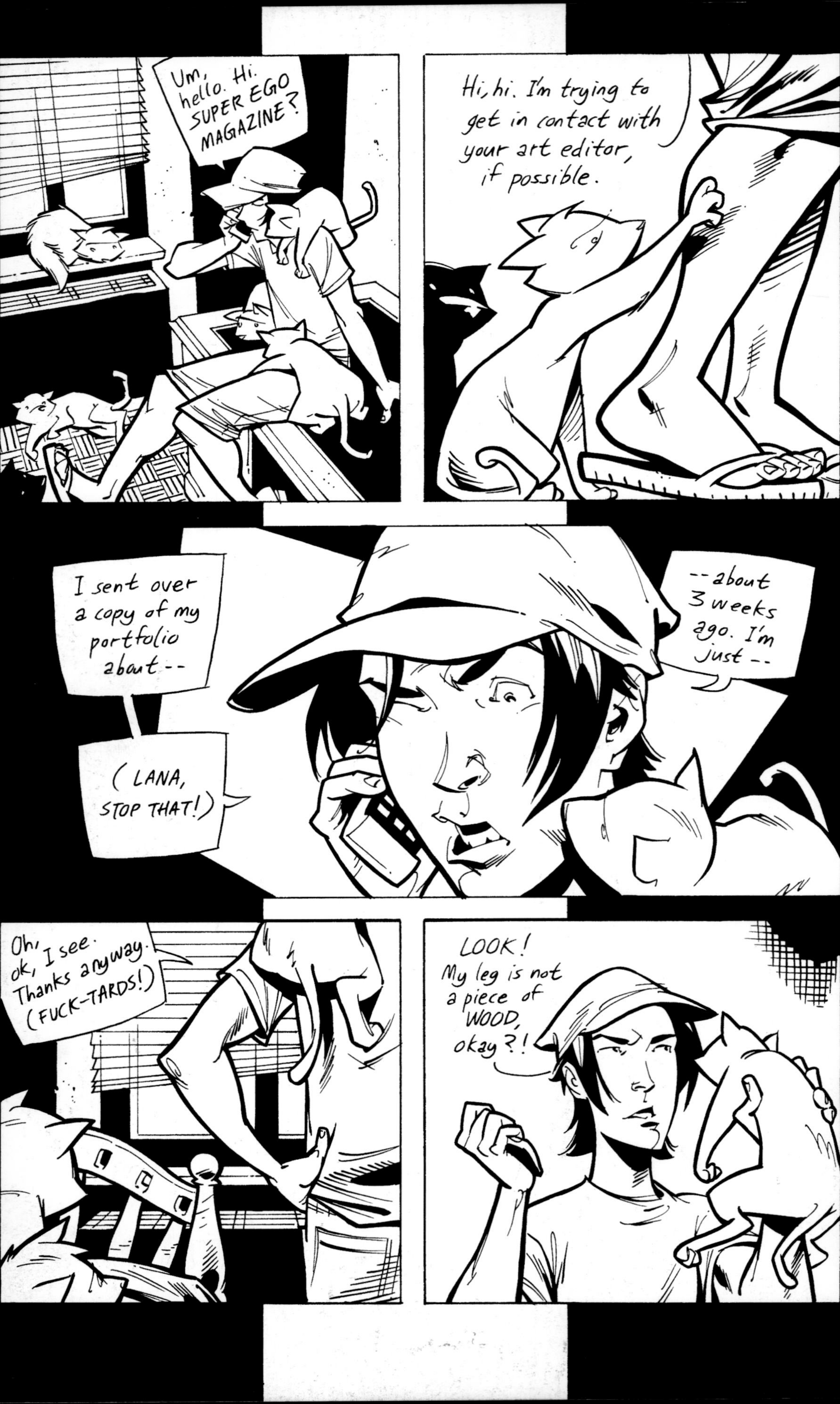
Um, hello. Hi. SUPER EGO MAGAZINE?
Hi, hi. I'm trying to get in contact with your art editor, if possible.
I sent over a copy of my portfolio about --
(LANA, STOP THAT!)
-- about 3 weeks ago. I'm just --
Oh, ok, I see. Thanks anyway. (FUCK-TARDS!)
LOOK! My leg is not a piece of WOOD, okay?!

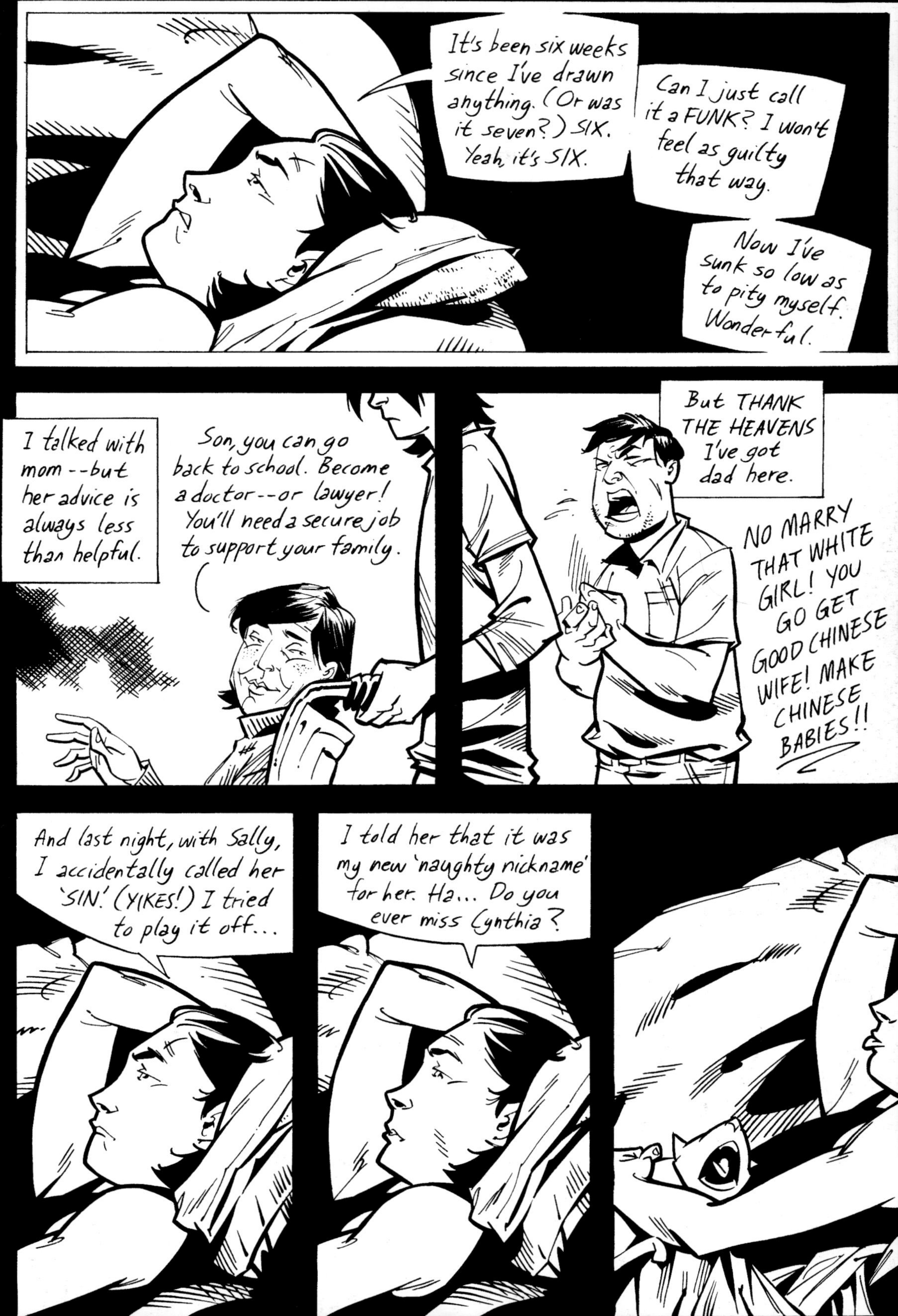
It's been six weeks since I've drawn anything. (Or was it seven?) SIX. Yeah, it's SIX.
Can I just call it a FUNK? I won't feel as guilty that way.
Now I've sunk so low as to pity myself. Wonderful.
I talked with mom --but her advice is always less than helpful.
Son, you can go back to school. Become a doctor--or lawyer! You'll need a secure job to support your family.
But THANK THE HEAVENS I've got dad here.
NO MARRY THAT WHITE GIRL! YOU GO GET GOOD CHINESE WIFE! MAKE CHINESE BABIES!!
And last night, with Sally, I accidentally called her 'SIN.' (YIKES!) I tried to play it off...
I told her that it was my new 'naughty nickname' for her. Ha... Do you ever miss Cynthia?

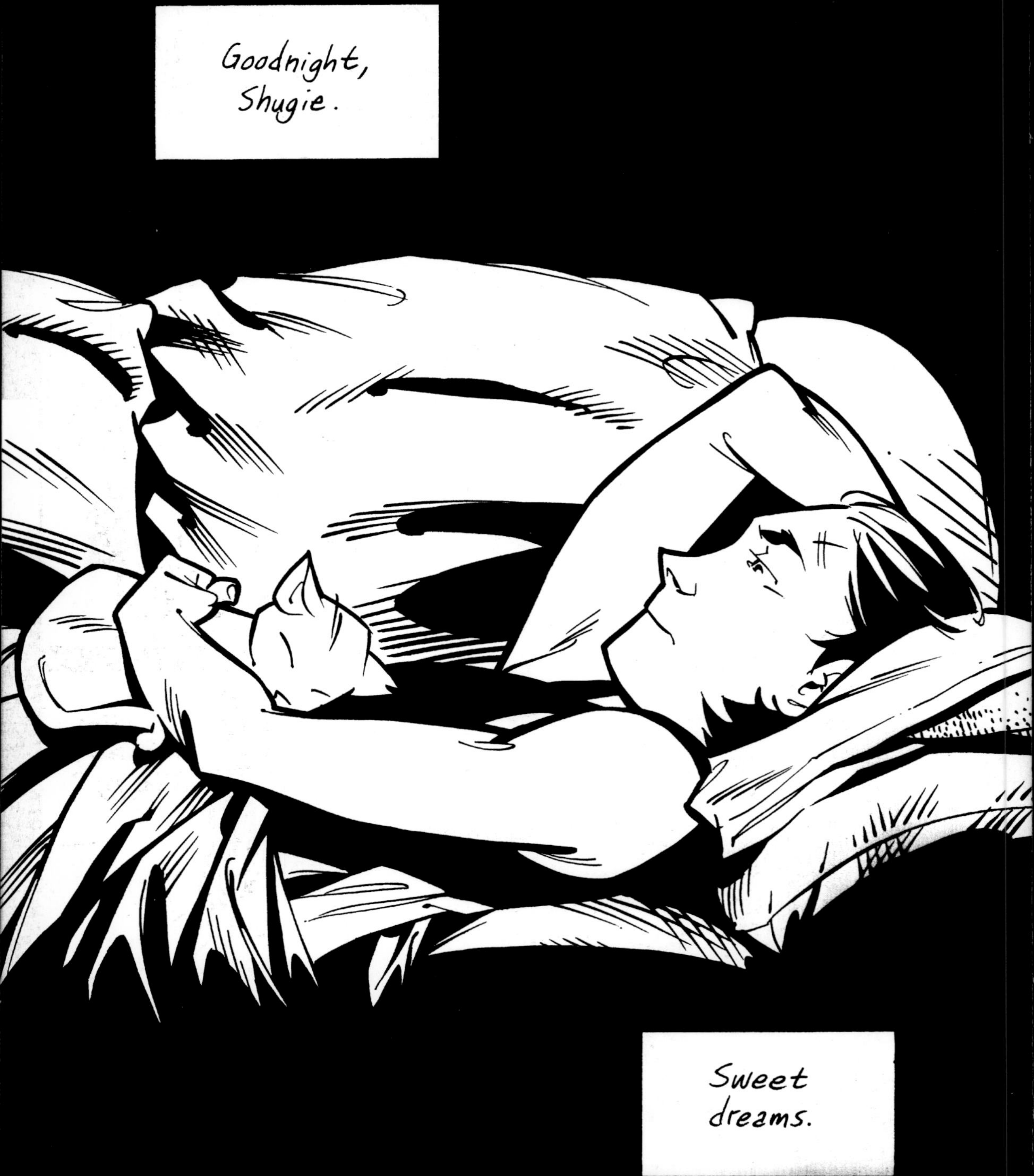
Goodnight, Shugie.
Sweet dreams.

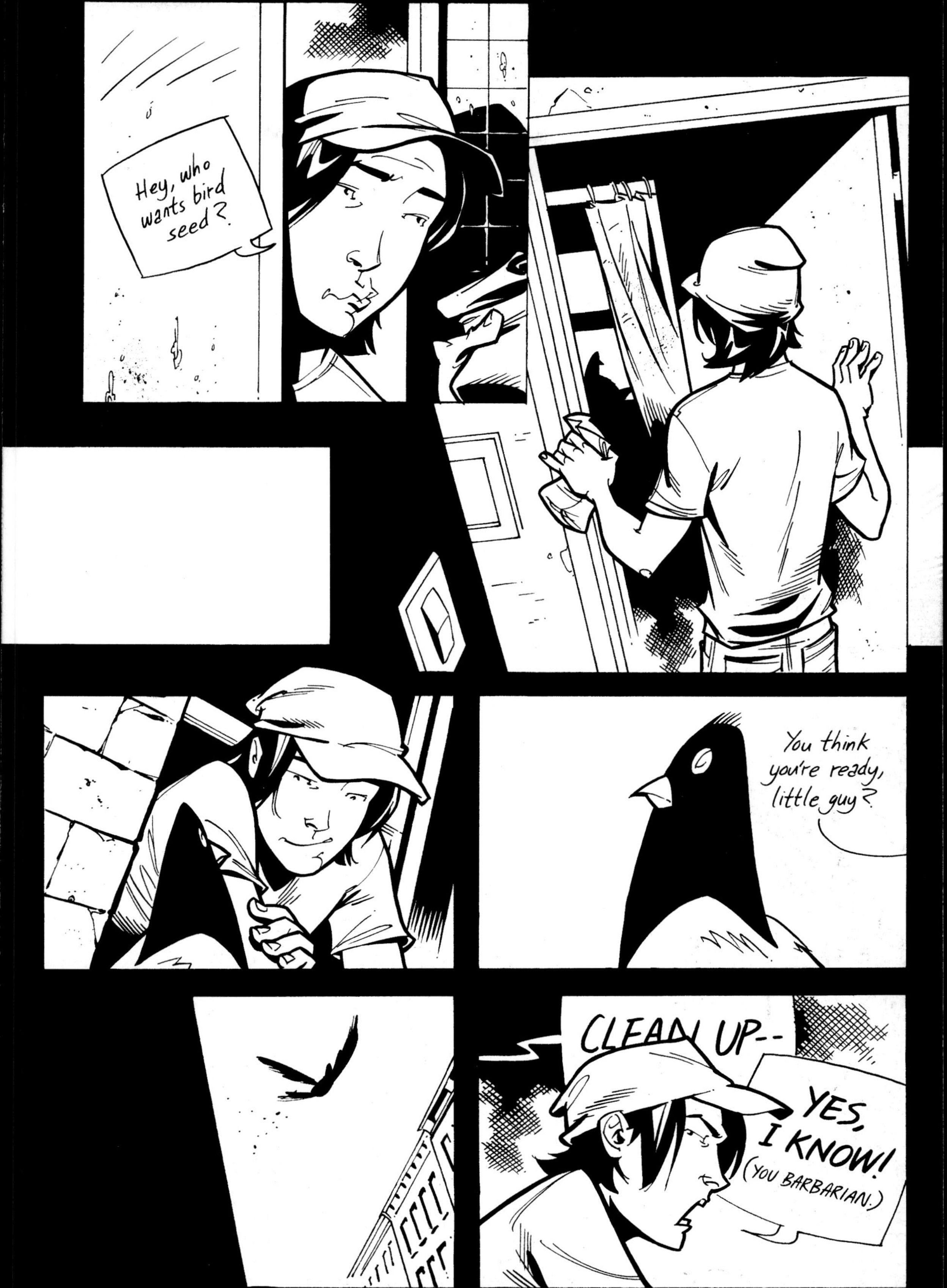
Hey, who wants bird seed?
You think you're ready, little guy?
CLEAN UP--
YES, I KNOW!
(YOU BARBARIAN.)

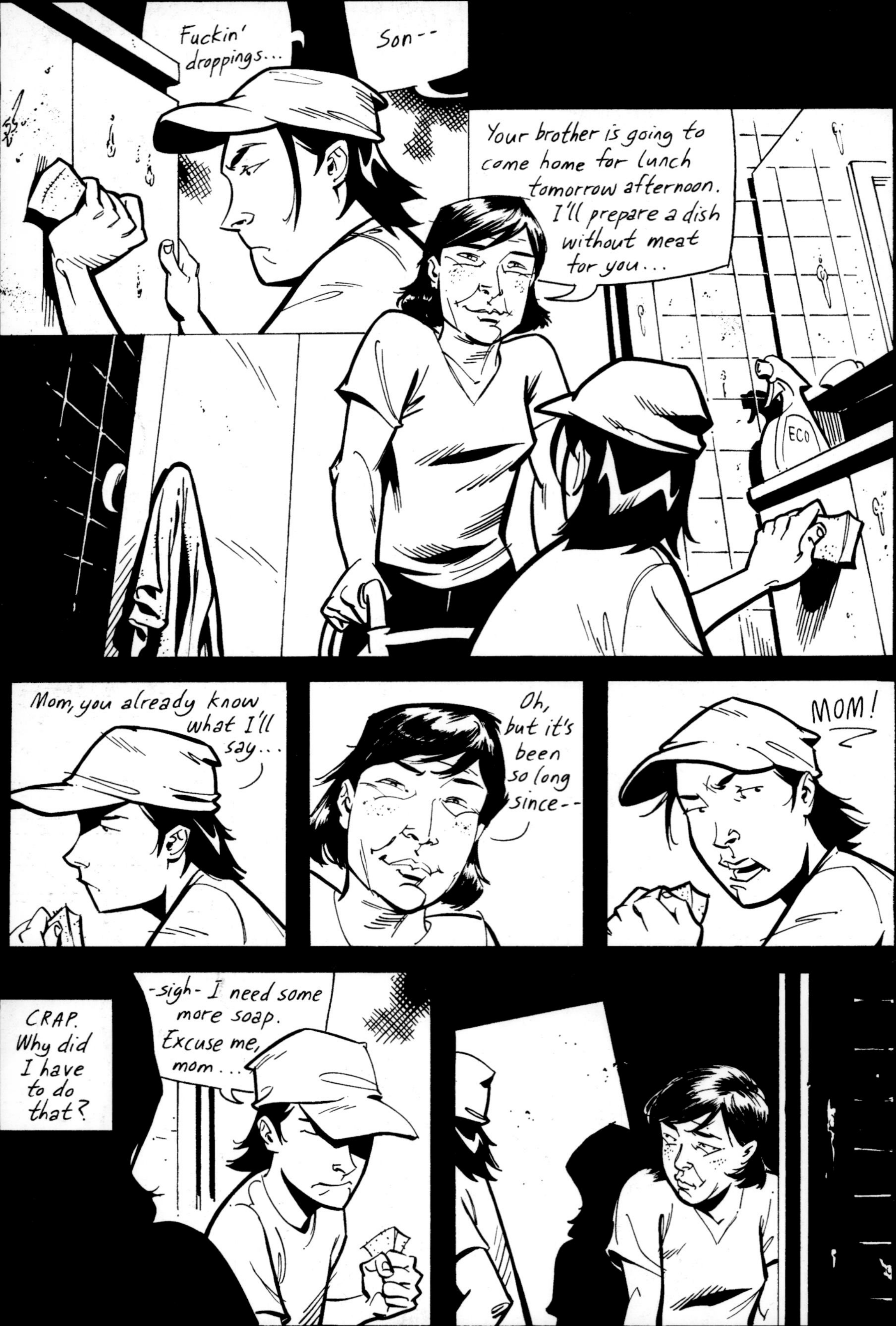
Fuckin' droppings...
Son--
Your brother is going to come home for lunch tomorrow afternoon. I'll prepare a dish without meat for you...
ECO
Mom, you already know what I'll say...
Oh, but it's been so long since--
MOM!
CRAP. Why did I have to do that?
-sigh- I need some more soap. Excuse me, mom...

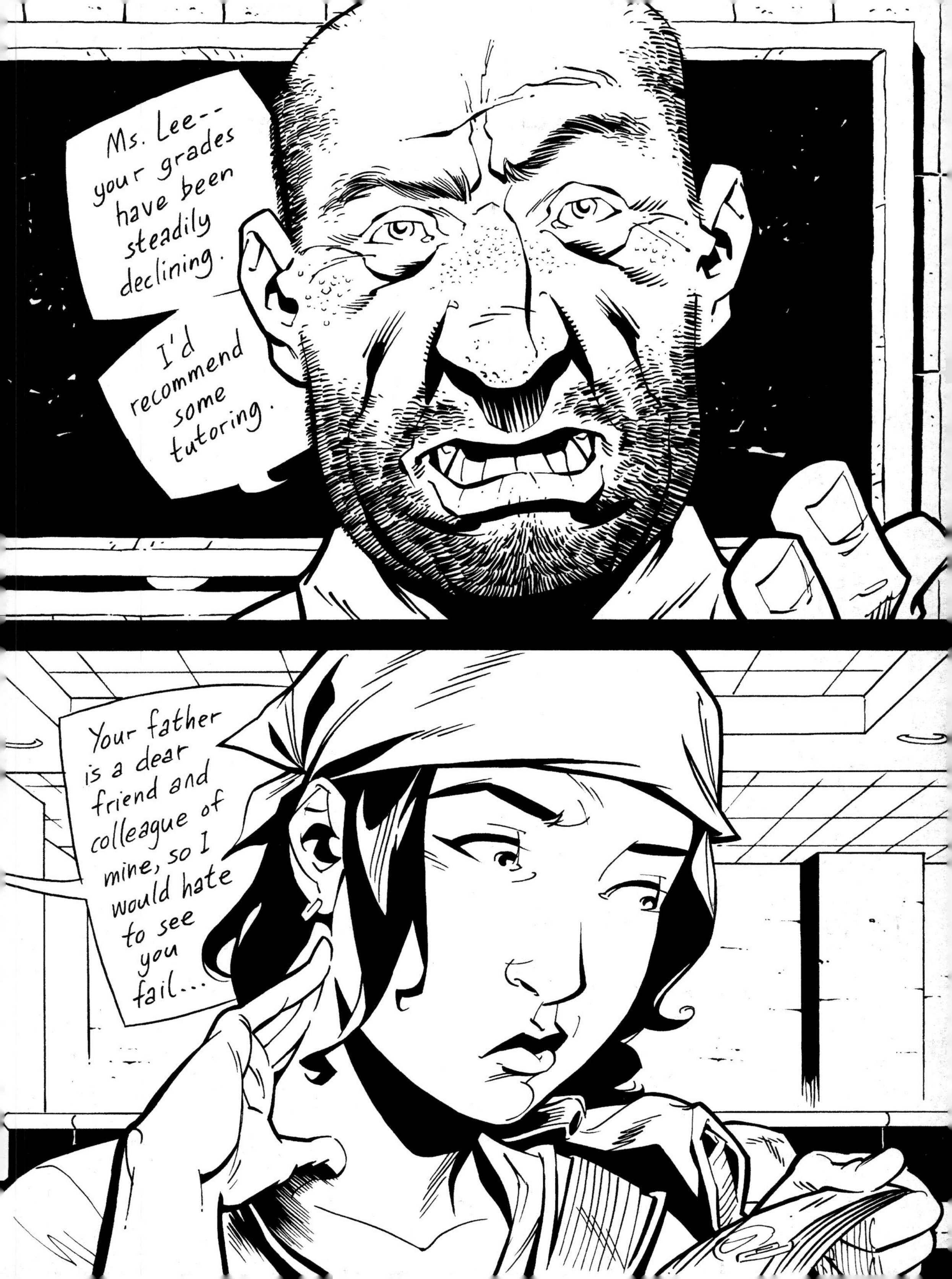
Ms. Lee-- your grades have been steadily declining.
I'd recommend some tutoring.
Your father is a dear friend and colleague of mine, so I would hate to see you fail...

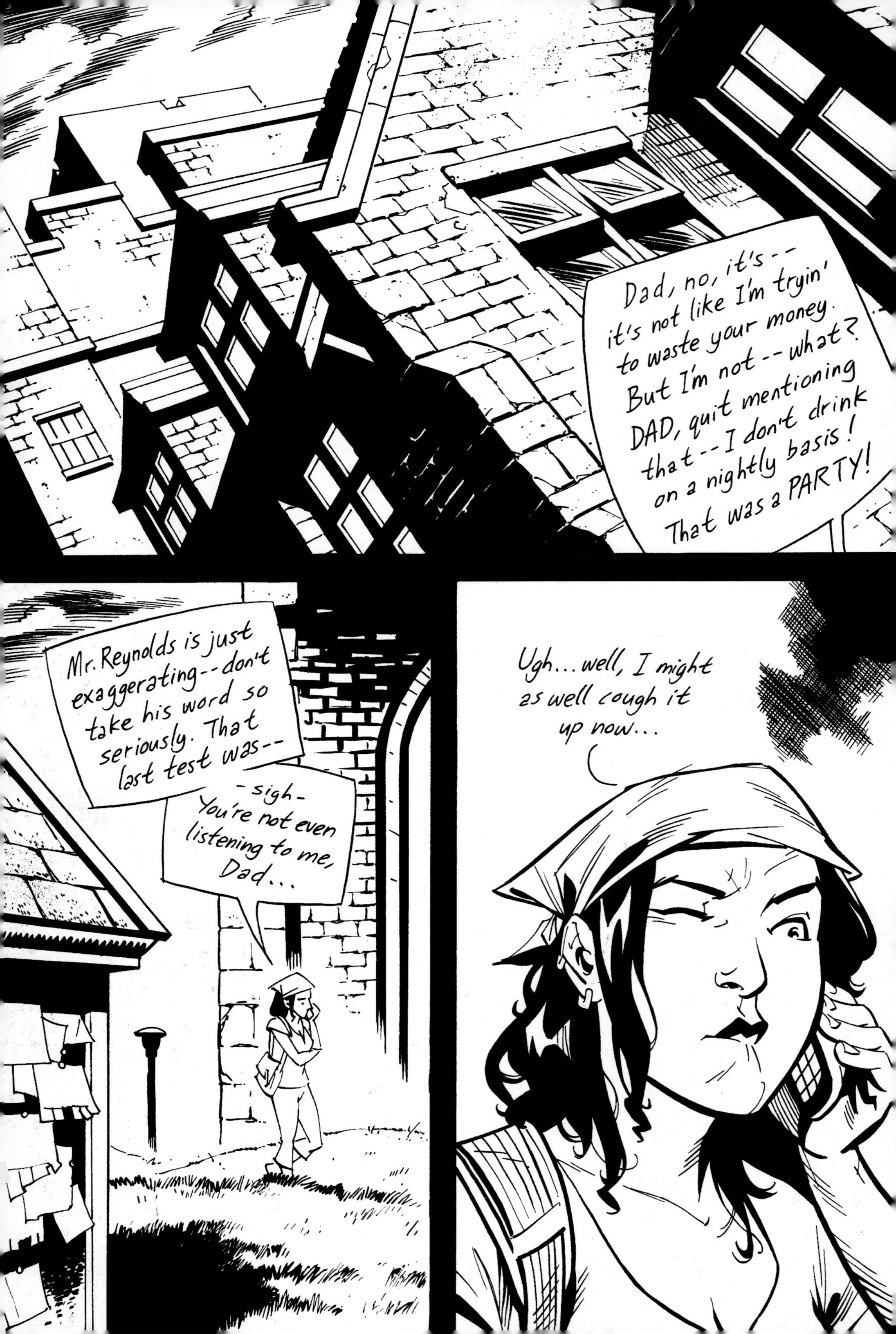
Dad, no, it's -- it's not like I'm tryin' to waste your money. But I'm not -- what? But I'm not -- what? DAD, quit mentioning that -- I don't drink on a nightly basis! That was a PARTY!
Mr. Reynolds is just exaggerating -- don't take his word so seriously. That last test was--
-sigh- You're not even listening to me, Dad...
Ugh... well, I might as well cough it up now...

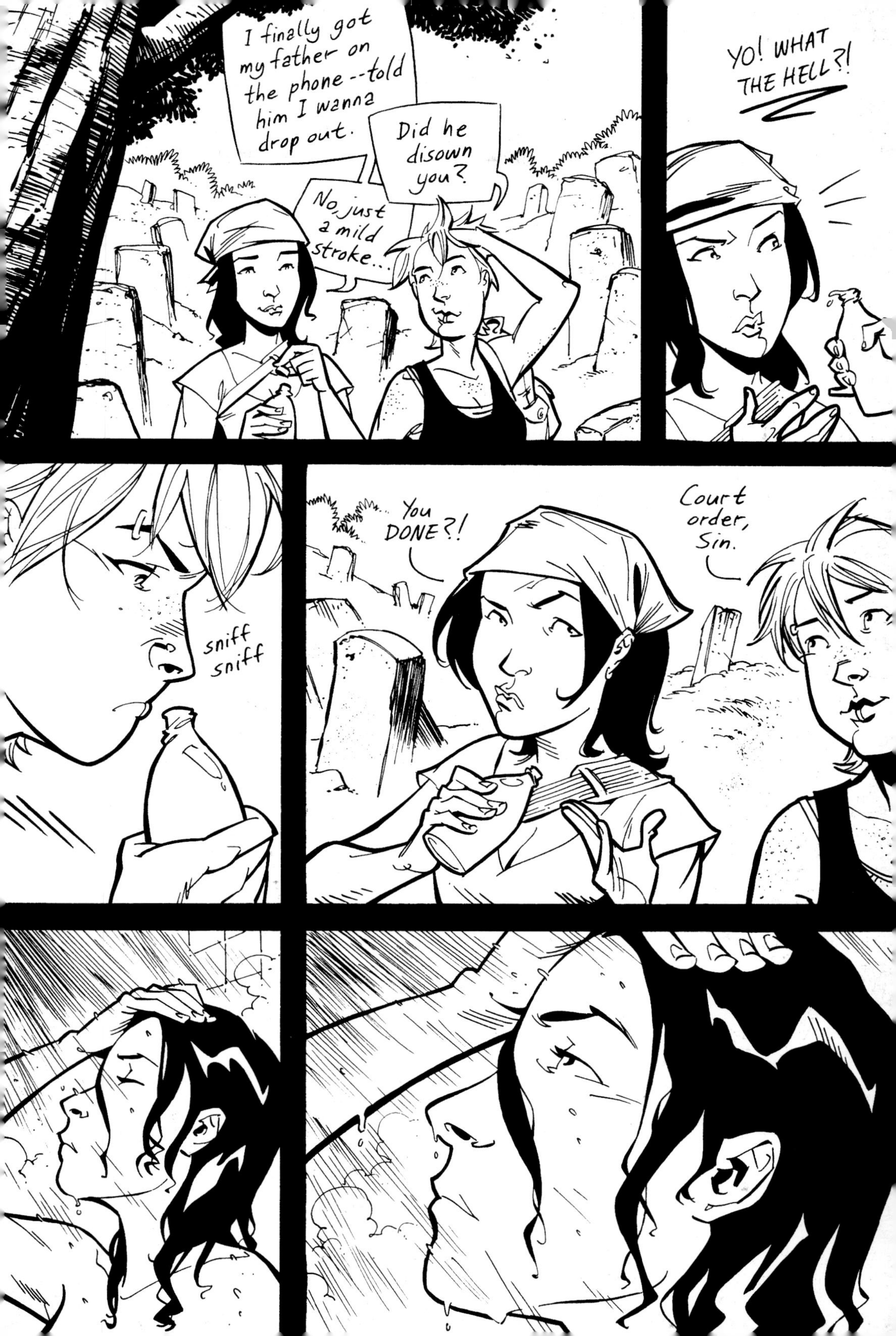
I finally got my father on the phone --told him I wanna drop out.
Did he disown you?
No, just a mild stroke...
YO! WHAT THE HELL?!
sniff sniff
You DONE?!
Court order, Sin.

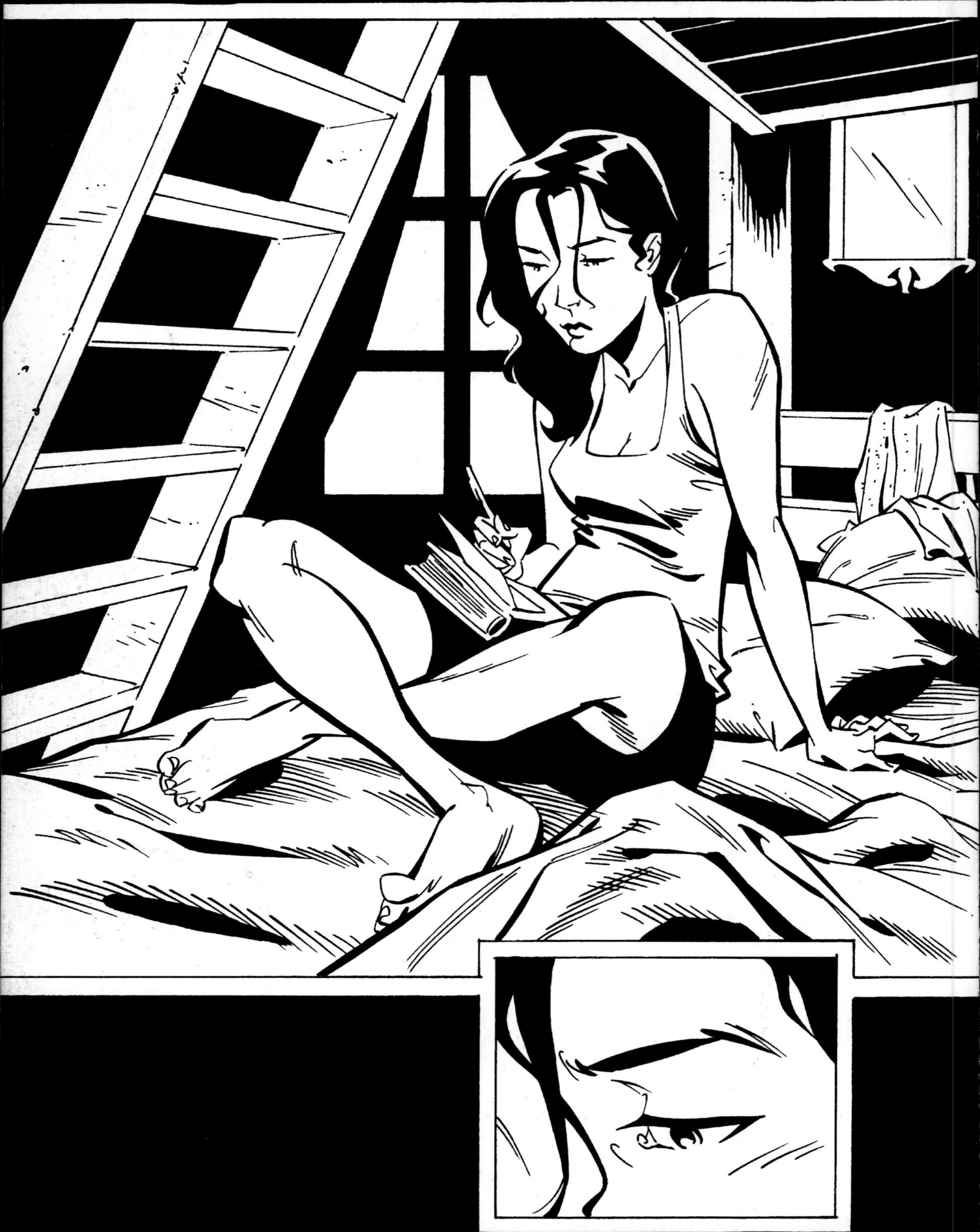

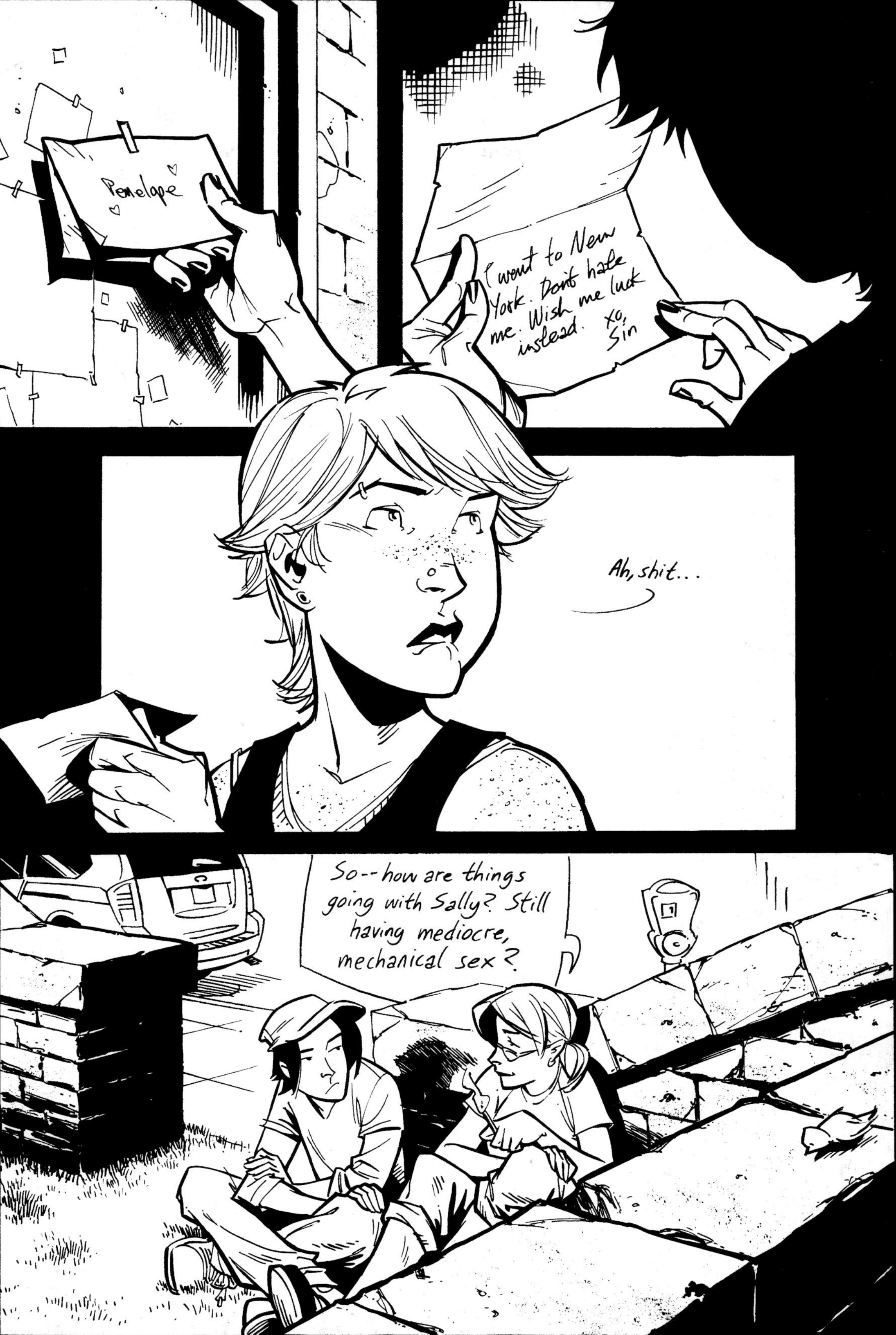
Penelope
I went to New York. Don't hate me. Wish me luck instead. xo, Sin
Ah, shit...
So--how are things going with Sally? Still having mediocre, mechanical sex?

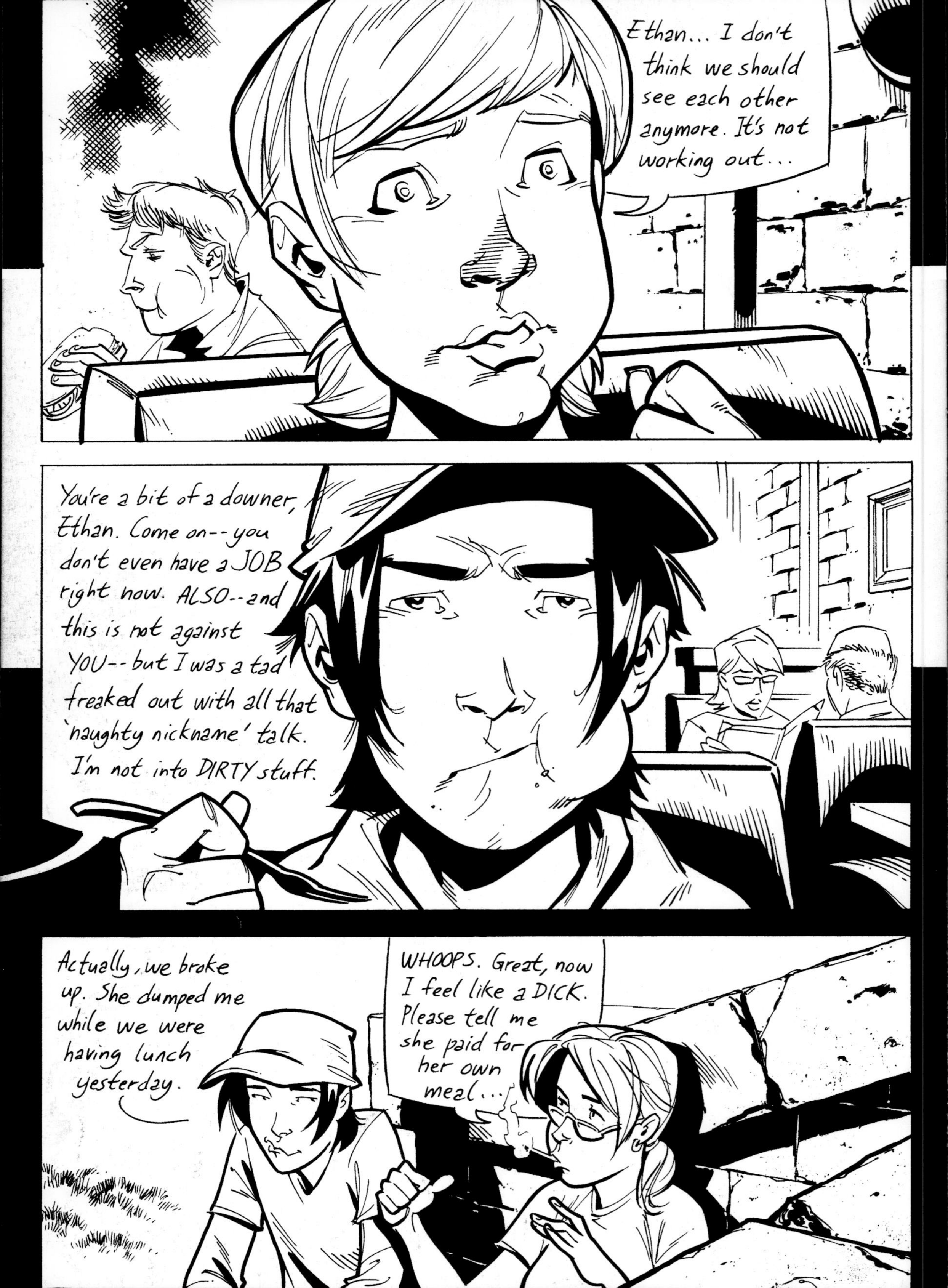

Ethan... I don't think we should see each other anymore. It's not working out...
You're a bit of a downer, Ethan. Come on--you don't even have a JOB right now. ALSO--and this is not against YOU--but I was a tad freaked out with all that 'naughty nickname' talk. I'm not into DIRTY stuff.
Actually, we broke up. She dumped me while we were having lunch yesterday.
WHOOPS. Great, now I feel like a DICK. Please tell me she paid for her own meal...

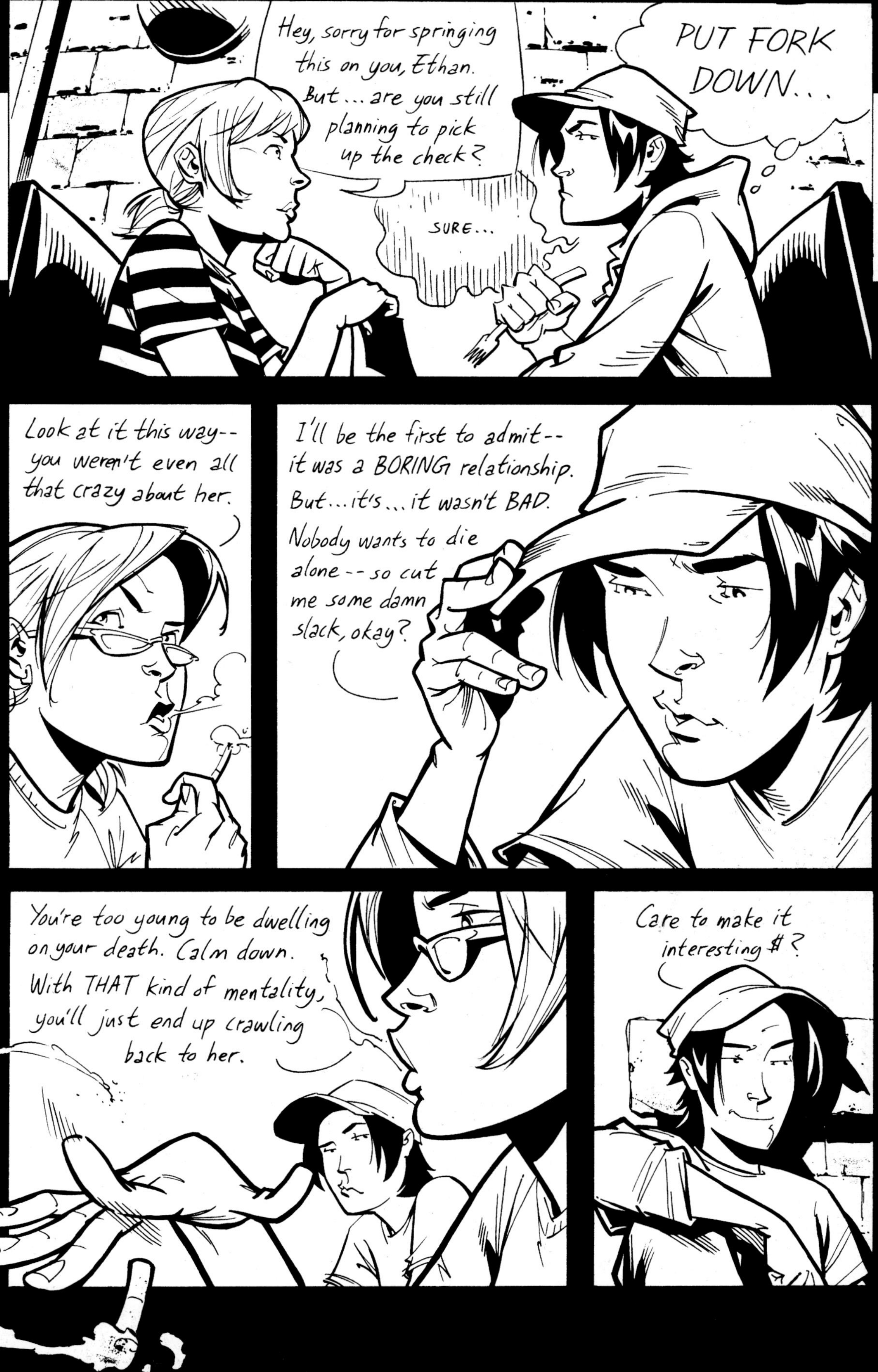
Hey, sorry for springing this on you, Ethan. But... are you still planning to pick up the check?
SURE...
PUT FORK DOWN...
Look at it this way-- you weren't even all that crazy about her.
I'll be the first to admit-- it was a BORING relationship. But...it's... it wasn't BAD. Nobody wants to die alone -- so cut me some damn slack, okay?
You're too young to be dwelling on your death. Calm down. With THAT kind of mentality, you'll just end up crawling back to her.
Care to make it interesting $?

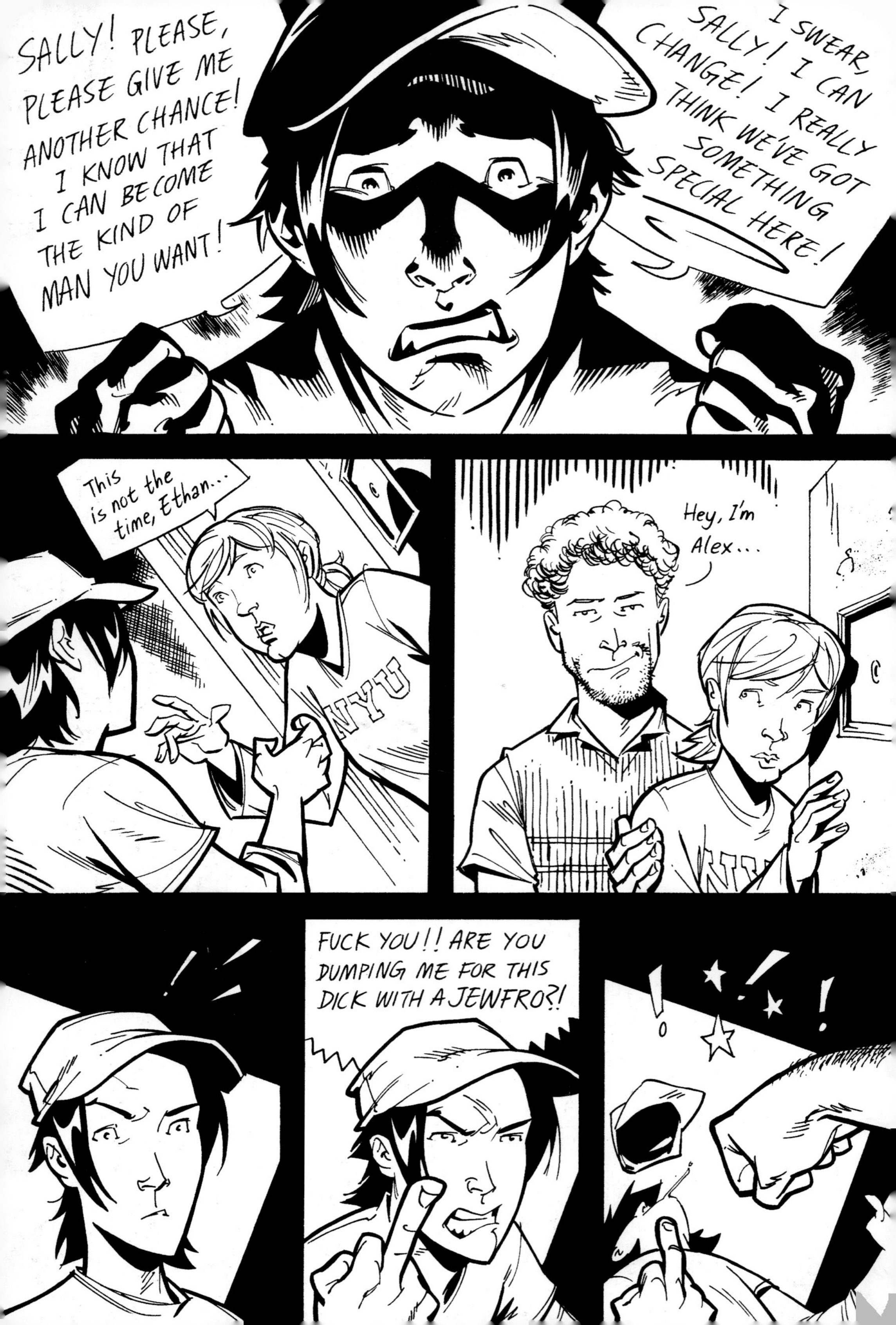
SALLY! PLEASE, PLEASE GIVE ME ANOTHER CHANCE! I KNOW THAT I CAN BECOME THE KIND OF MAN YOU WANT!
I SWEAR, SALLY! I CAN CHANGE! I REALLY THINK WE'VE GOT SOMETHING SPECIAL HERE!
This is not the time, Ethan...
Hey, I'm Alex...
FUCK YOU!! ARE YOU DUMPING ME FOR THIS DICK WITH A JEWFRO?!

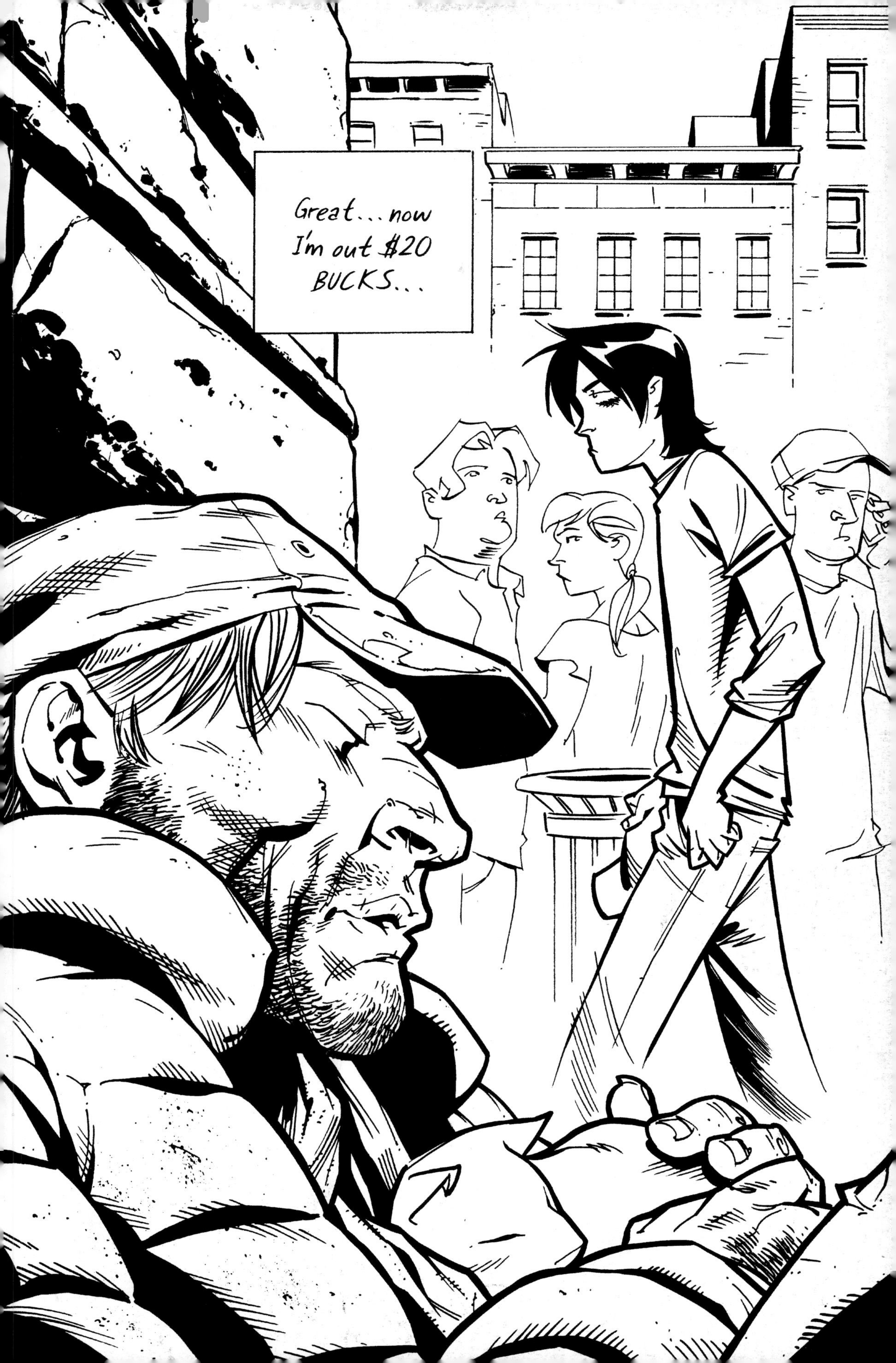
Great...now I'm out $20 BUCKS...

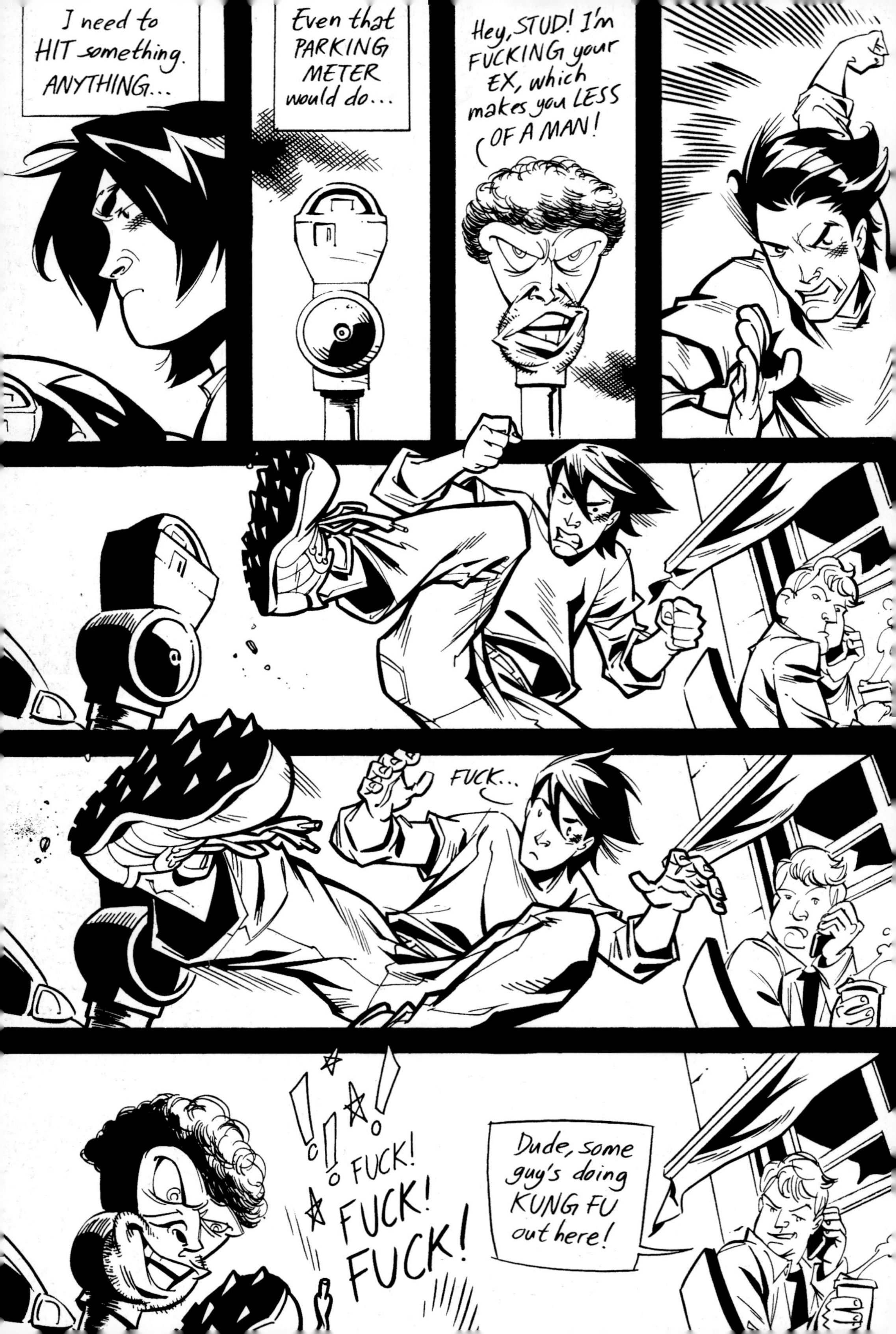
I need to HIT something. ANYTHING...
Even that PARKING METER would do...
Hey, STUD! I'm FUCKING your EX, which makes you LESS OF A MAN!
FUCK...
FUCK! FUCK! FUCK!
Dude, some guy's doing KUNG FU out here!

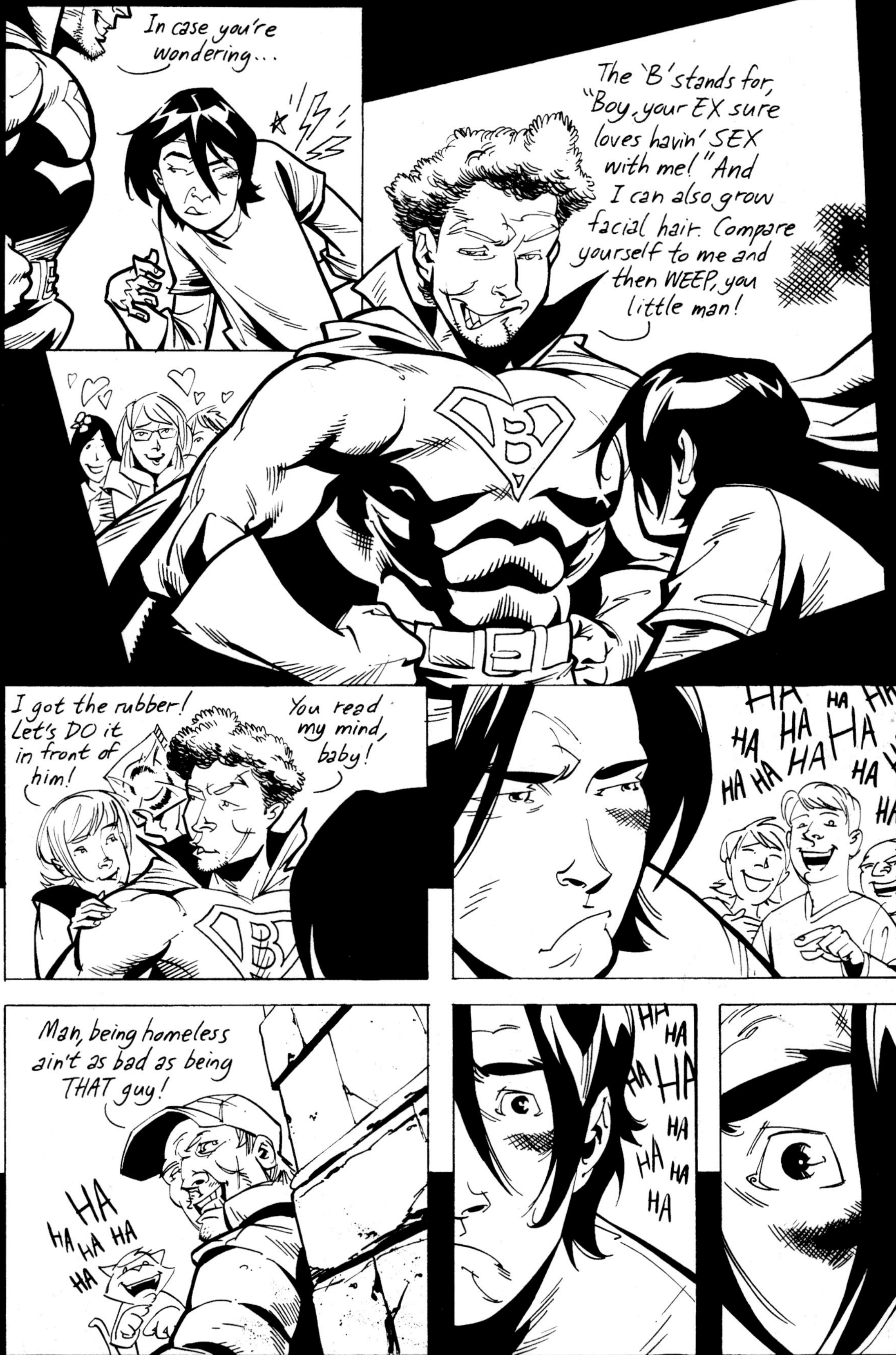
In case you're wondering...
The 'B' stands for, "Boy, your EX sure loves havin' SEX with me!" And I can also grow facial hair. Compare yourself to me and then WEEP, you little man!
I got the rubber! Let's DO it in front of him!
You read my mind, baby!
HA HA HA HA HA HA HA HA HA HA HA HA
Man, being homeless ain't as bad as being THAT guy!
HA HA HA HA HA
HA HA HA HA HA HA HA HA HA

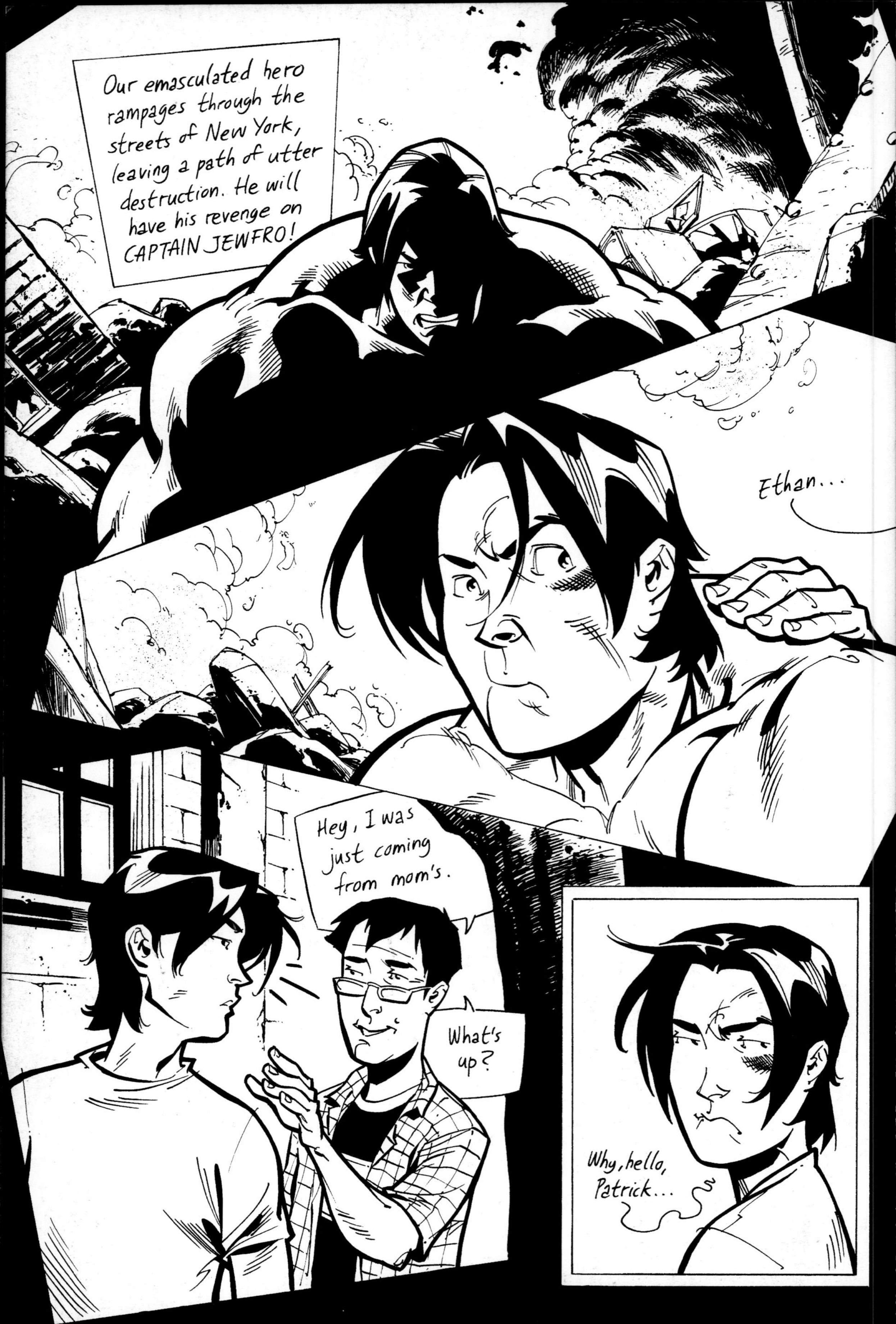
Our emasculated hero rampages through the streets of New York, leaving a path of utter destruction. He will have his revenge on CAPTAIN JEWFRO!
Ethan...
Hey, I was just coming from mom's.
What's up?
Why, hello, Patrick...

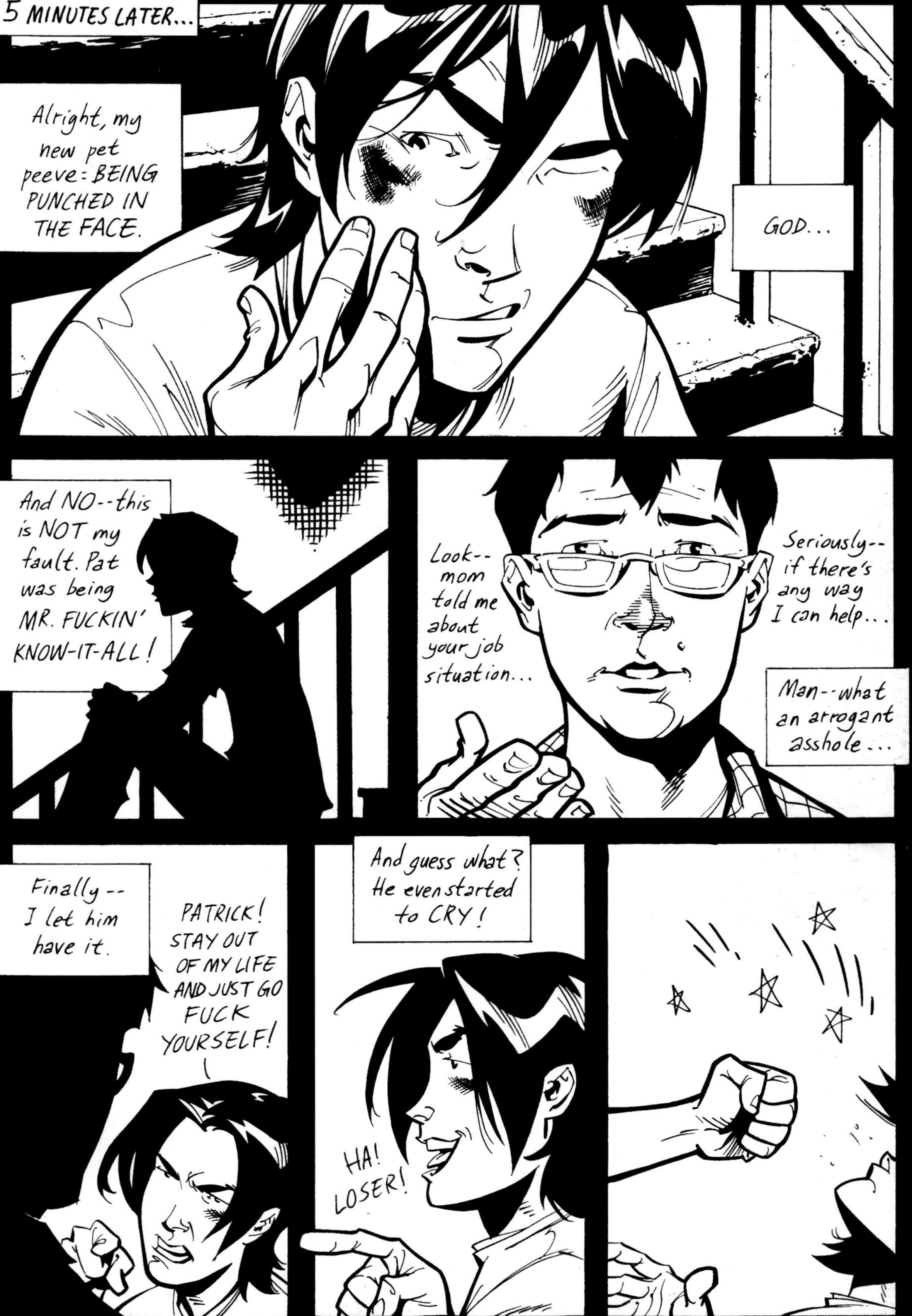
5 MINUTES LATER...
Alright, my new pet peeve: BEING PUNCHED IN THE FACE.
GOD...
And NO--this is NOT my fault. Pat was being MR. FUCKIN' KNOW-IT-ALL!
Look--mom told me about your job situation...
Seriously--if there's any way I can help...
Man--what an arrogant asshole...
Finally--I let him have it.
PATRICK! STAY OUT OF MY LIFE AND JUST GO FUCK YOURSELF!
And guess what? He even started to CRY!
HA! LOSER!

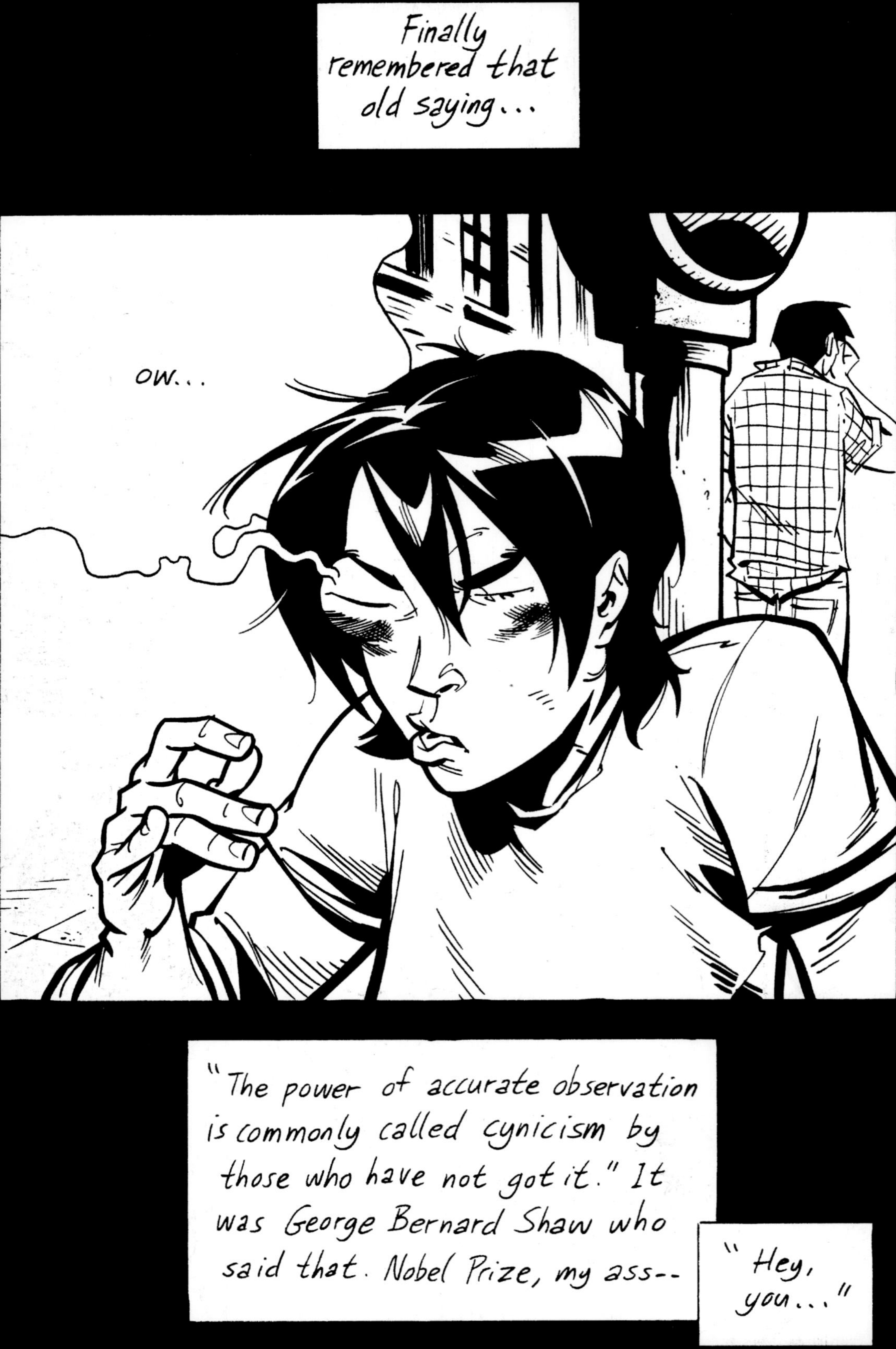
Finally remembered that old saying...
OW...
"The power of accurate observation is commonly called cynicism by those who have not got it." It was George Bernard Shaw who said that. Nobel Prize, my ass--
"Hey, you..."

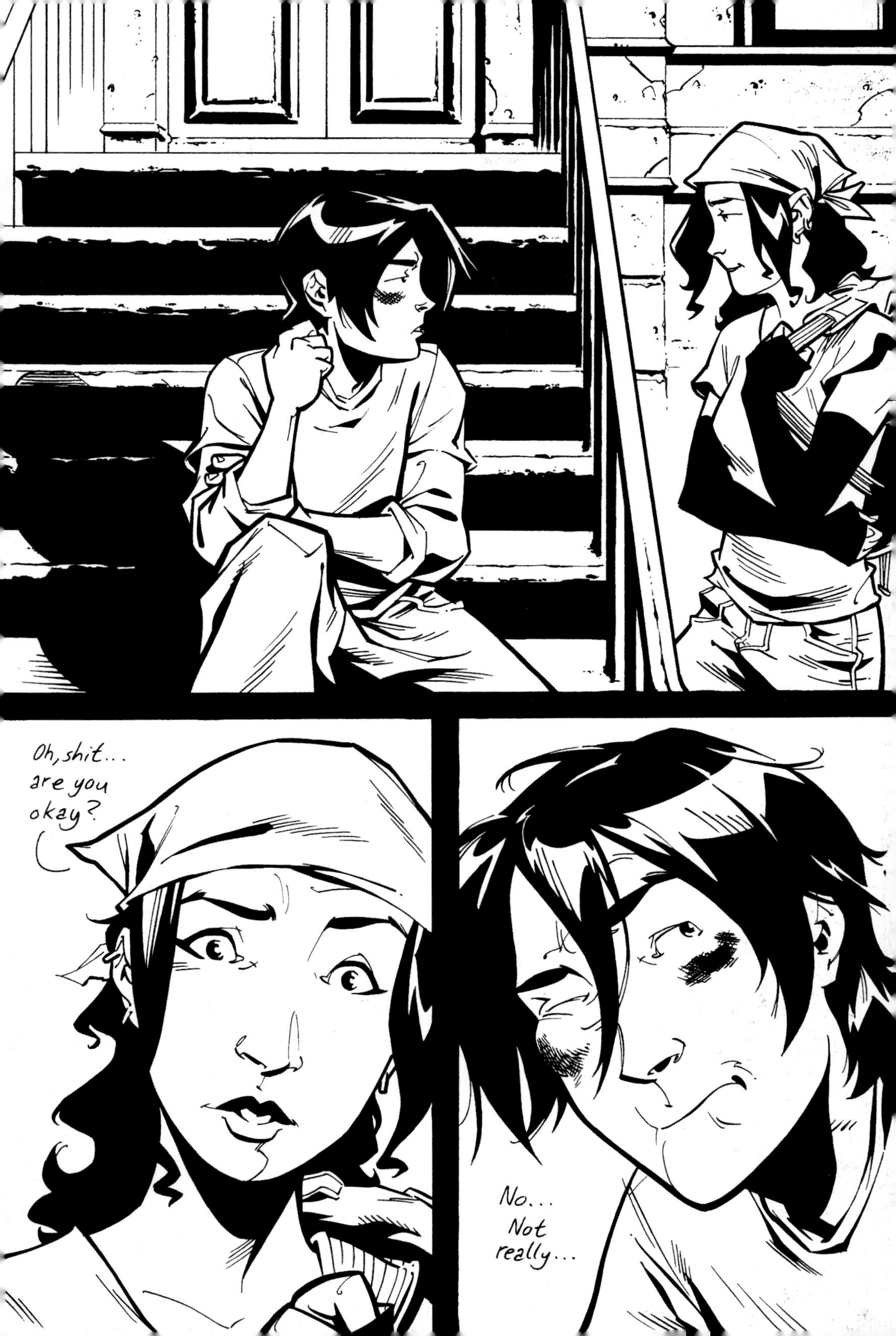
Oh, shit... are you okay?
No... Not really...

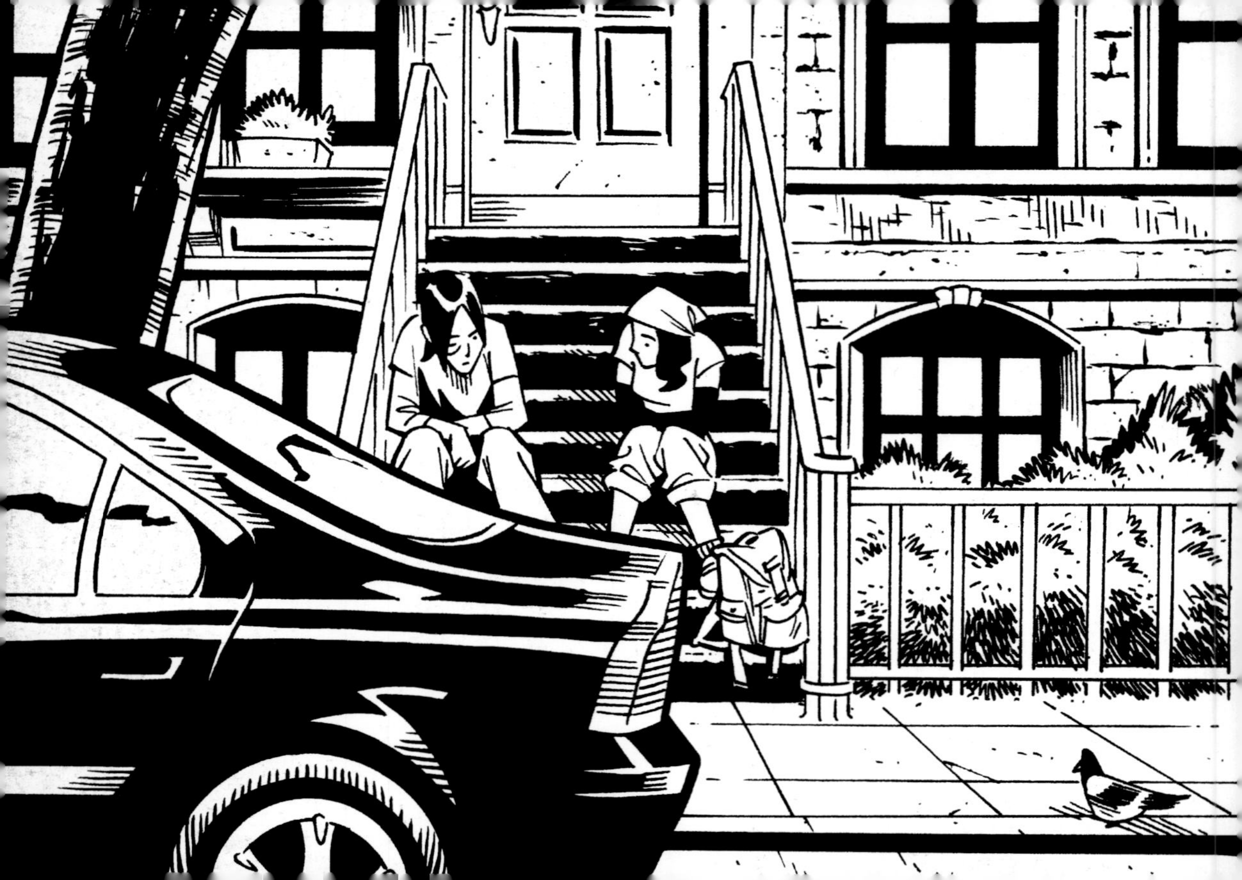

ETHAN, THE INCREDIBLE

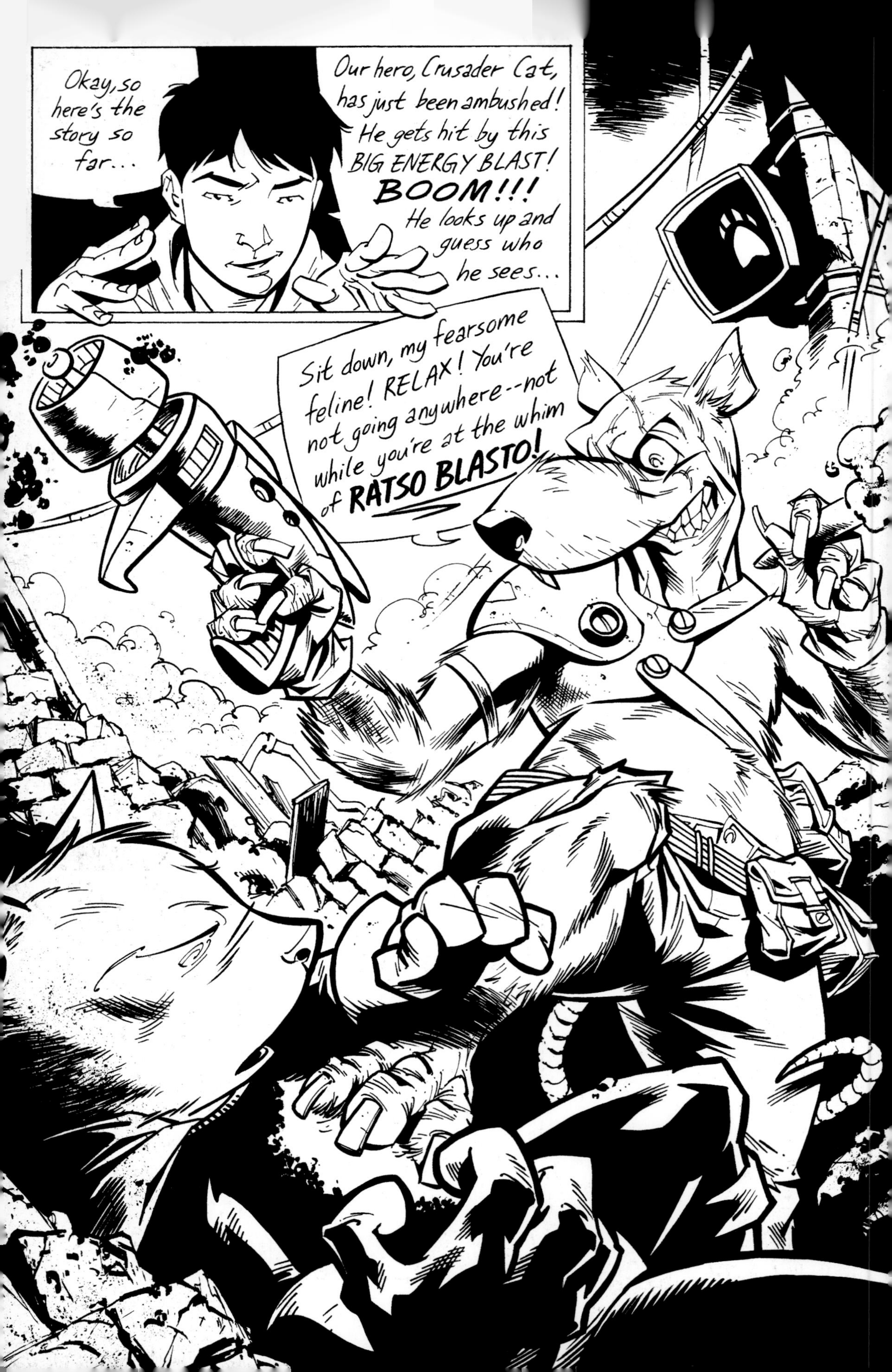

Okay, so here's the story so far...
Our hero, Crusader Cat, has just been ambushed! He gets hit by this BIG ENERGY BLAST! BOOM!!! He looks up and guess who he sees...
Sit down, my fearsome feline! RELAX! You're not going anywhere--not while you're at the whim of RATSO BLASTO!

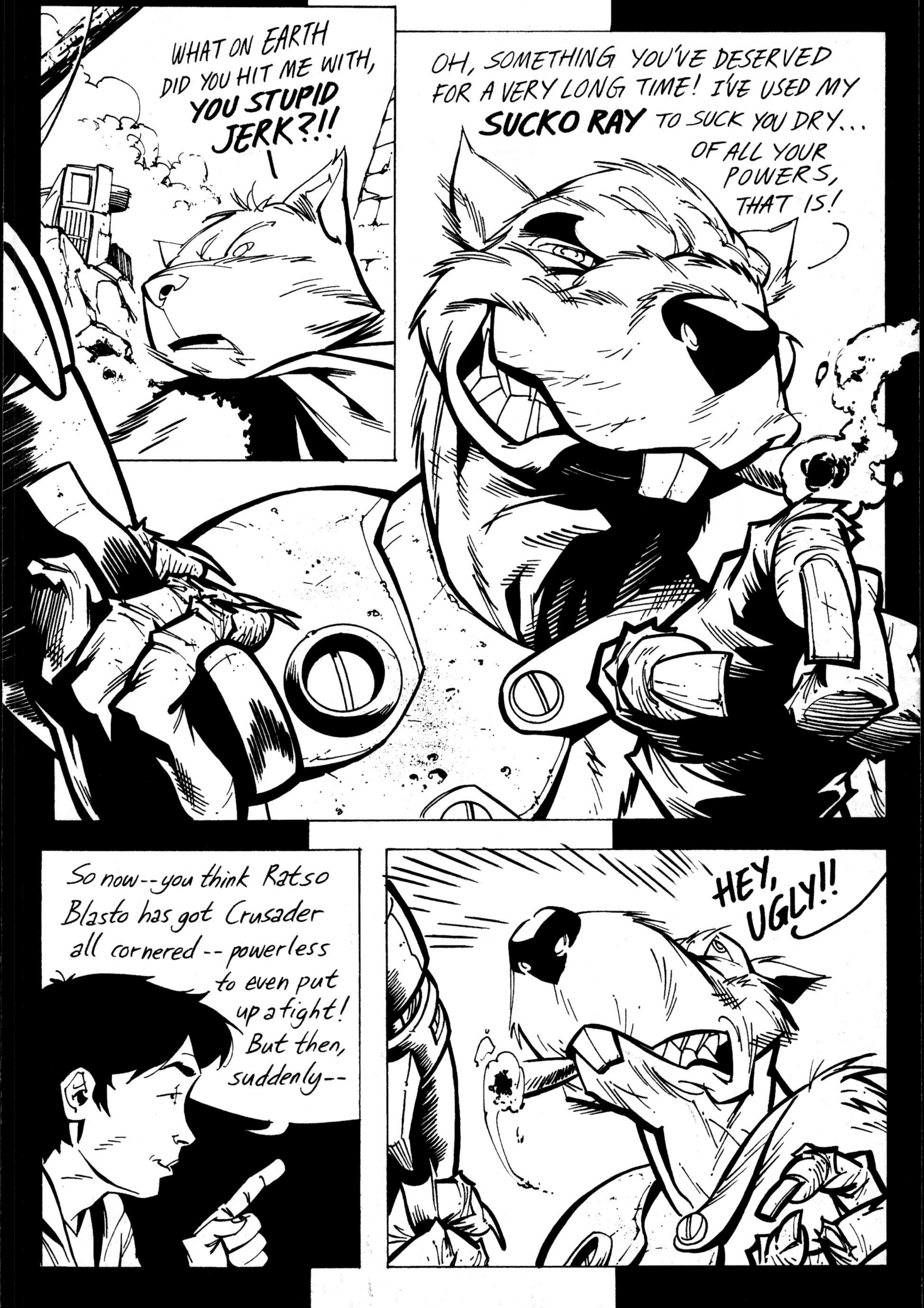

WHAT ON EARTH DID YOU HIT ME WITH, YOU STUPID JERK?!!
OH, SOMETHING YOU'VE DESERVED FOR A VERY LONG TIME! I'VE USED MY SUCKO RAY TO SUCK YOU DRY... OF ALL YOUR POWERS, THAT IS!
So now--you think Ratso Blasto has got Crusader all cornered--powerless to even put up a fight! But then, suddenly--
HEY, UGLY!!

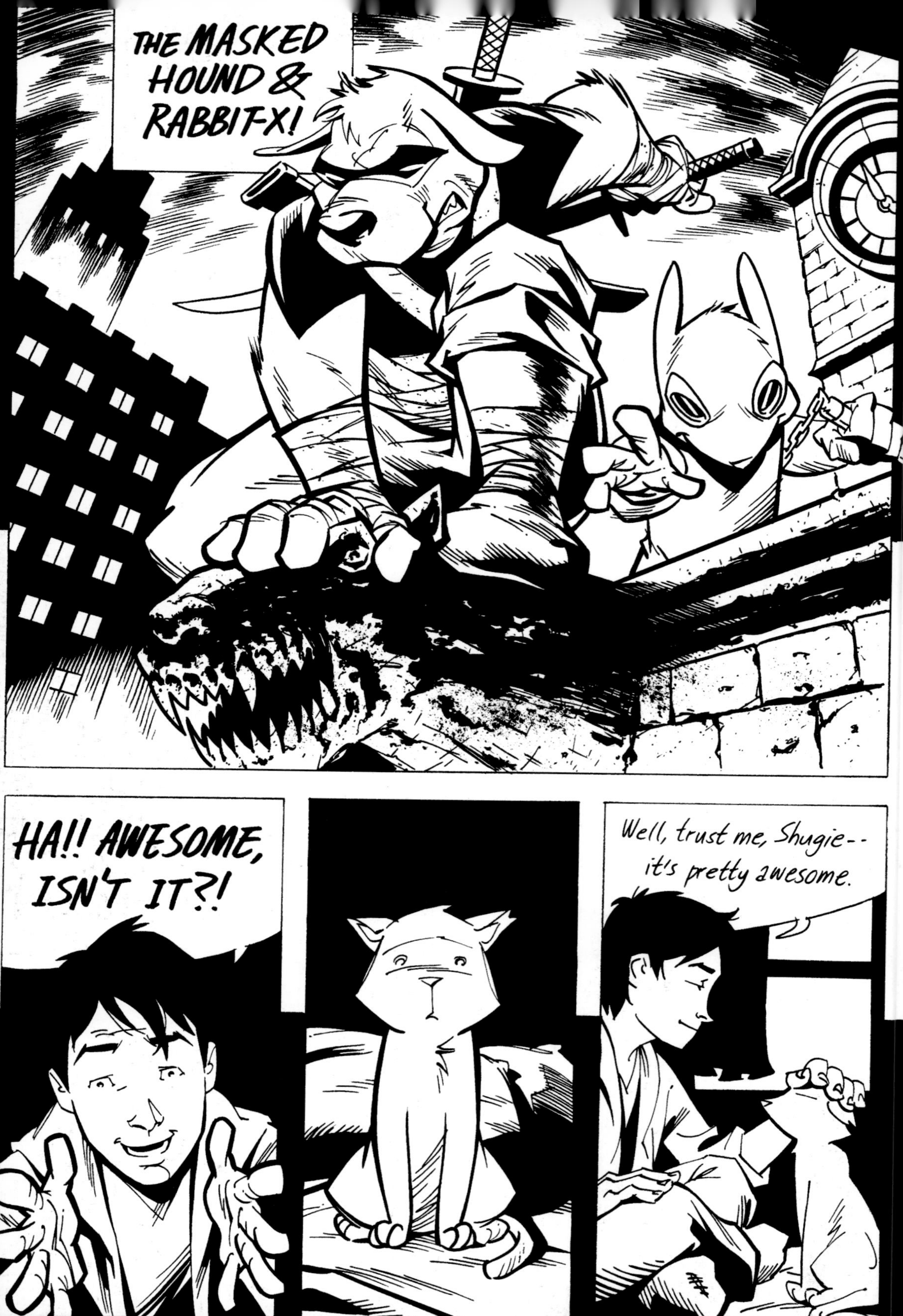
THE MASKED HOUND & RABBIT-X!
HA!! AWESOME, ISN'T IT?!
Well, trust me, Shugie--
it's pretty awesome.

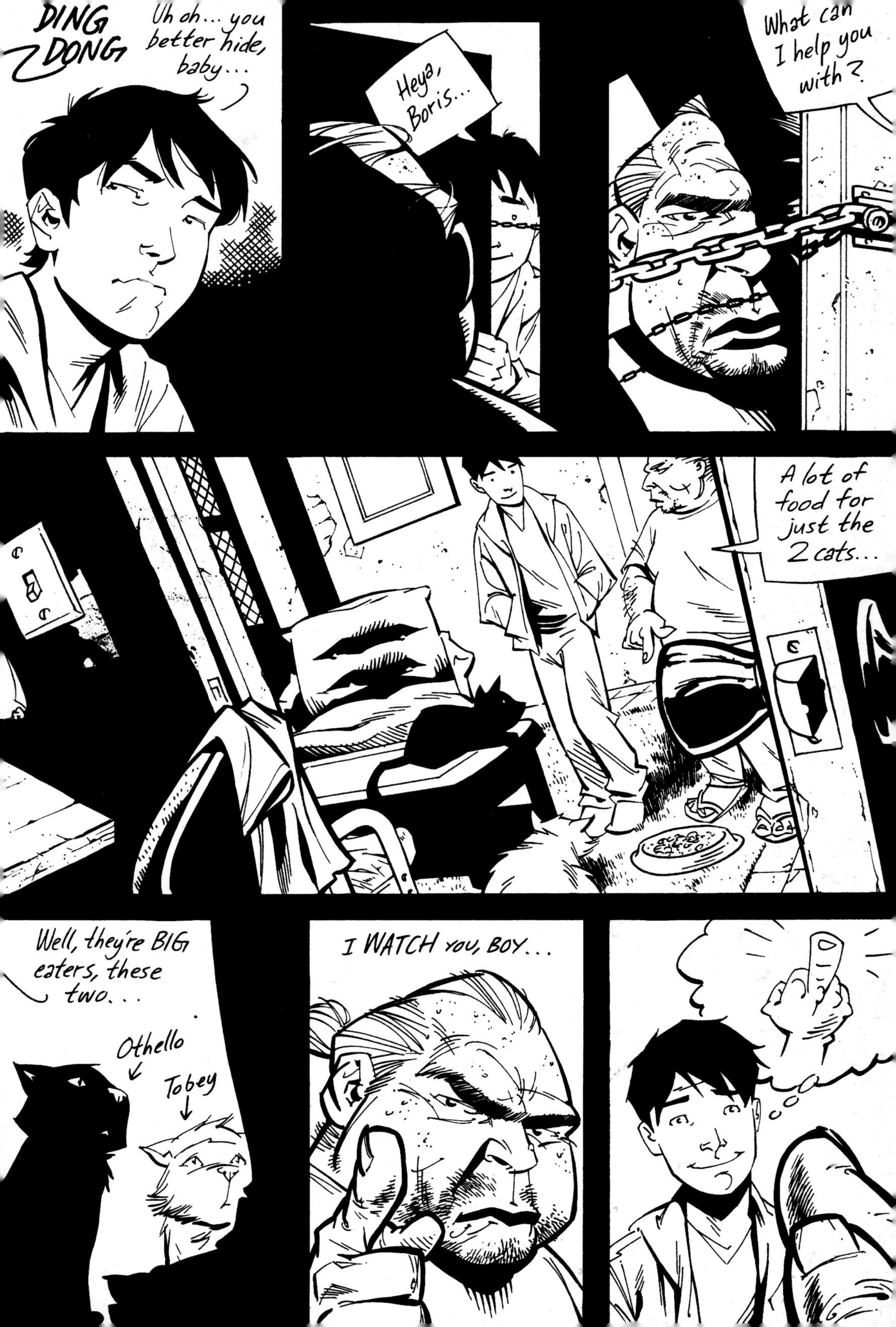
DING DONG
Uh oh... you better hide, baby...
Heya, Boris...
What can I help you with?
A lot of food for just the 2 cats...
Well, they're BIG eaters, these two...
Othello
Tobey
I WATCH you, BOY...

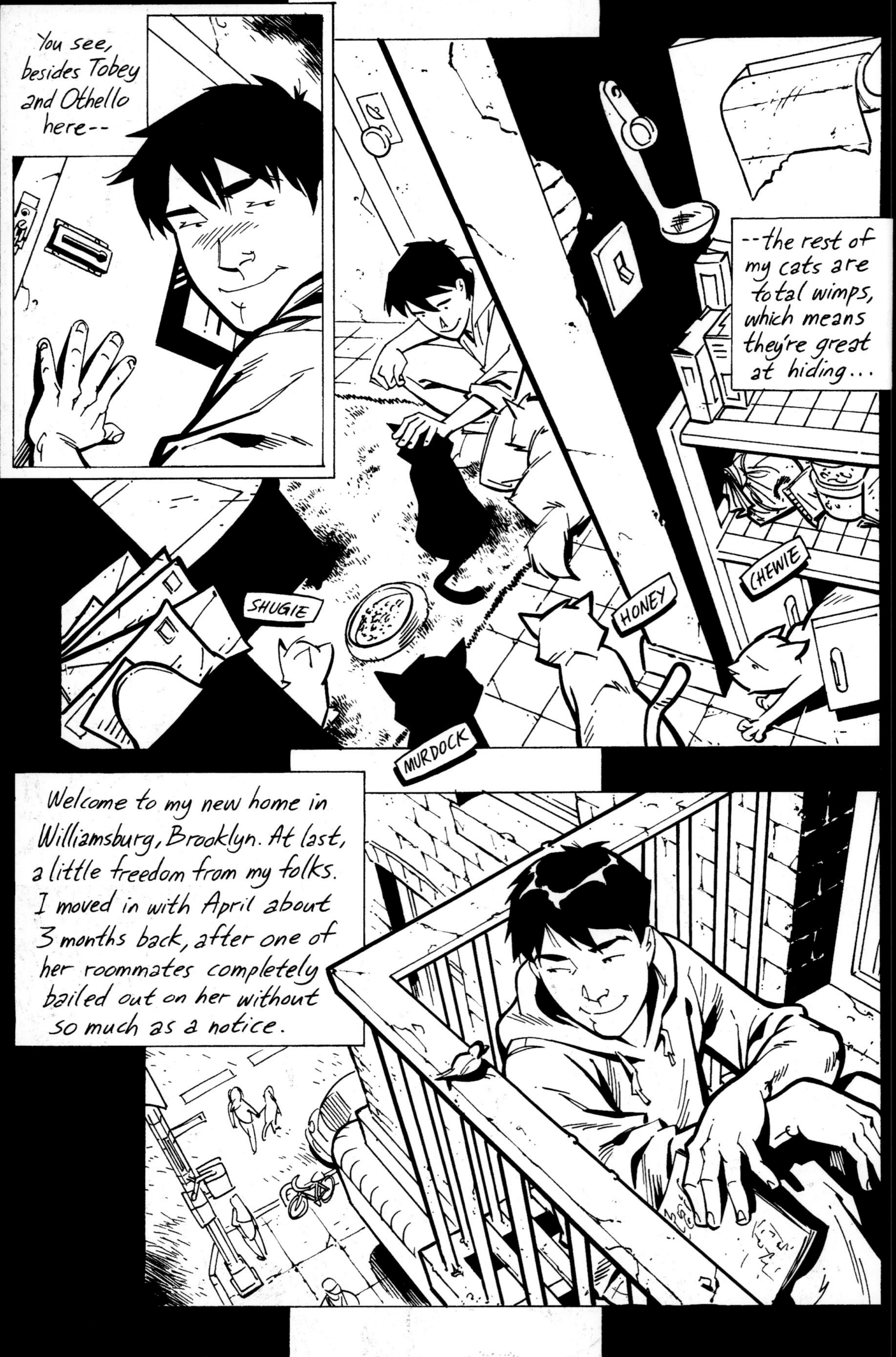
You see, besides Tobey and Othello here--
--the rest of my cats are total wimps, which means they're great at hiding...
SHUGIE
HONEY
CHEWIE
MURDOCK
Welcome to my new home in Williamsburg, Brooklyn. At last, a little freedom from my folks. I moved in with April about 3 months back, after one of her roommates completely bailed out on her without so much as a notice.

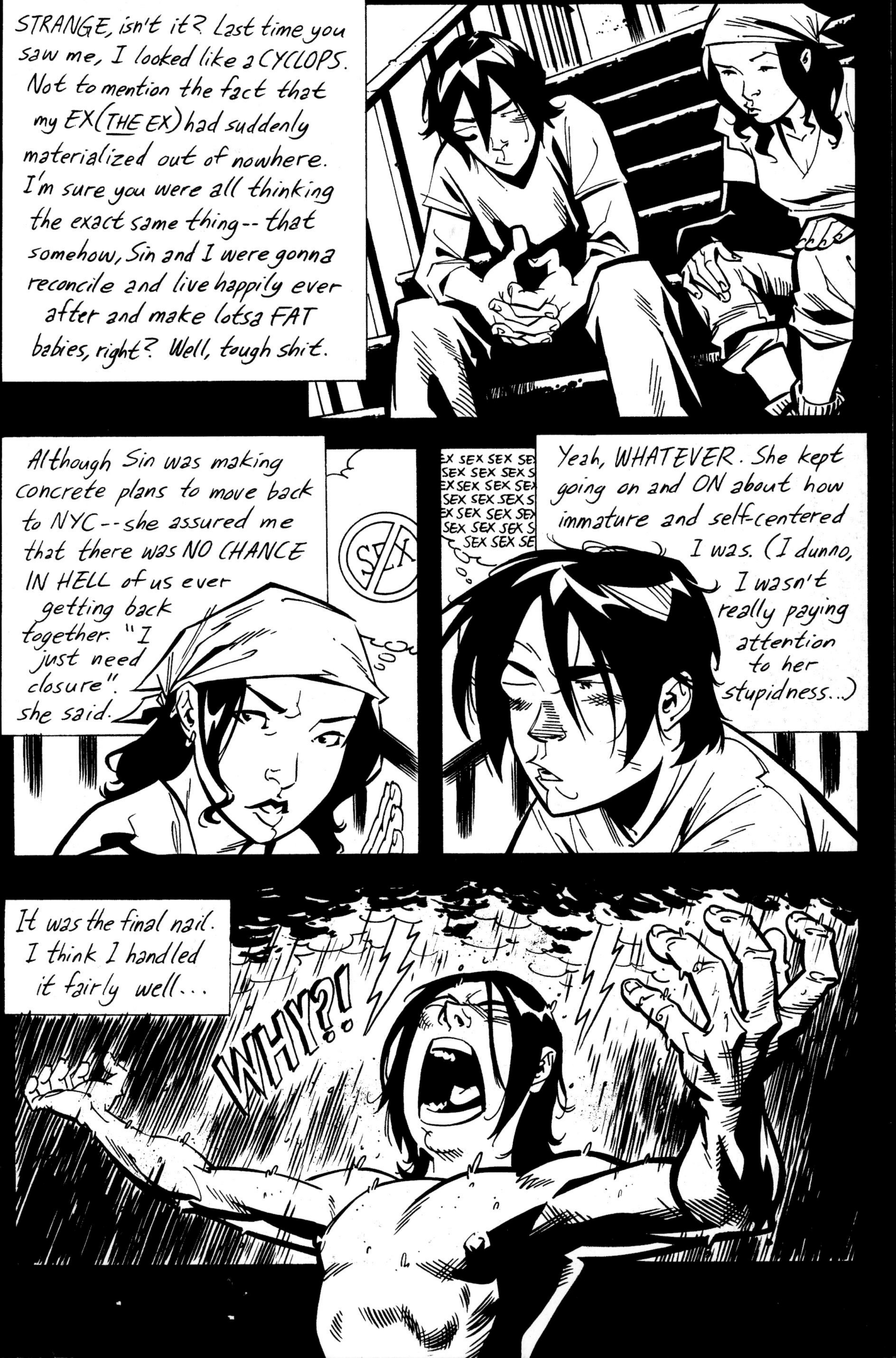
STRANGE, isn't it? Last time you saw me, I looked like a CYCLOPS. Not to mention the fact that my EX (THE EX) had suddenly materialized out of nowhere. I'm sure you were all thinking the exact same thing-- that somehow, Sin and I were gonna reconcile and live happily ever after and make lotsa FAT babies, right? Well, tough shit.
Although Sin was making concrete plans to move back to NYC--she assured me that there was NO CHANCE IN HELL of us ever getting back together. "I just need closure". she said.
SEX
SEX SEX SEX SEX SEX SEX SEX SEX SEX SEX SEX SEX SEX SEX SEX SEX SEX SEX SEX SEX SEX SEX
Yeah, WHATEVER. She kept going on and ON about how immature and self-centered I was. (I dunno, I wasn't really paying attention to her stupidness...)
It was the final nail. I think I handled it fairly well...
WHY?!

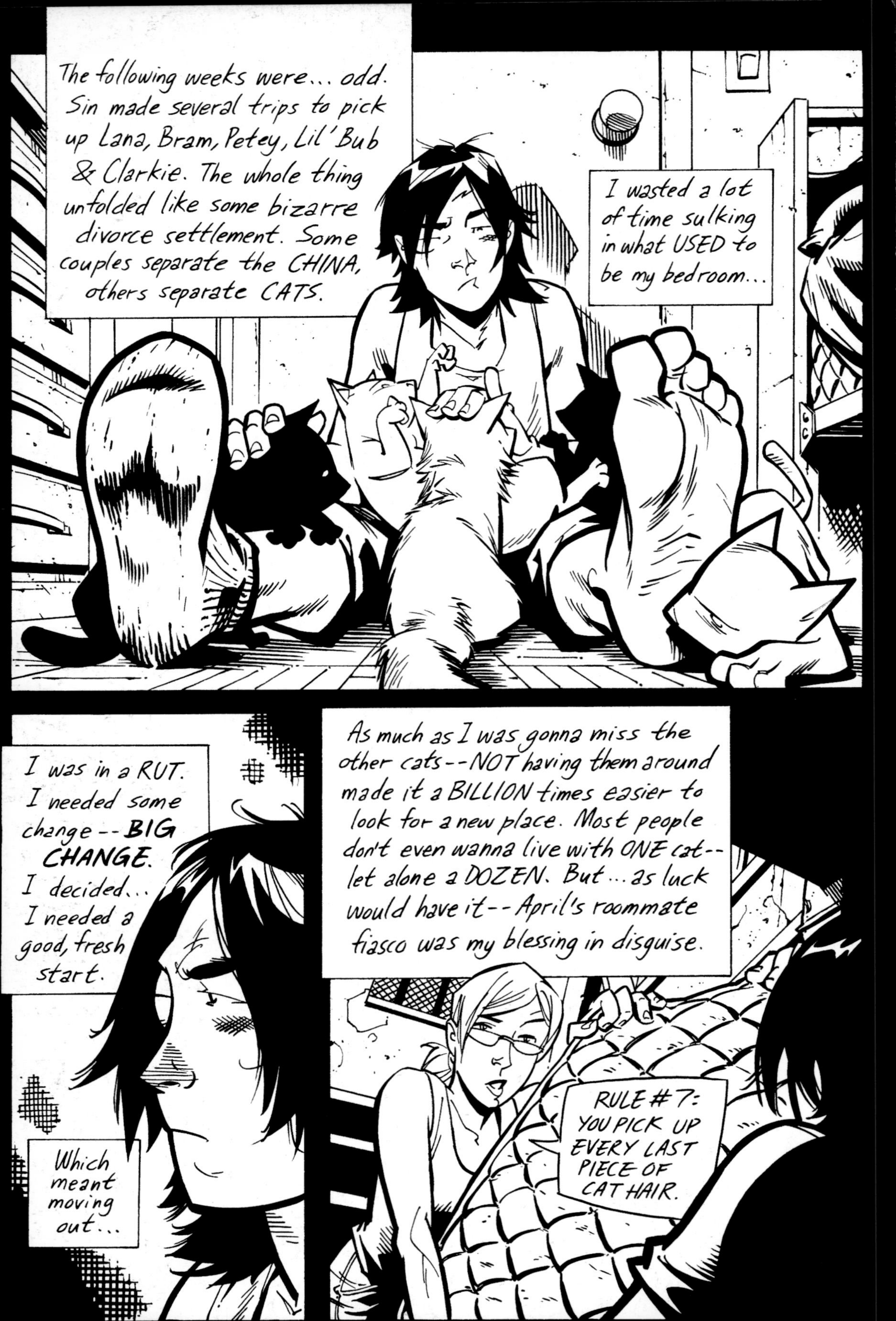

The following weeks were... odd. Sin made several trips to pick up Lana, Bram, Petey, Lil' Bub & Clarkie. The whole thing unfolded like some bizarre divorce settlement. Some couples separate the CHINA, others separate CATS.
I wasted a lot of time sulking in what USED to be my bedroom...
I was in a RUT. I needed some change -- **BIG CHANGE**. I decided... I needed a good, fresh start.
Which meant moving out...
As much as I was gonna miss the other cats--NOT having them around made it a BILLION times easier to look for a new place. Most people don't even wanna live with ONE cat-- let alone a DOZEN. But... as luck would have it-- April's roommate fiasco was my blessing in disguise.
RULE #7: YOU PICK UP EVERY LAST PIECE OF CAT HAIR.

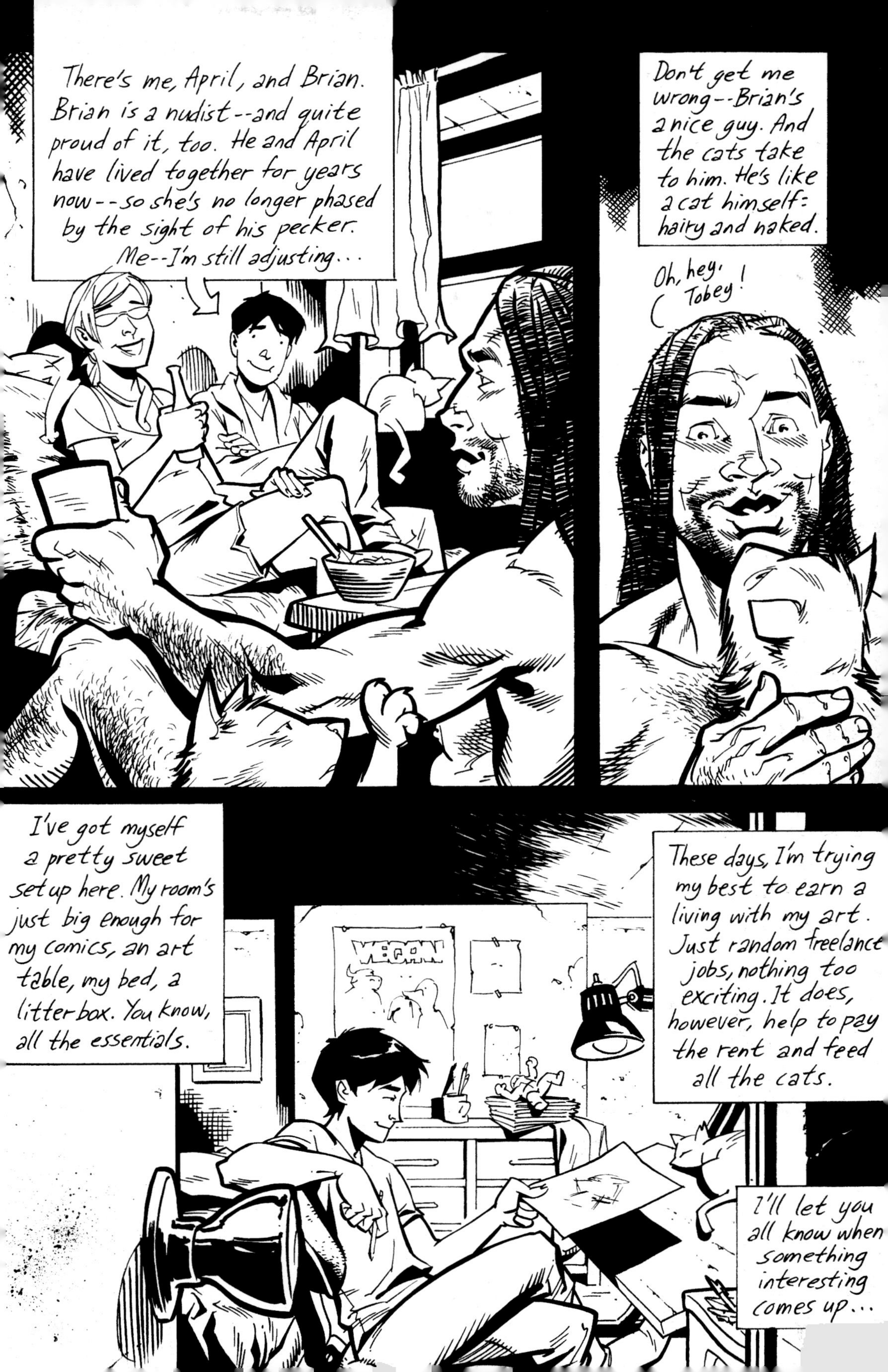
There's me, April, and Brian. Brian is a nudist--and quite proud of it, too. He and April have lived together for years now--so she's no longer phased by the sight of his pecker. Me--I'm still adjusting...
Don't get me wrong--Brian's a nice guy. And the cats take to him. He's like a cat himself: hairy and naked.
Oh, hey, Tobey!
I've got myself a pretty sweet set up here. My room's just big enough for my comics, an art table, my bed, a litter box. You know, all the essentials.
These days, I'm trying my best to earn a living with my art. Just random freelance jobs, nothing too exciting. It does, however, help to pay the rent and feed all the cats.
I'll let you all know when something interesting comes up...

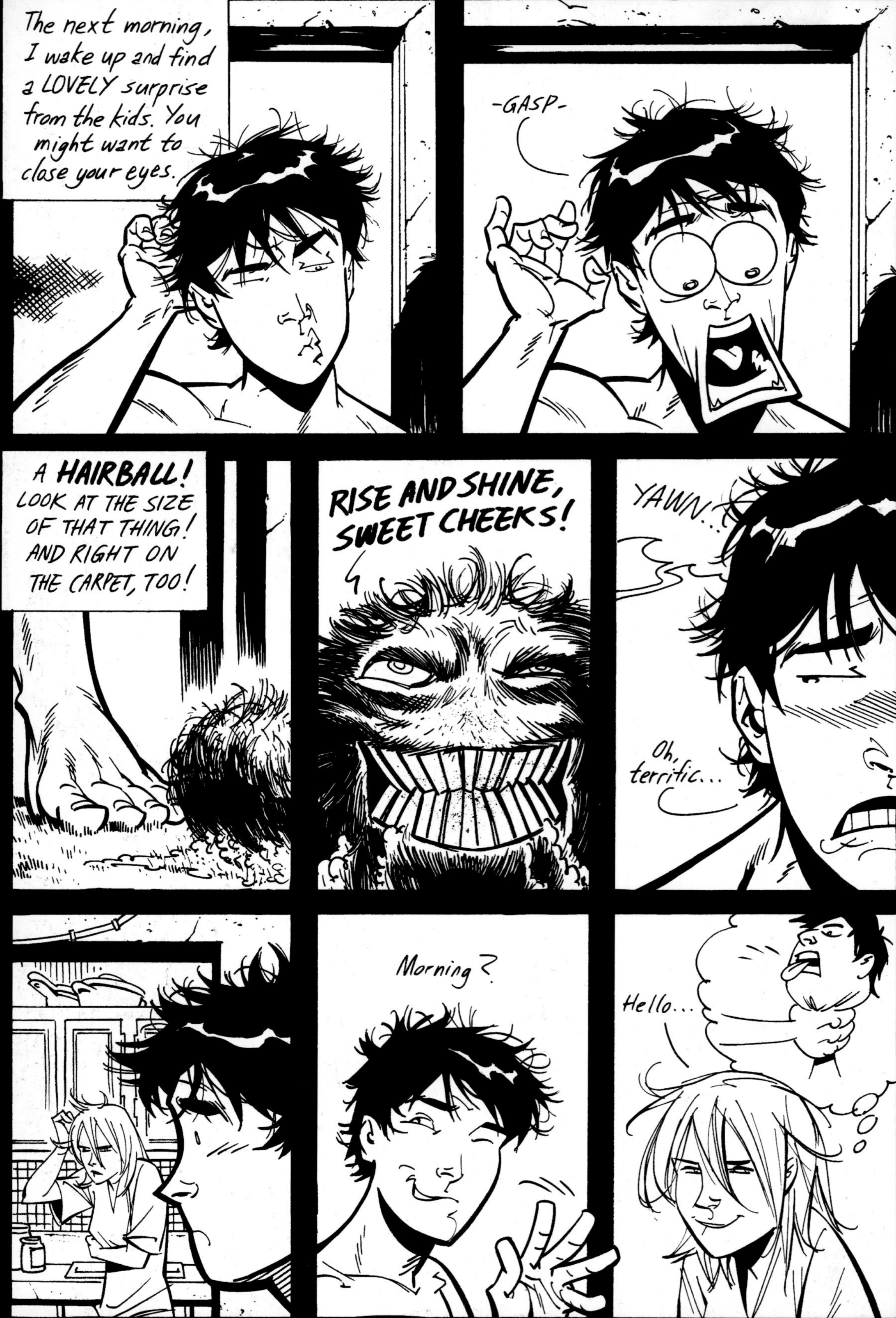

The next morning, I wake up and find a LOVELY surprise from the kids. You might want to close your eyes.
-GASP-
A **HAIRBALL!** LOOK AT THE SIZE OF THAT THING! AND RIGHT ON THE CARPET, TOO!
RISE AND SHINE, SWEET CHEEKS!
YAWN...
Oh, terrific...
Morning?
Hello...

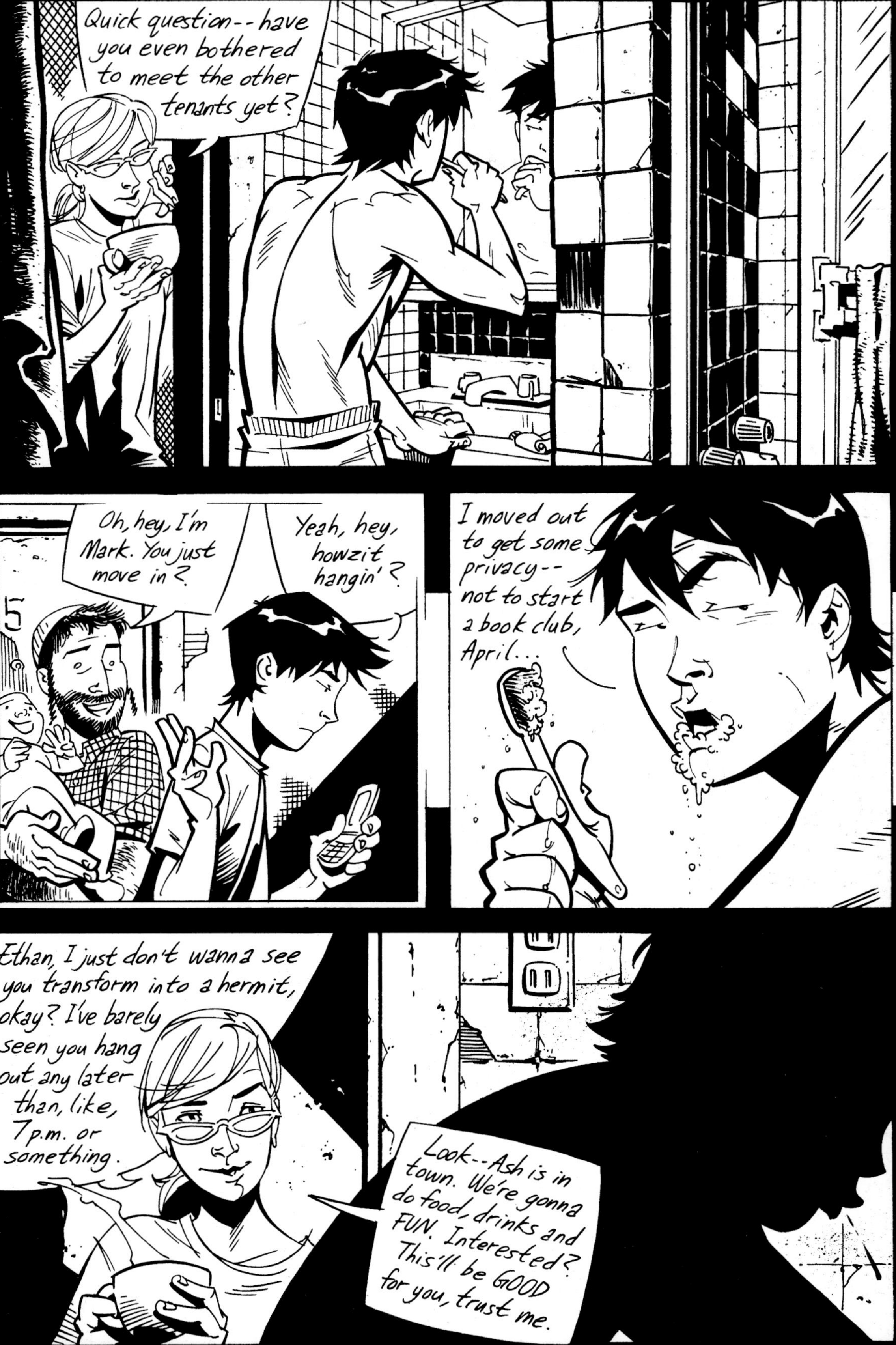
Quick question--have you even bothered to meet the other tenants yet?
Oh, hey, I'm Mark. You just move in?
Yeah, hey, howzit hangin'?
I moved out to get some privacy--not to start a book club, April...
Ethan, I just don't wanna see you transform into a hermit, okay? I've barely seen you hang out any later than, like, 7 p.m. or something.
Look--Ash is in town. We're gonna do food, drinks and FUN. Interested? This'll be GOOD for you, trust me.

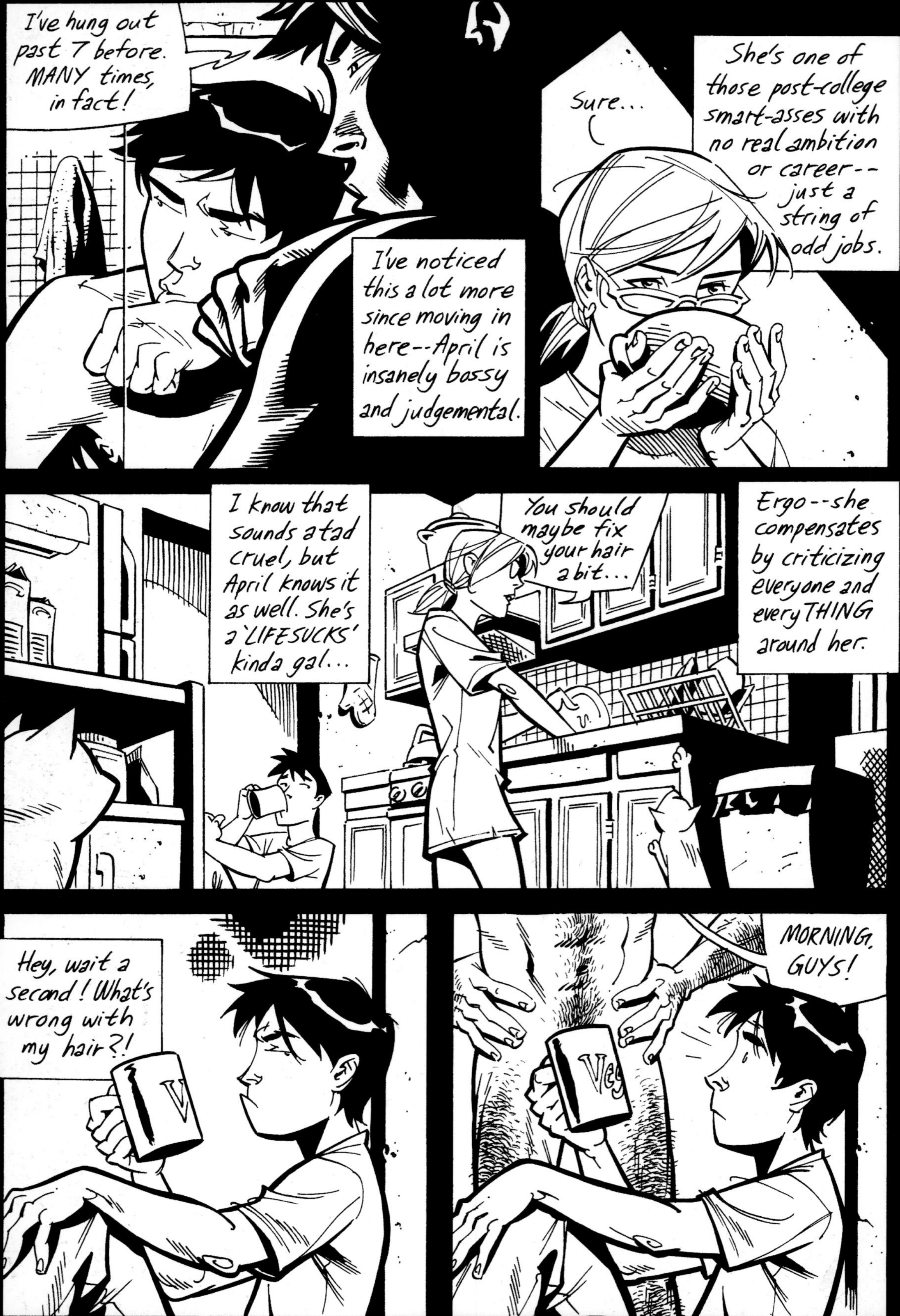

I've hung out past 7 before. MANY times, in fact!
I've noticed this a lot more since moving in here--April is insanely bossy and judgemental.
Sure...
She's one of those post-college smart-asses with no real ambition or career--just a string of odd jobs.
I know that sounds a tad cruel, but April knows it as well. She's a 'LIFESUCKS' kinda gal...
You should maybe fix your hair a bit...
Ergo--she compensates by criticizing everyone and everyTHING around her.
Hey, wait a second! What's wrong with my hair?!
V
MORNING, GUYS!
Veg

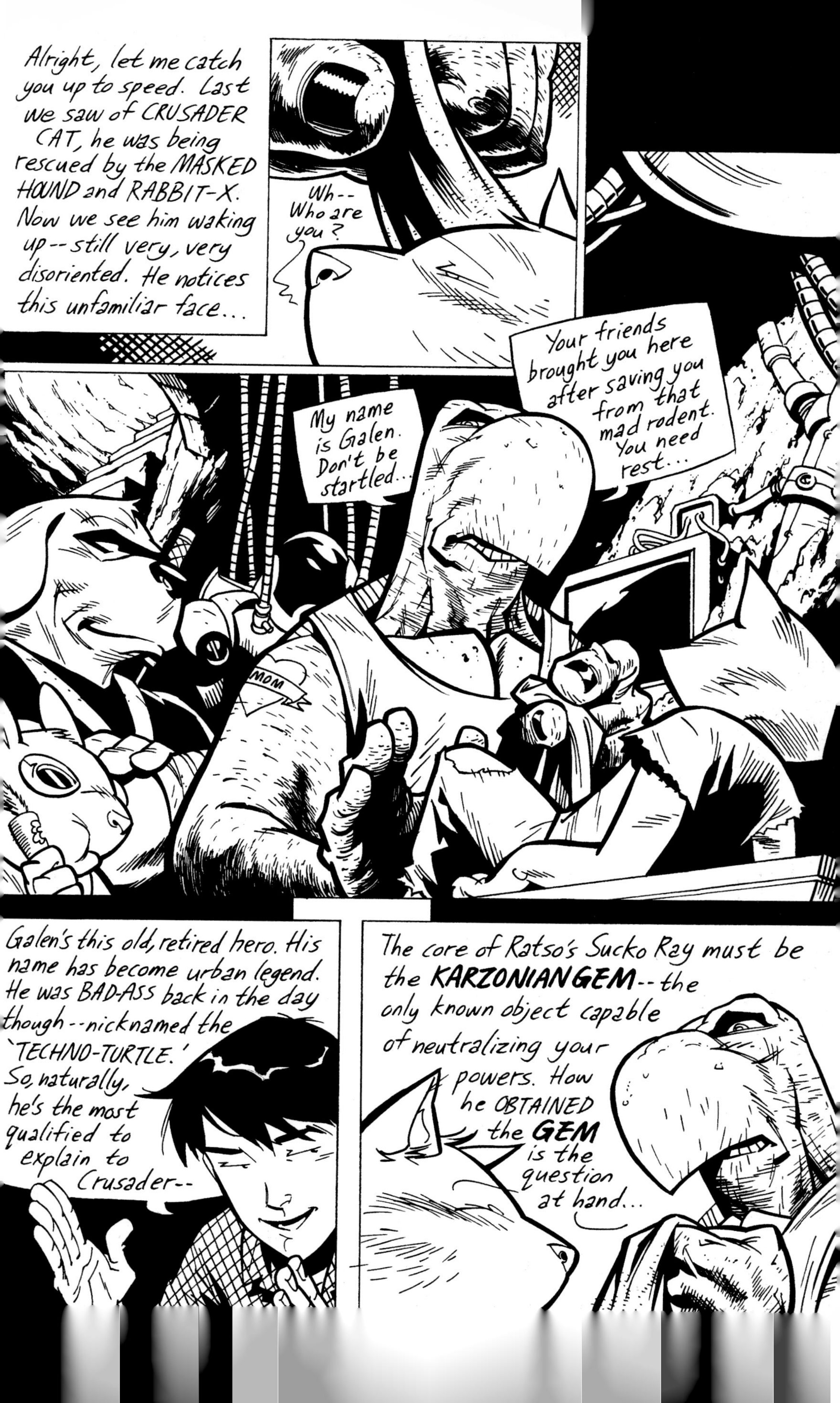

Alright, let me catch you up to speed. Last we saw of CRUSADER CAT, he was being rescued by the MASKED HOUND and RABBIT-X. Now we see him waking up--still very, very disoriented. He notices this unfamiliar face...
Wh-- Who are you?
My name is Galen. Don't be startled...
Your friends brought you here after saving you from that mad rodent. You need rest...
MOM
Galen's this old, retired hero. His name has become urban legend. He was BAD-ASS back in the day though--nicknamed the 'TECHNO-TURTLE.' So, naturally, he's the most qualified to explain to Crusader--
The core of Ratso's Sucko Ray must be the KARZONIAN GEM--the only known object capable of neutralizing your powers. How he OBTAINED the GEM is the question at hand...

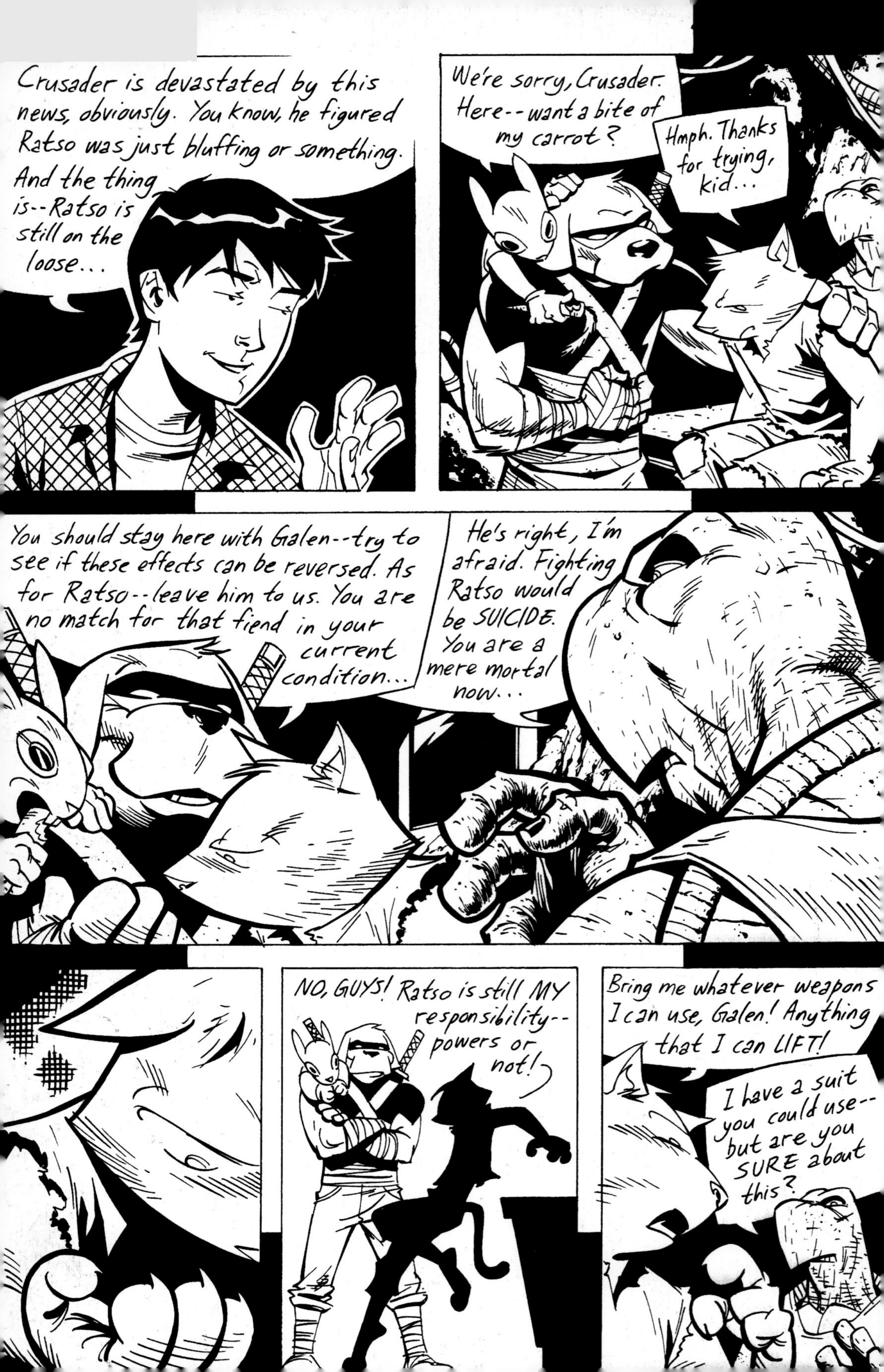
Crusader is devastated by this news, obviously. You know, he figured Ratso was just bluffing or something. And the thing is--Ratso is still on the loose...
We're sorry, Crusader. Here--want a bite of my carrot?
Hmph. Thanks for trying, kid...
You should stay here with Galen--try to see if these effects can be reversed. As for Ratso--leave him to us. You are no match for that fiend in your current condition...
He's right, I'm afraid. Fighting Ratso would be SUICIDE. You are a mere mortal now...
NO, GUYS! Ratso is still MY responsibility--powers or not!
Bring me whatever weapons I can use, Galen! Anything that I can LIFT!
I have a suit you could use--but are you SURE about this?

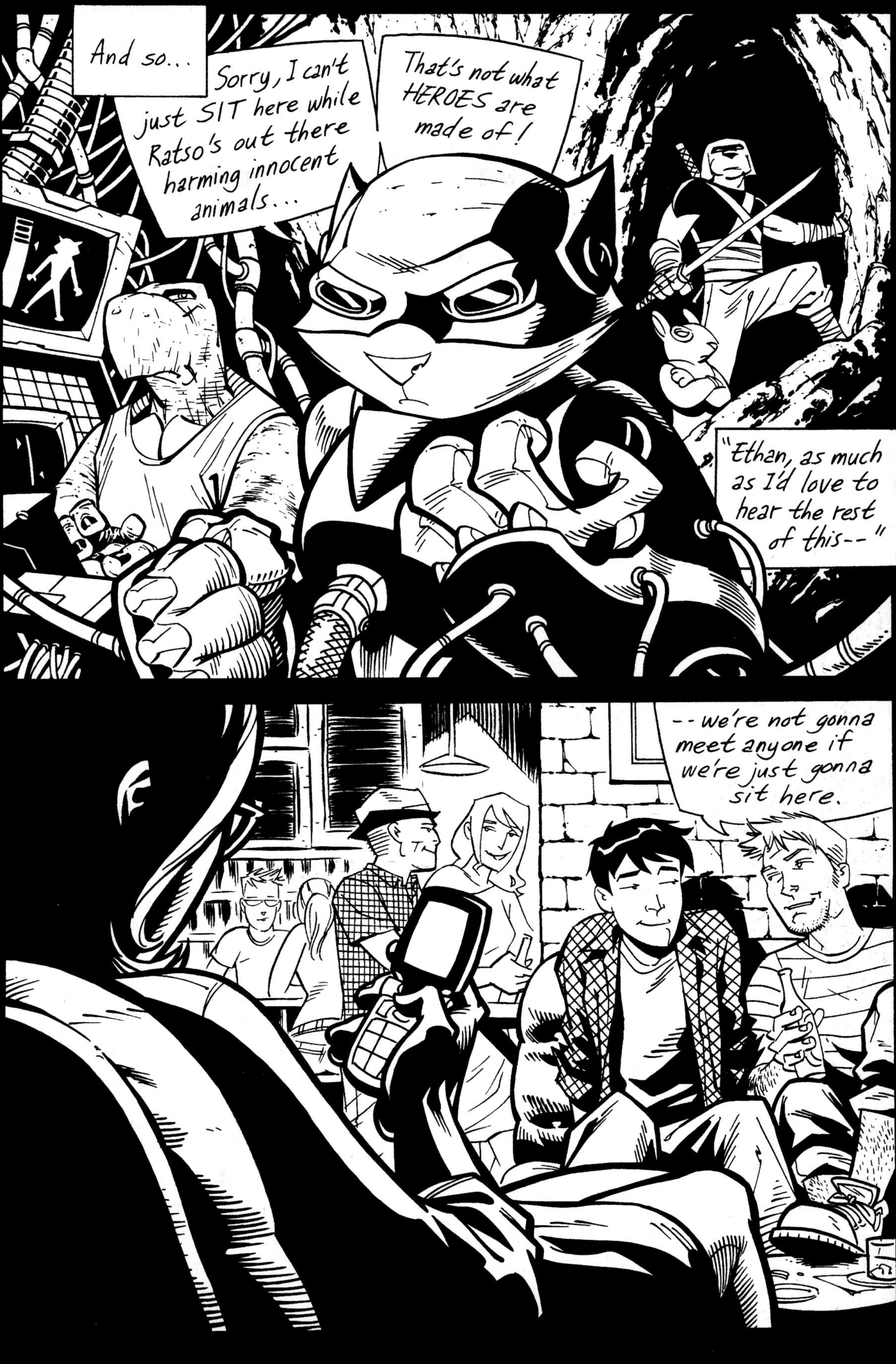
And so...
Sorry, I can't just SIT here while Ratso's out there harming innocent animals...
That's not what HEROES are made of!
"Ethan, as much as I'd love to hear the rest of this--"
--we're not gonna meet anyone if we're just gonna sit here.

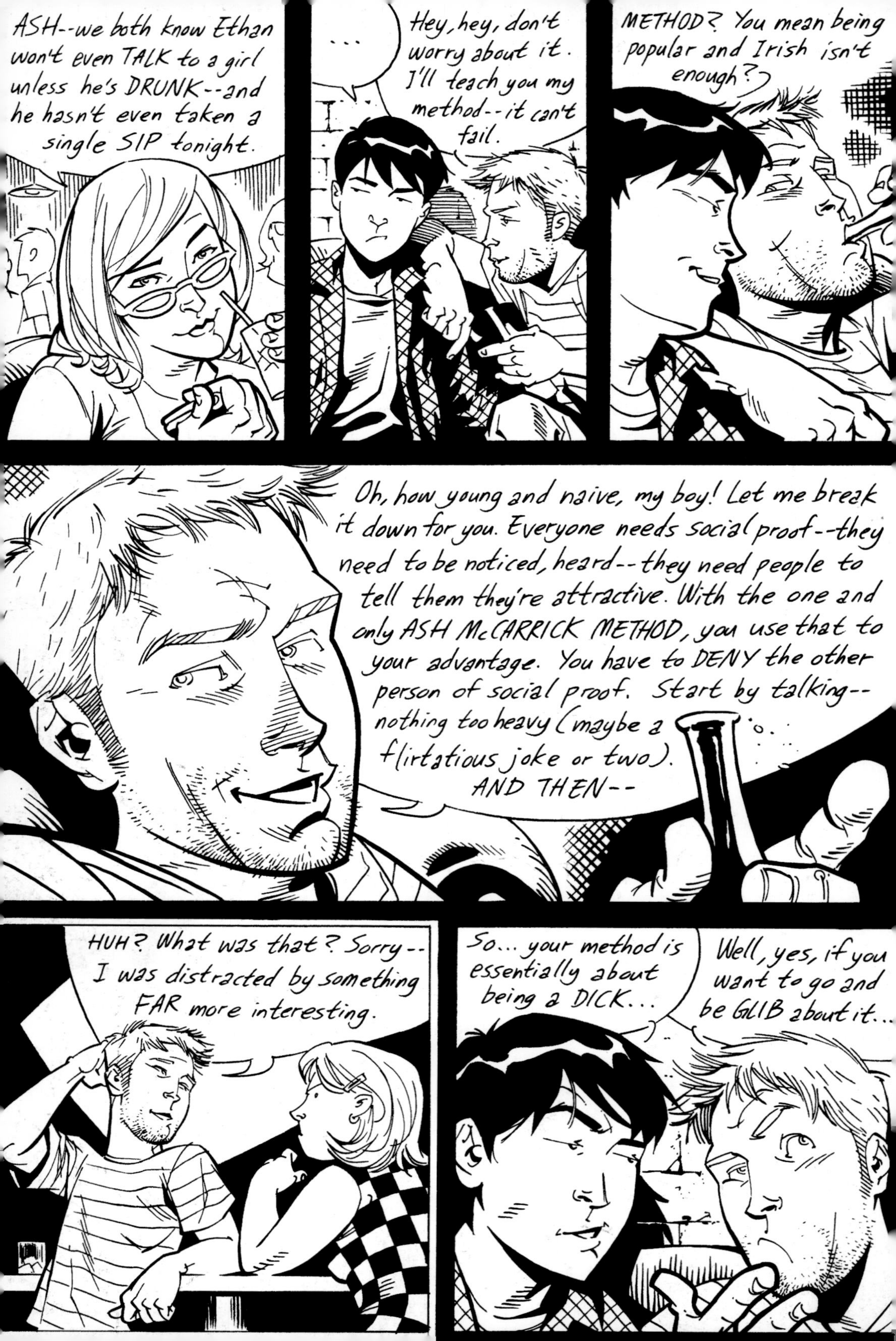
ASH--we both know Ethan won't even TALK to a girl unless he's DRUNK--and he hasn't even taken a single SIP tonight.
...
Hey, hey, don't worry about it. I'll teach you my method--it can't fail.
METHOD? You mean being popular and Irish isn't enough?
Oh, how young and naive, my boy! Let me break it down for you. Everyone needs social proof--they need to be noticed, heard--they need people to tell them they're attractive. With the one and only ASH McCARRICK METHOD, you use that to your advantage. You have to DENY the other person of social proof. Start by talking--nothing too heavy (maybe a flirtatious joke or two). AND THEN--
HUH? What was that? Sorry--I was distracted by something FAR more interesting.
So... your method is essentially about being a DICK...
Well, yes, if you want to go and be GLIB about it...

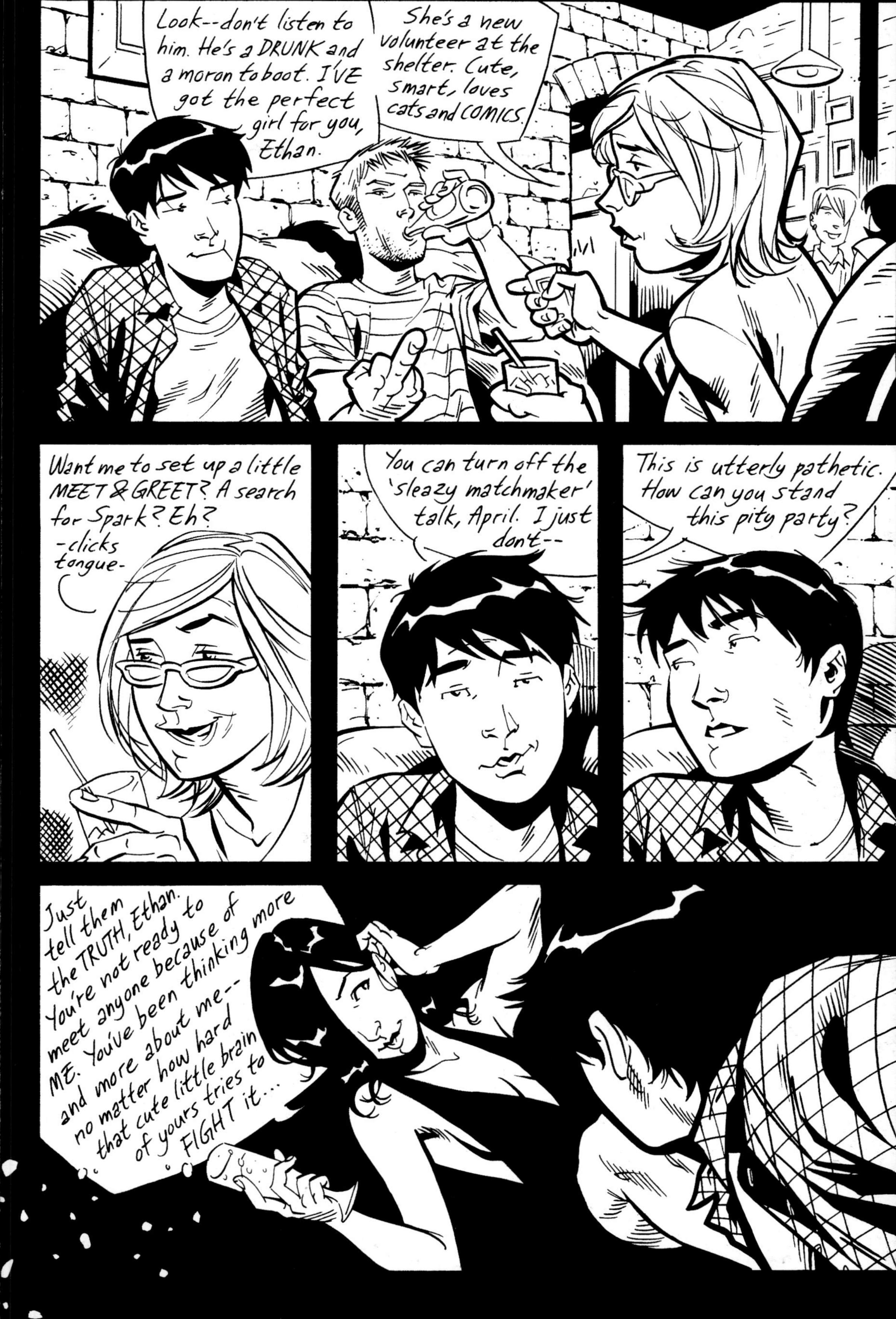
Look--don't listen to him. He's a DRUNK and a moron to boot. I'VE got the perfect girl for you, Ethan.
She's a new volunteer at the shelter. Cute, smart, loves cats and COMICS.
Want me to set up a little MEET & GREET? A search for Spark? Eh?
-clicks tongue-
You can turn off the 'sleazy matchmaker' talk, April. I just don't--
This is utterly pathetic. How can you stand this pity party?
Just tell them the TRUTH, Ethan. You're not ready to meet anyone because of ME. You've been thinking more and more about me-- no matter how hard that cute little brain of yours tries to FIGHT it...

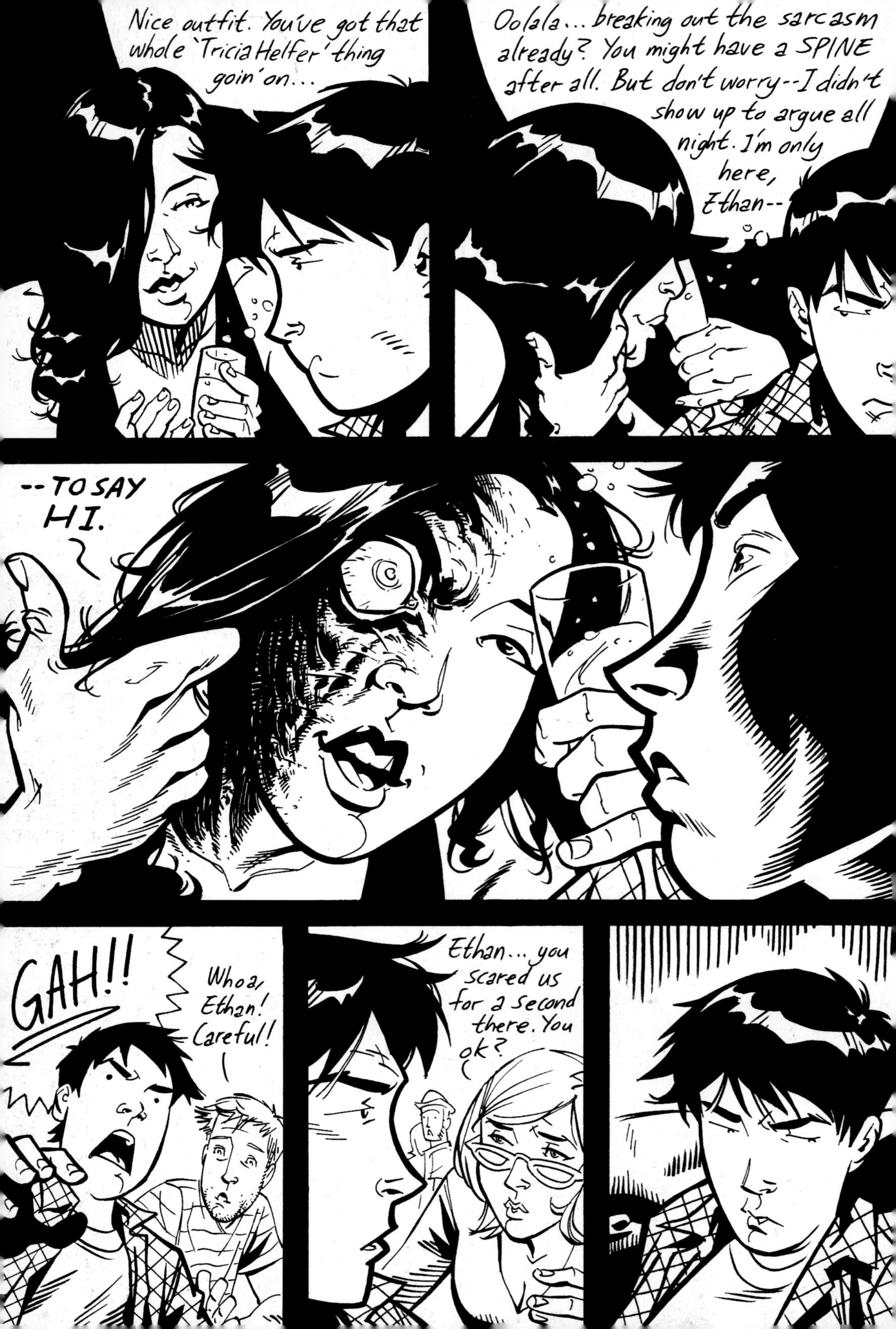
Nice outfit. You've got that whole 'Tricia Helfer' thing goin' on...
Oolala... breaking out the sarcasm already? You might have a SPINE after all. But don't worry--I didn't show up to argue all night. I'm only here, Ethan--
--TO SAY HI.
GAH!!
Whoa, Ethan! Careful!
Ethan... you scared us for a second there. You ok?

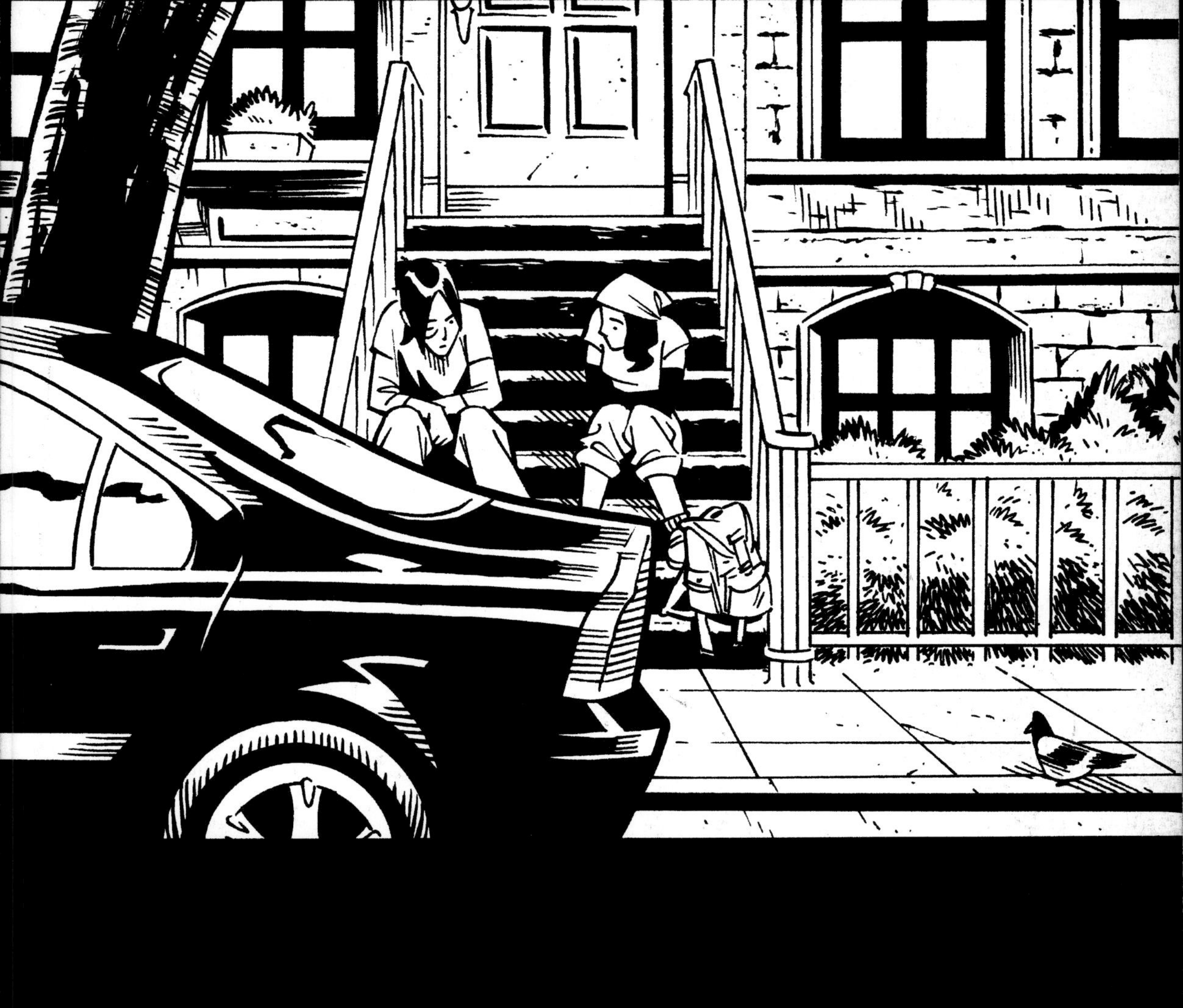

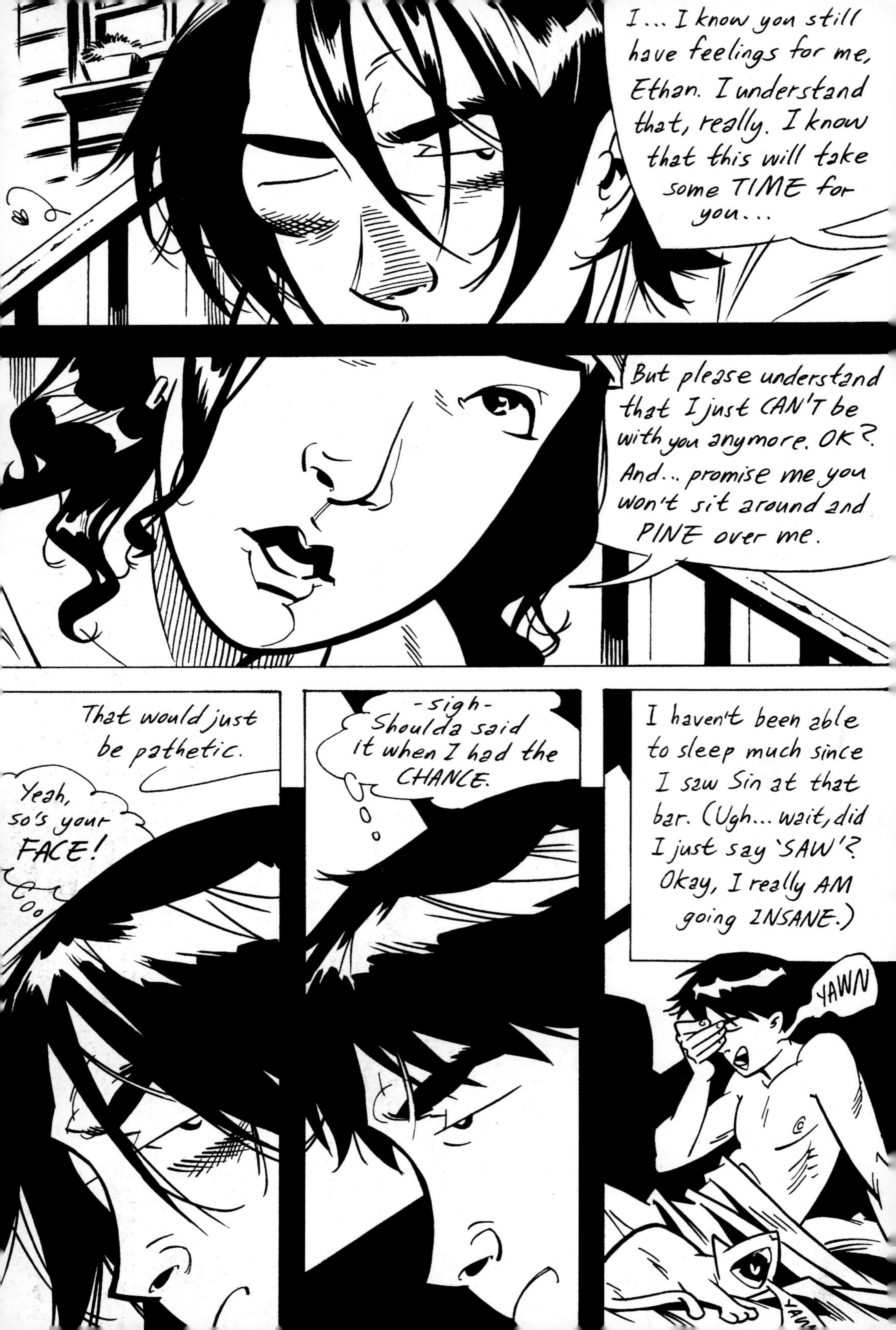
I... I know you still have feelings for me, Ethan. I understand that, really. I know that this will take some TIME for you...
But please understand that I just CAN'T be with you anymore. OK? And... promise me you won't sit around and PINE over me.
That would just be pathetic.
Yeah, so's your FACE!
-sigh- Shoulda said it when I had the CHANCE.
I haven't been able to sleep much since I saw Sin at that bar. (Ugh... wait, did I just say 'SAW'? Okay, I really AM going INSANE.)
YAWN

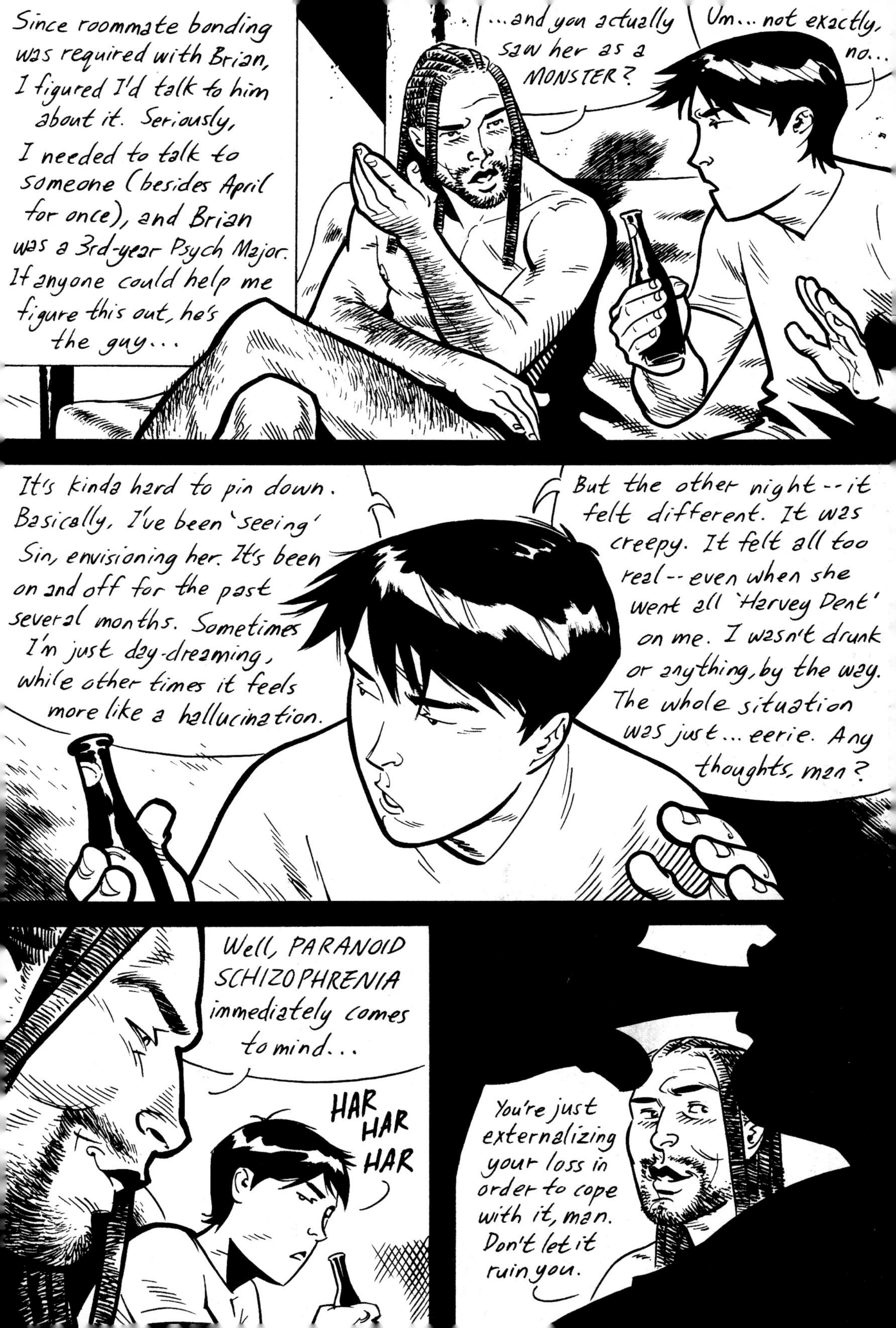
Since roommate bonding was required with Brian, I figured I'd talk to him about it. Seriously, I needed to talk to someone (besides April for once), and Brian was a 3rd-year Psych Major. If anyone could help me figure this out, he's the guy...
...and you actually saw her as a MONSTER?
Um... not exactly, no...
It's kinda hard to pin down. Basically, I've been 'seeing' Sin, envisioning her. It's been on and off for the past several months. Sometimes I'm just day-dreaming, while other times it feels more like a hallucination.
But the other night--it felt different. It was creepy. It felt all too real--even when she went all 'Harvey Dent' on me. I wasn't drunk or anything, by the way. The whole situation was just... eerie. Any thoughts, man?
Well, PARANOID SCHIZOPHRENIA immediately comes to mind...
HAR HAR HAR
You're just externalizing your loss in order to cope with it, man. Don't let it ruin you.

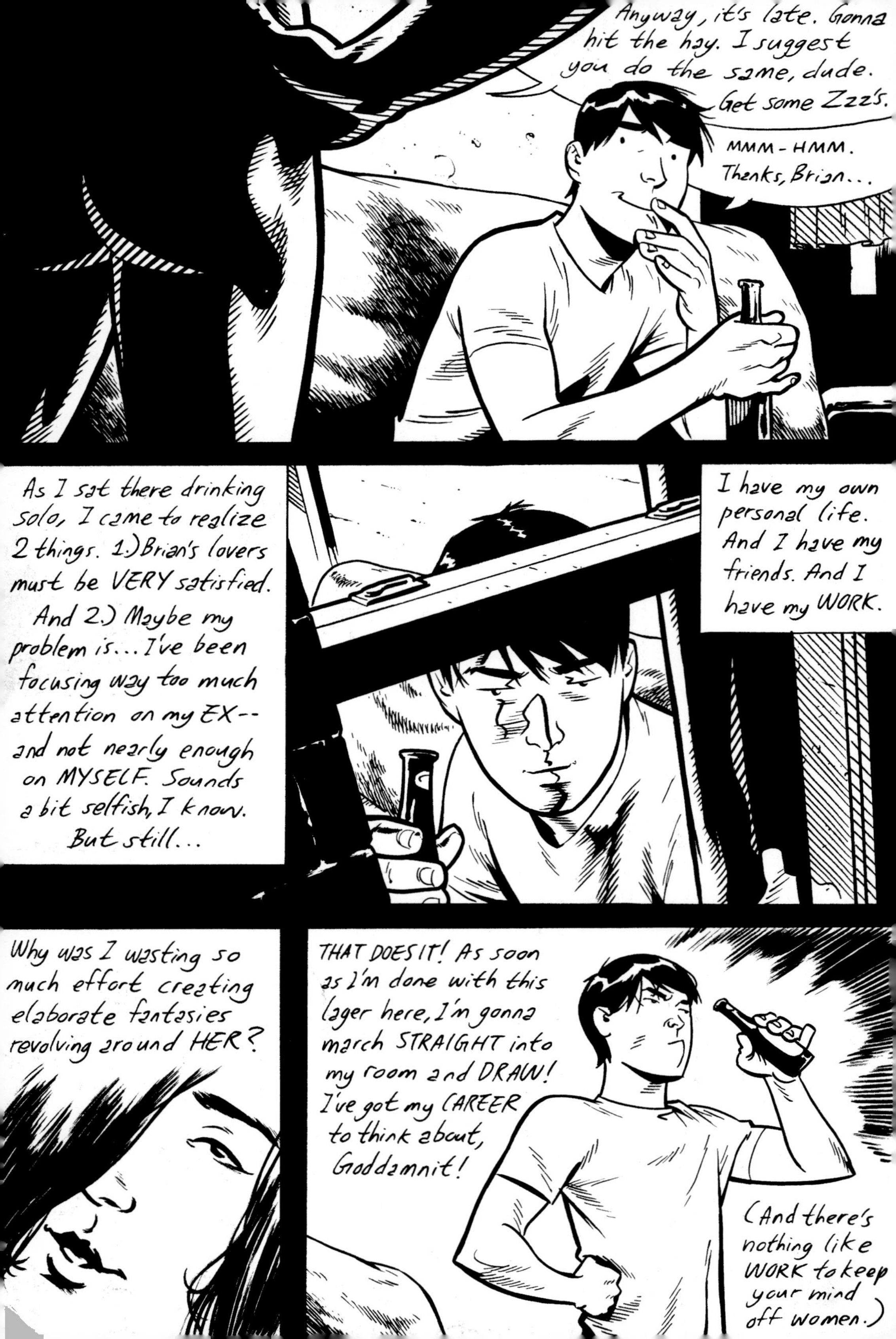

Anyway, it's late. Gonna hit the hay. I suggest you do the same, dude. Get some Zzz's.
MMM-HMM. Thanks, Brian...
As I sat there drinking solo, I came to realize 2 things. 1.) Brian's lovers must be VERY satisfied. And 2.) Maybe my problem is... I've been focusing way too much attention on my EX-- and not nearly enough on MYSELF. Sounds a bit selfish, I know. But still...
I have my own personal life. And I have my friends. And I have my WORK.
Why was I wasting so much effort creating elaborate fantasies revolving around HER?
THAT DOES IT! As soon as I'm done with this lager here, I'm gonna march STRAIGHT into my room and DRAW! I've got my CAREER to think about, Goddamnit!
(And there's nothing like WORK to keep your mind off women.)

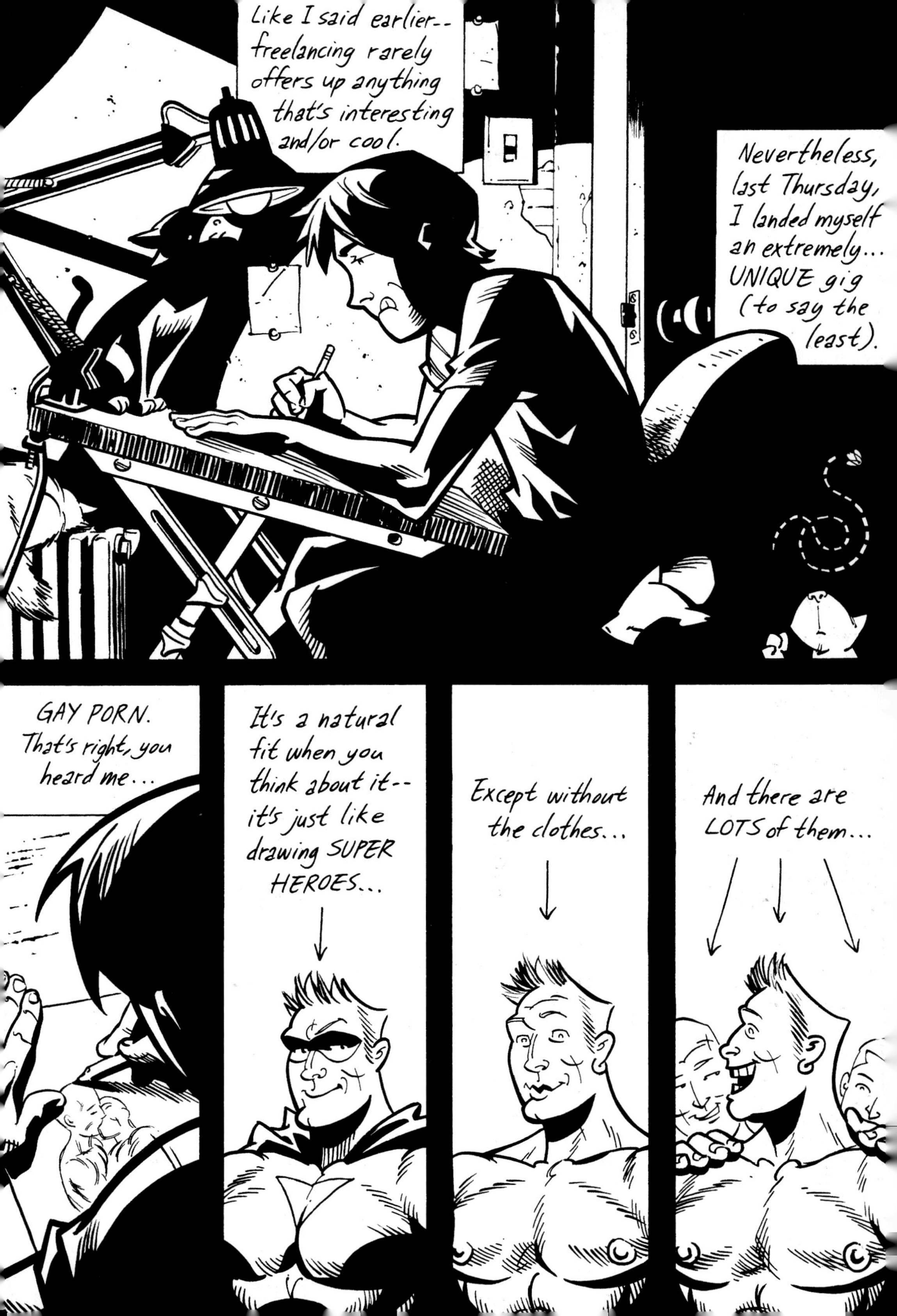
Like I said earlier-- freelancing rarely offers up anything that's interesting and/or cool.
Nevertheless, last Thursday, I landed myself an extremely... UNIQUE gig (to say the least).
GAY PORN. That's right, you heard me...
It's a natural fit when you think about it-- it's just like drawing SUPER HEROES...
Except without the clothes...
And there are LOTS of them...

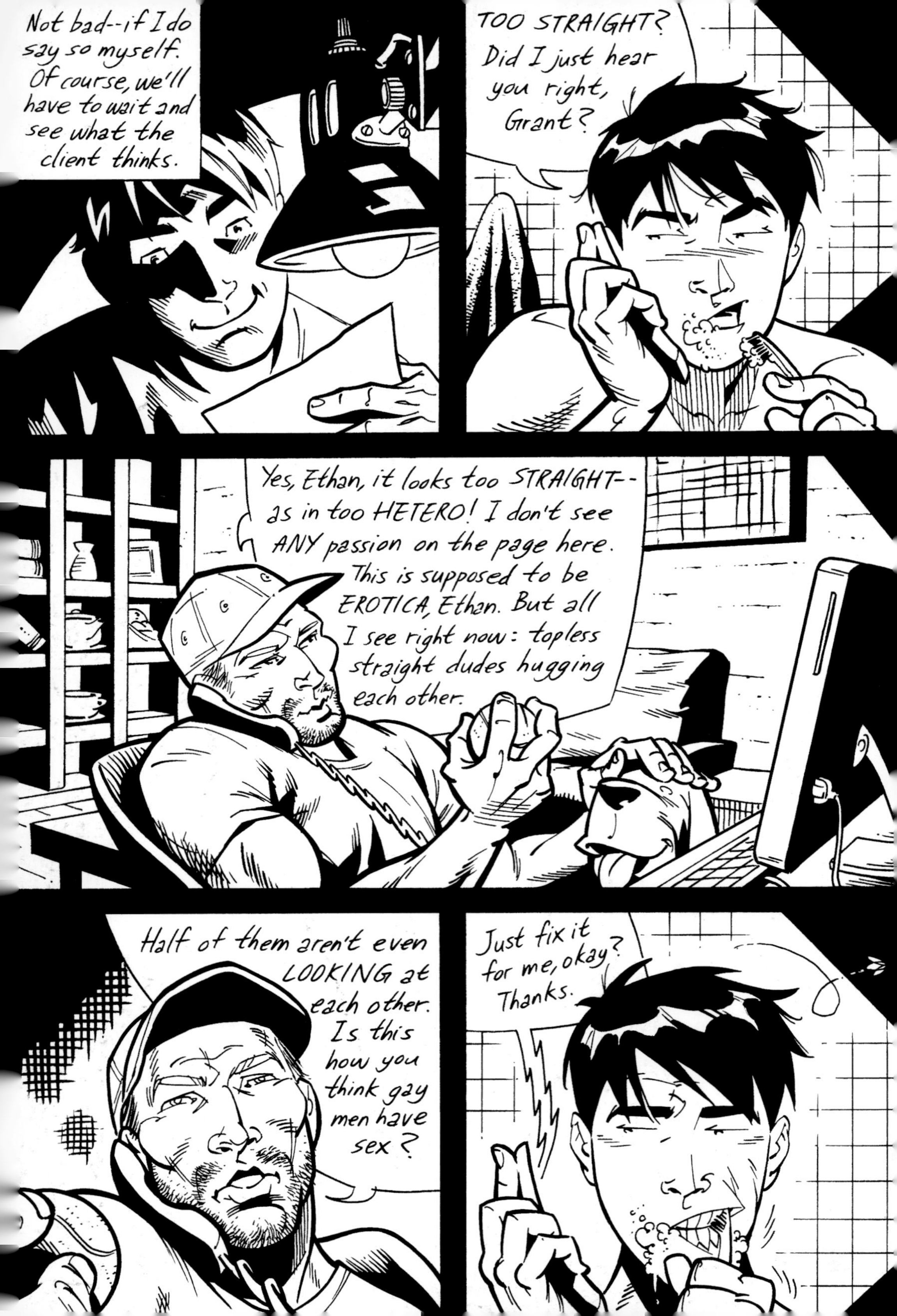
Not bad--if I do say so myself. Of course, we'll have to wait and see what the client thinks.
TOO STRAIGHT? Did I just hear you right, Grant?
Yes, Ethan, it looks too STRAIGHT--as in too HETERO! I don't see ANY passion on the page here. This is supposed to be EROTICA, Ethan. But all I see right now: topless straight dudes hugging each other.
Half of them aren't even LOOKING at each other. Is this how you think gay men have sex?
Just fix it for me, okay? Thanks.

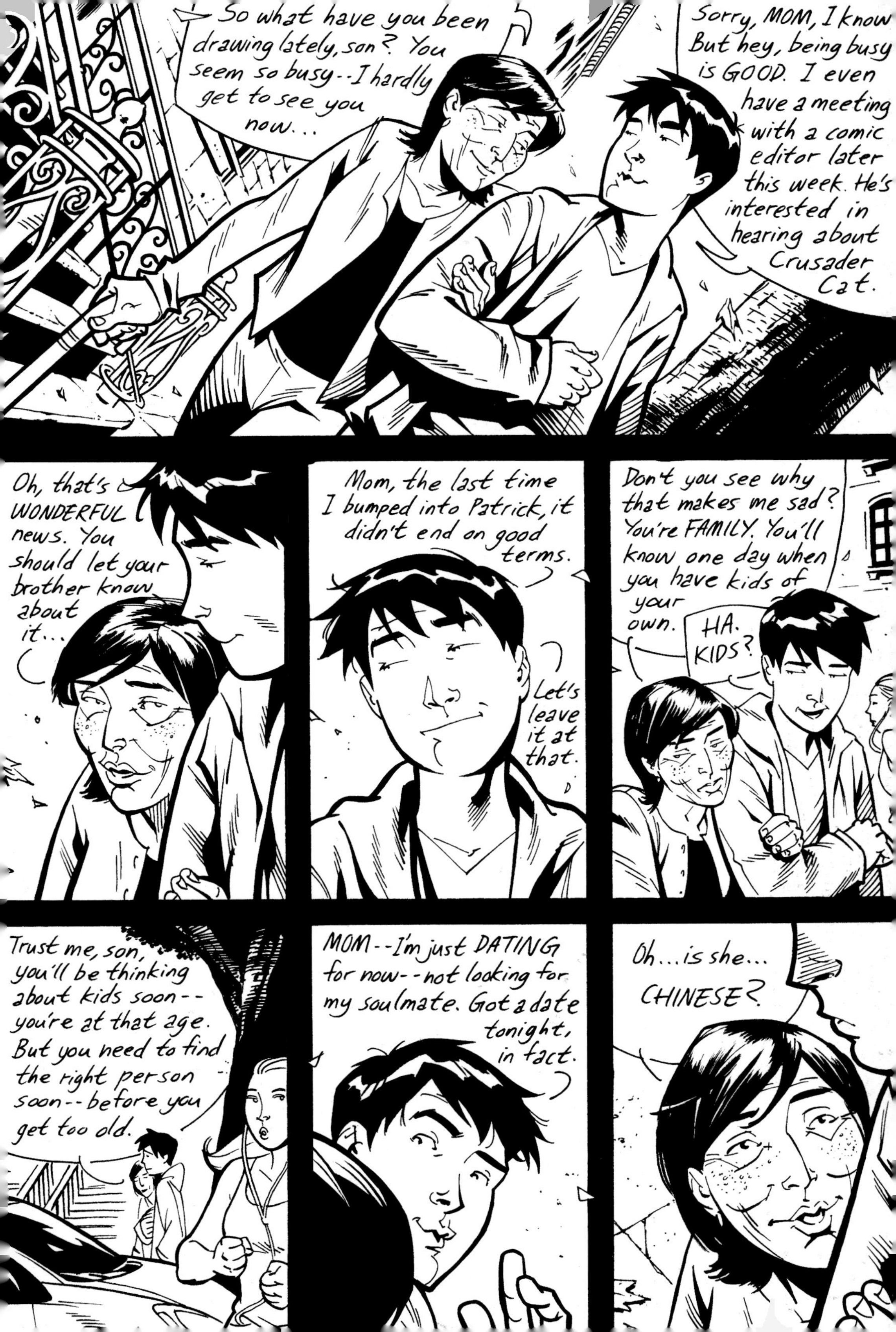
So what have you been drawing lately, son? You seem so busy--I hardly get to see you now...
Sorry, MOM, I know But hey, being busy is GOOD. I even have a meeting with a comic editor later this week. He's interested in hearing about Crusader Cat.
Oh, that's WONDERFUL news. You should let your brother know about it...
Mom, the last time I bumped into Patrick, it didn't end on good terms.
Let's leave it at that.
Don't you see why that makes me sad? You're FAMILY. You'll know one day when you have kids of your own.
HA. KIDS?
Trust me, son, you'll be thinking about kids soon--you're at that age. But you need to find the right person soon--before you get too old.
MOM--I'm just DATING for now--not looking for my soulmate. Got a date tonight, in fact.
Oh...is she... CHINESE?

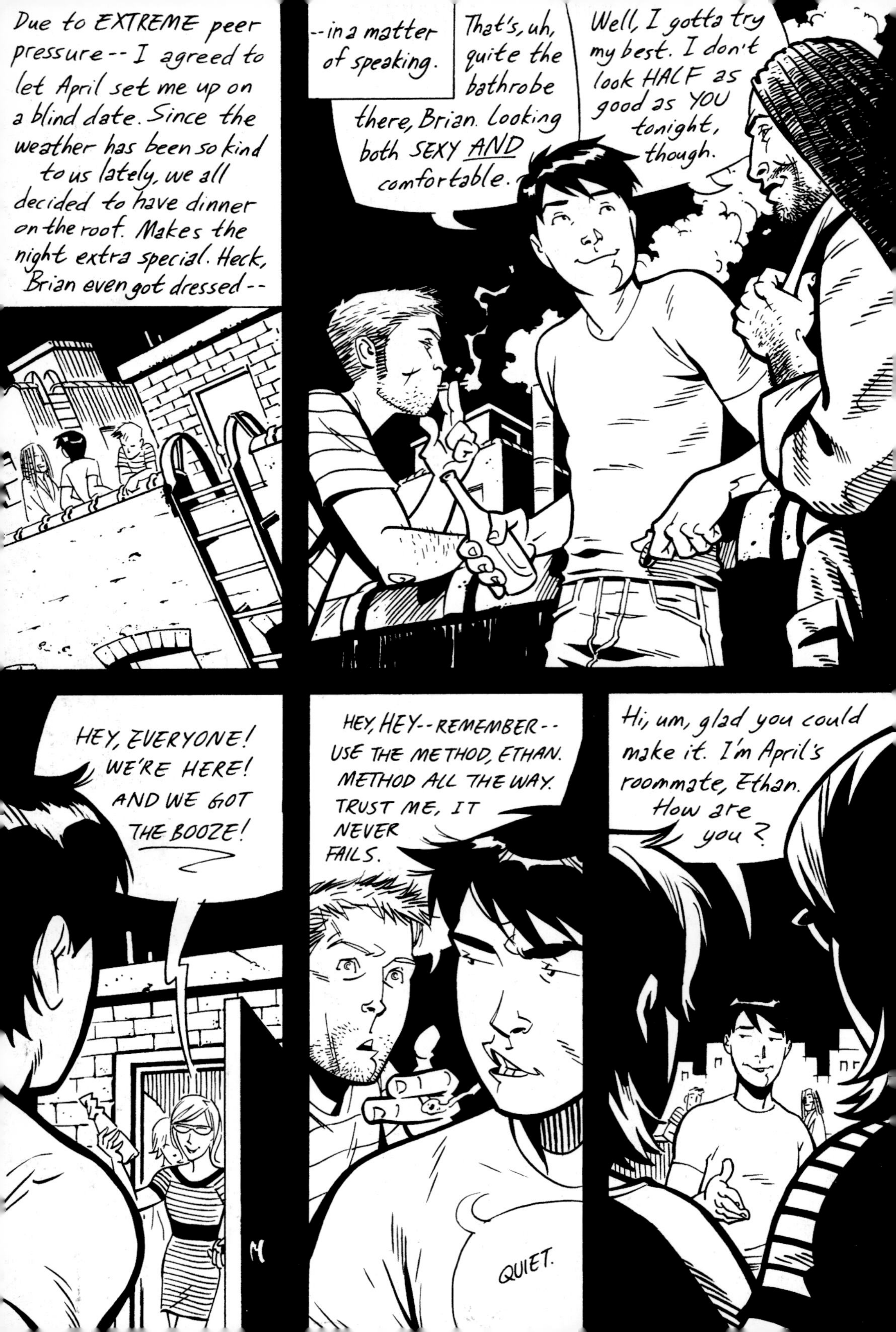
Due to EXTREME peer pressure -- I agreed to let April set me up on a blind date. Since the weather has been so kind to us lately, we all decided to have dinner on the roof. Makes the night extra special. Heck, Brian even got dressed --
-- in a matter of speaking.
That's, uh, quite the bathrobe there, Brian. Looking both SEXY AND comfortable.
Well, I gotta try my best. I don't look HALF as good as YOU tonight, though.
HEY, EVERYONE! WE'RE HERE! AND WE GOT THE BOOZE!
HEY, HEY -- REMEMBER -- USE THE METHOD, ETHAN. METHOD ALL THE WAY. TRUST ME, IT NEVER FAILS.
QUIET.
Hi, um, glad you could make it. I'm April's roommate, Ethan. How are you?

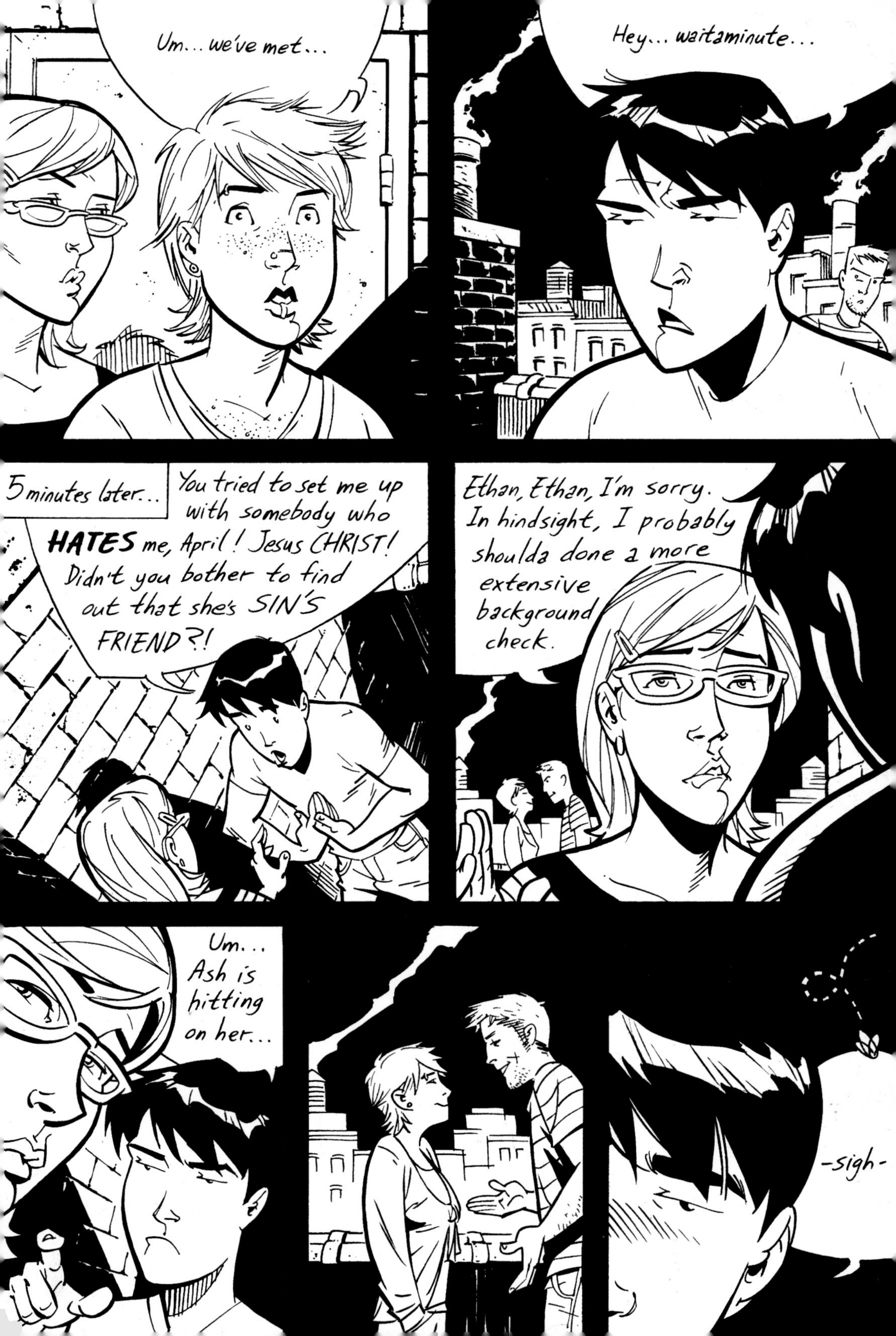
Um... we've met...
Hey... waitaminute...
5 minutes later...
You tried to set me up with somebody who HATES me, April! Jesus CHRIST! Didn't you bother to find out that she's SIN'S FRIEND?!
Ethan, Ethan, I'm sorry. In hindsight, I probably shoulda done a more extensive background check.
Um... Ash is hitting on her...
-sigh-

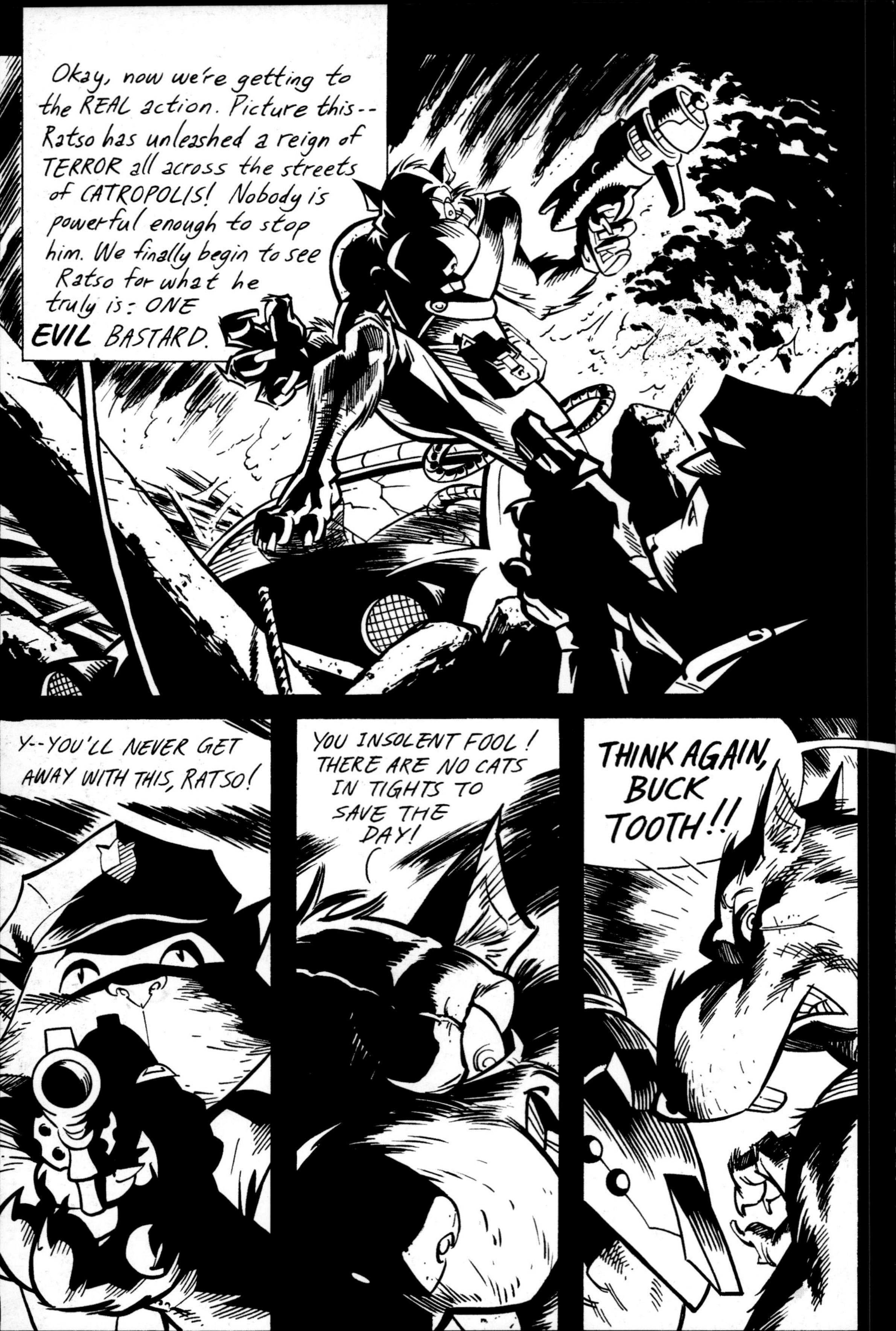
Okay, now we're getting to the REAL action. Picture this-- Ratso has unleashed a reign of TERROR all across the streets of CATROPOLIS! Nobody is powerful enough to stop him. We finally begin to see Ratso for what he truly is: ONE EVIL BASTARD.
Y--YOU'LL NEVER GET AWAY WITH THIS, RATSO!
YOU INSOLENT FOOL! THERE ARE NO CATS IN TIGHTS TO SAVE THE DAY!
THINK AGAIN, BUCK TOOTH!!

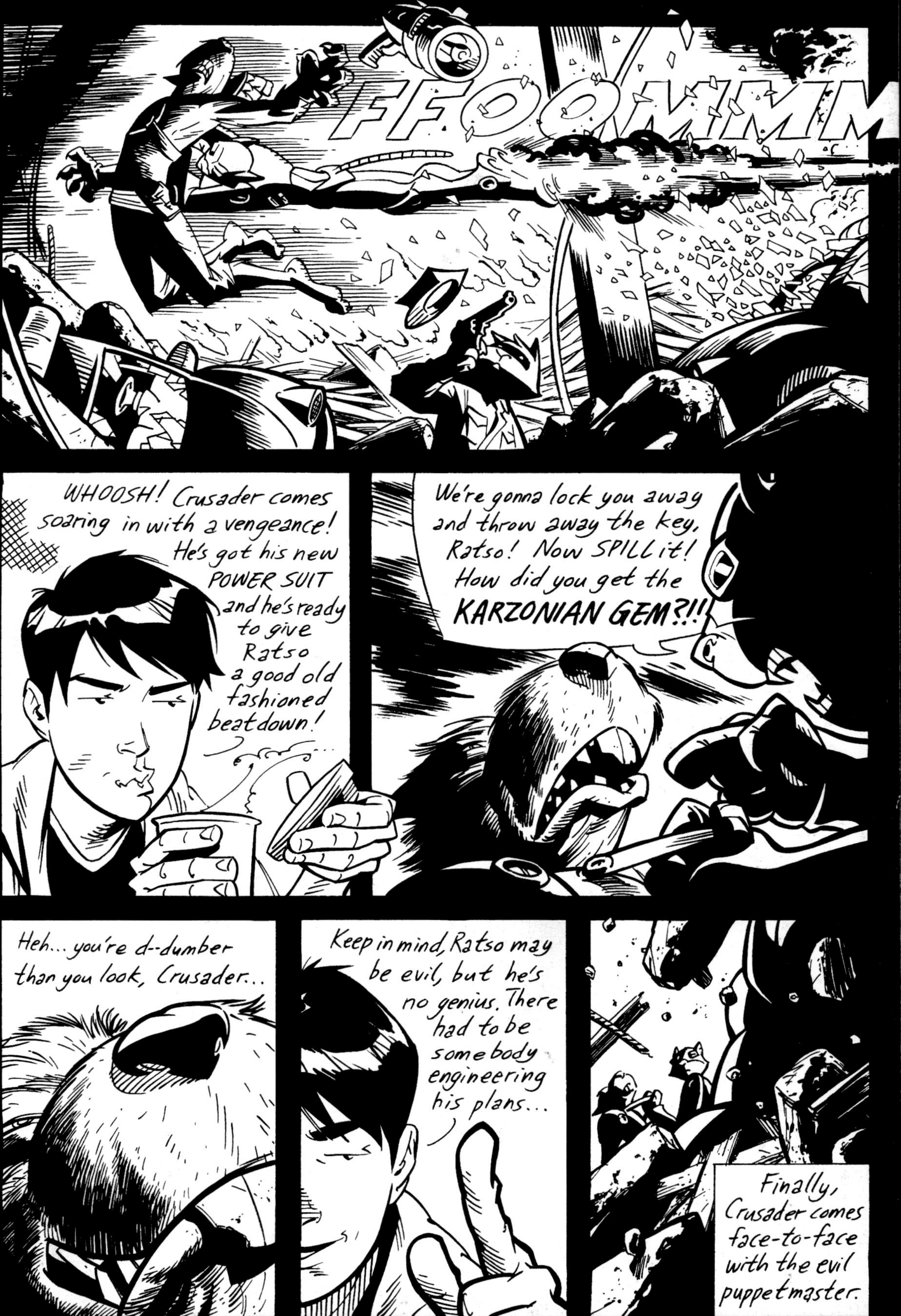
FFOOMMM
WHOOSH! Crusader comes soaring in with a vengeance! He's got his new POWER SUIT and he's ready to give Ratso a good old fashioned beatdown!
We're gonna lock you away and throw away the key, Ratso! Now SPILL it! How did you get the KARZONIAN GEM?!!
Heh... you're d--dumber than you look, Crusader...
Keep in mind, Ratso may be evil, but he's no genius. There had to be somebody engineering his plans...
Finally, Crusader comes face-to-face with the evil puppetmaster.

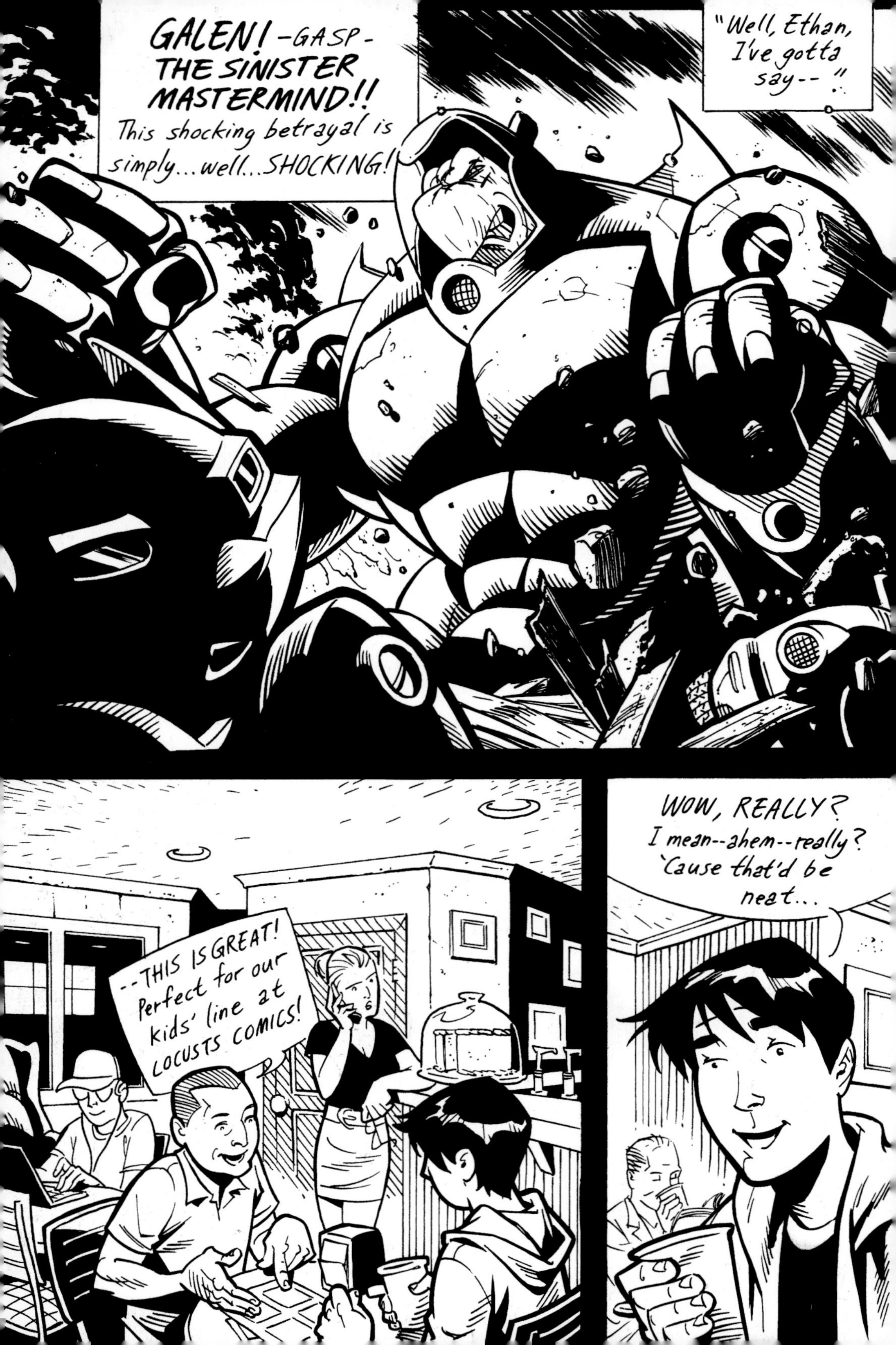
GALEN! -GASP- THE SINISTER MASTERMIND!! This shocking betrayal is simply...well...SHOCKING!
"Well, Ethan, I've gotta say--"
--THIS IS GREAT! Perfect for our kids' line at LOCUSTS COMICS!
WOW, REALLY? I mean--ahem--really? 'Cause that'd be neat...

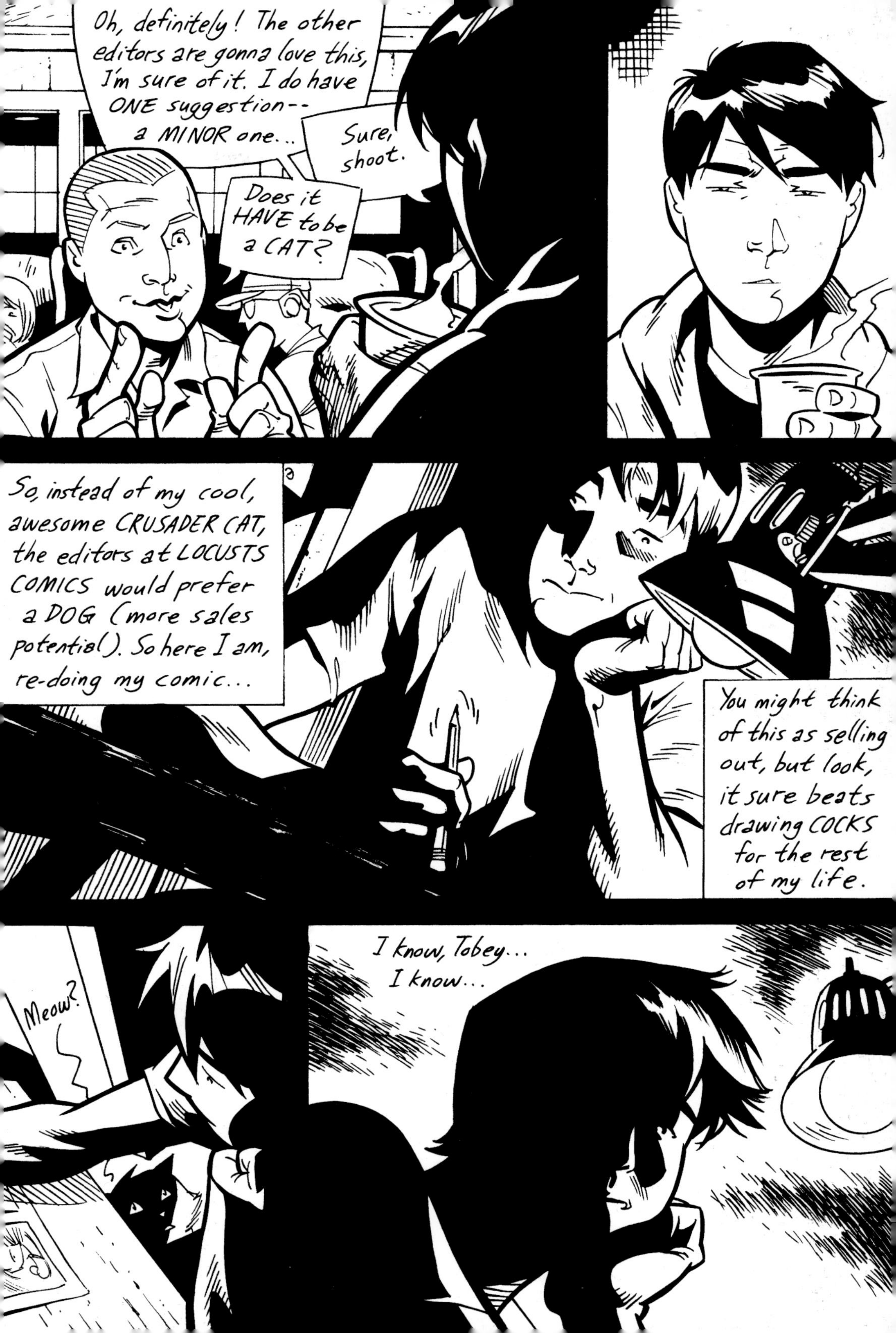
Oh, definitely! The other editors are gonna love this, I'm sure of it. I do have ONE suggestion-- a MINOR one...
Sure, shoot.
Does it HAVE to be a CAT?
So, instead of my cool, awesome CRUSADER CAT, the editors at LOCUSTS COMICS would prefer a DOG (more sales potential). So here I am, re-doing my comic...
You might think of this as selling out, but look, it sure beats drawing COCKS for the rest of my life.
Meow?
I know, Tobey... I know...

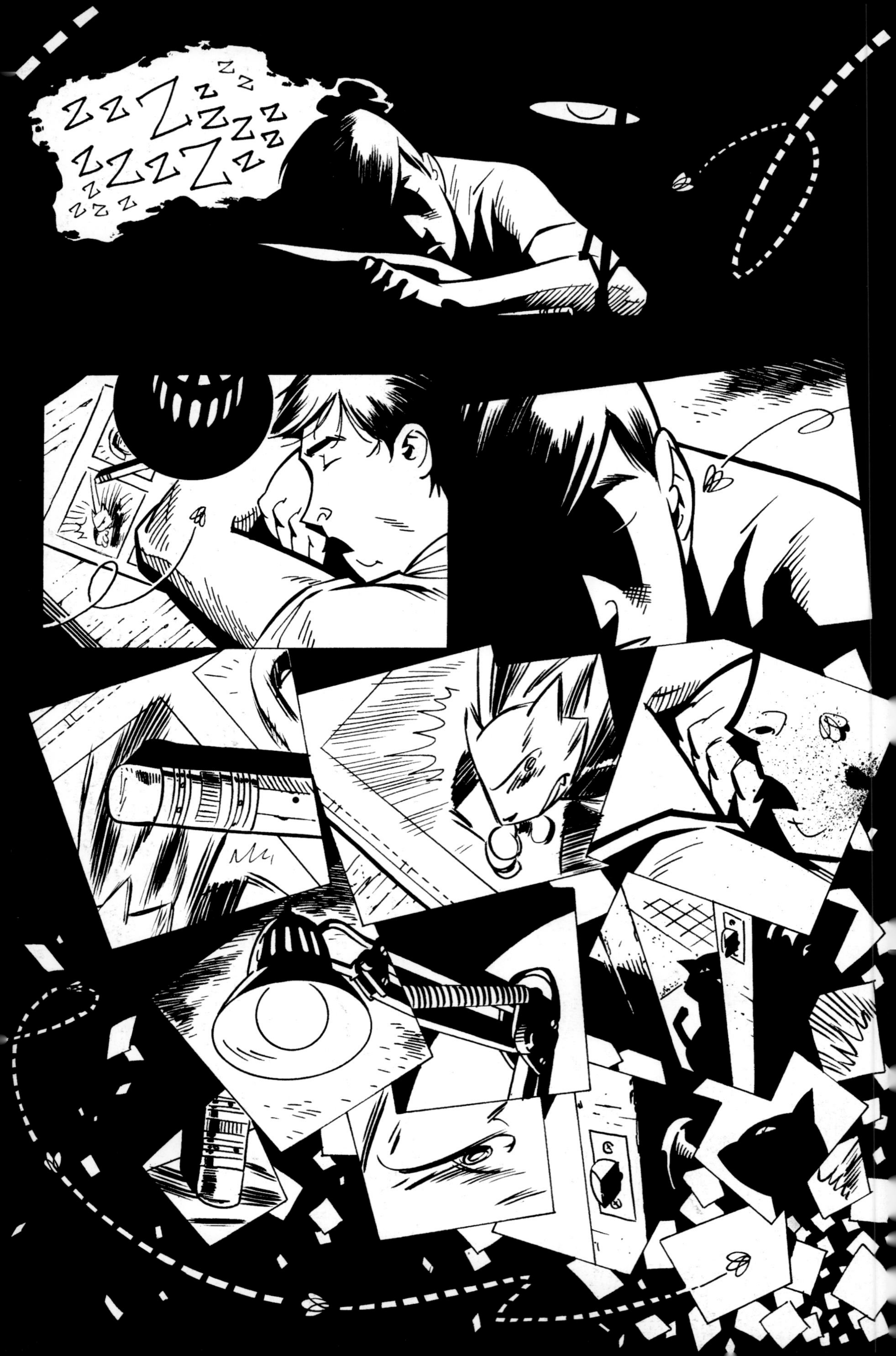
ZZ
ZZZZZZZZ
ZZZZZZ
ZZZZ

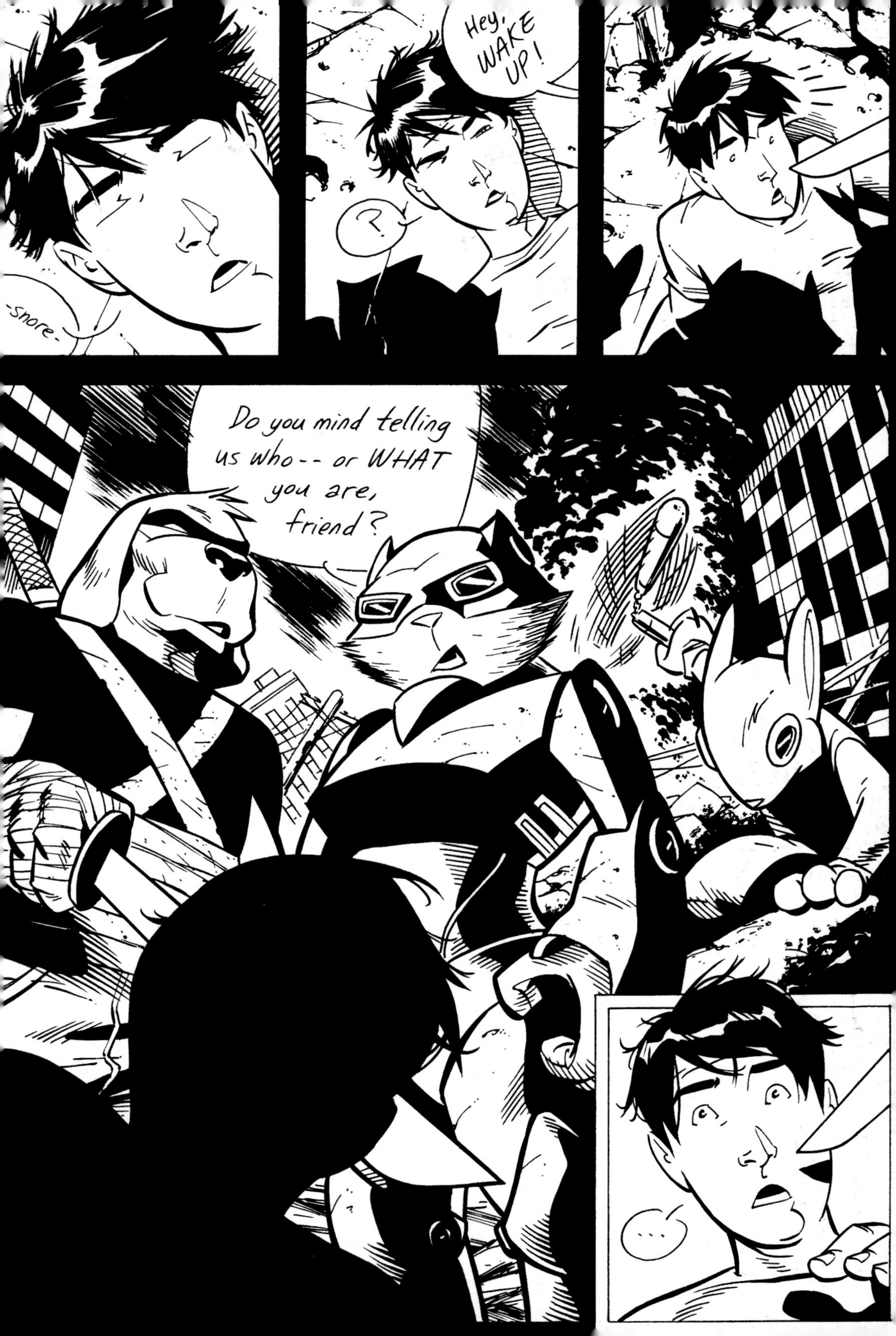

-snore-
Hey, WAKE UP!
?
Do you mind telling us who-- or WHAT you are, friend?
...

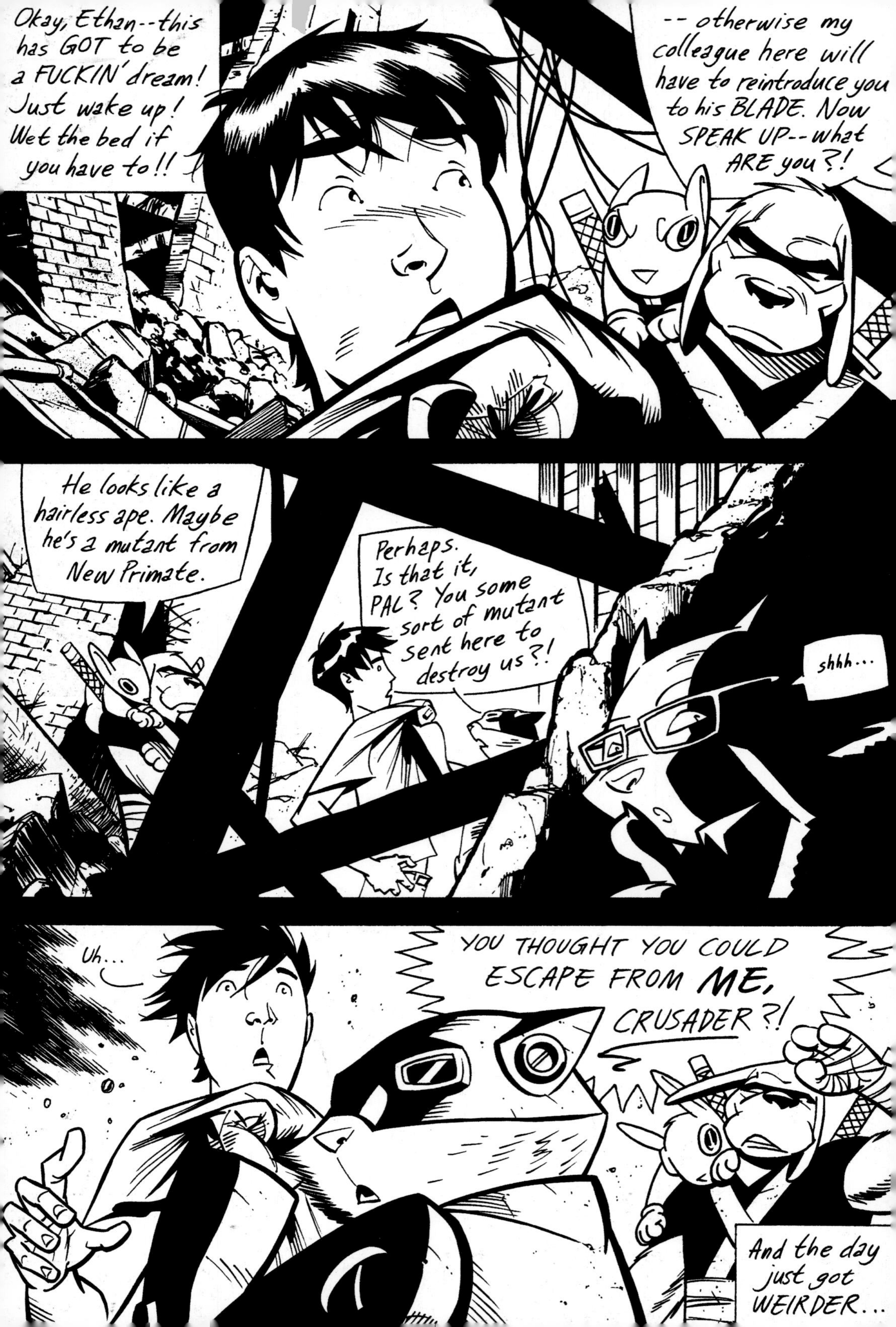
Okay, Ethan--this has GOT to be a FUCKIN' dream! Just wake up! Wet the bed if you have to!!
--otherwise my colleague here will have to reintroduce you to his BLADE. Now SPEAK UP--what ARE you?!
He looks like a hairless ape. Maybe he's a mutant from New Primate.
Perhaps. Is that it, PAL? You some sort of mutant sent here to destroy us?!
shhh...
Uh...
YOU THOUGHT YOU COULD ESCAPE FROM ME, CRUSADER?!
And the day just got WEIRDER...

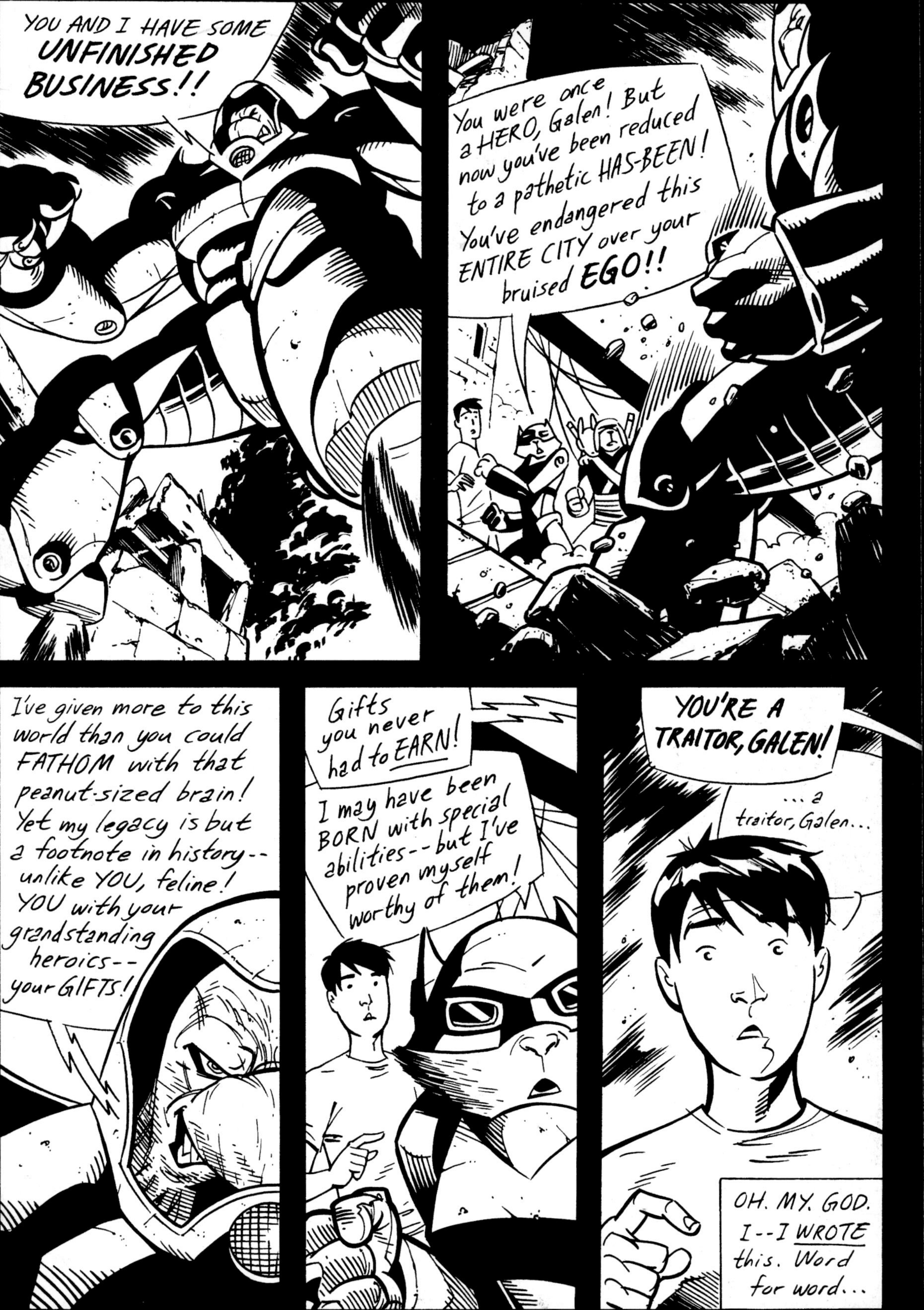

YOU AND I HAVE SOME UNFINISHED BUSINESS!!
You were once a HERO, Galen! But now you've been reduced to a pathetic HAS-BEEN! You've endangered this ENTIRE CITY over your bruised EGO!!
I've given more to this world than you could FATHOM with that peanut-sized brain! Yet my legacy is but a footnote in history-- unlike YOU, feline! YOU with your grandstanding heroics-- your GIFTS!
Gifts you never had to EARN!
I may have been BORN with special abilities--but I've proven myself worthy of them!
YOU'RE A TRAITOR, GALEN!
...a traitor, Galen...
OH. MY. GOD. I--I WROTE this. Word for word...

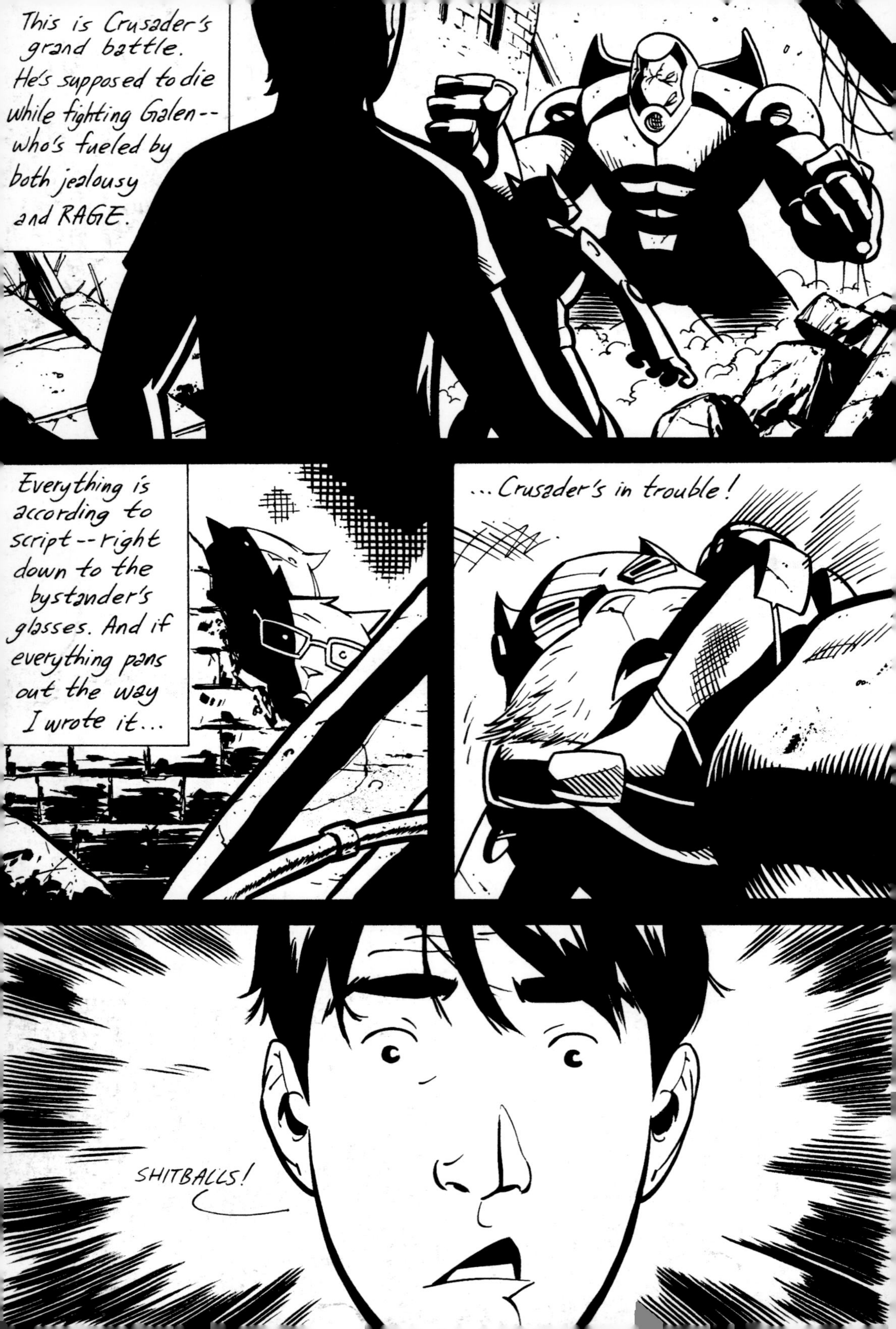
This is Crusader's grand battle. He's supposed to die while fighting Galen-- who's fueled by both jealousy and RAGE.
Everything is according to script--right down to the bystander's glasses. And if everything pans out the way I wrote it...
...Crusader's in trouble!
SHITBALLS!

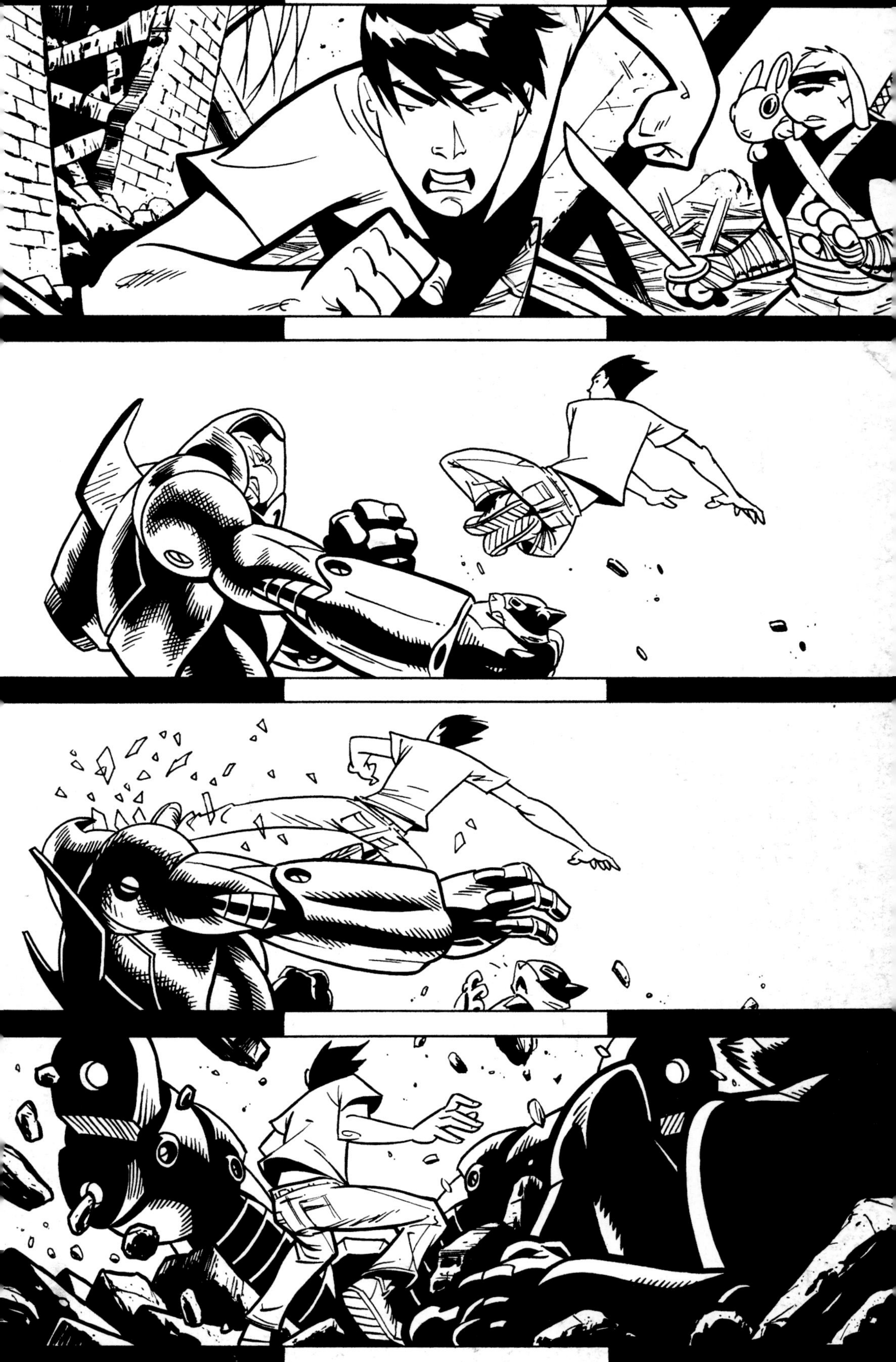

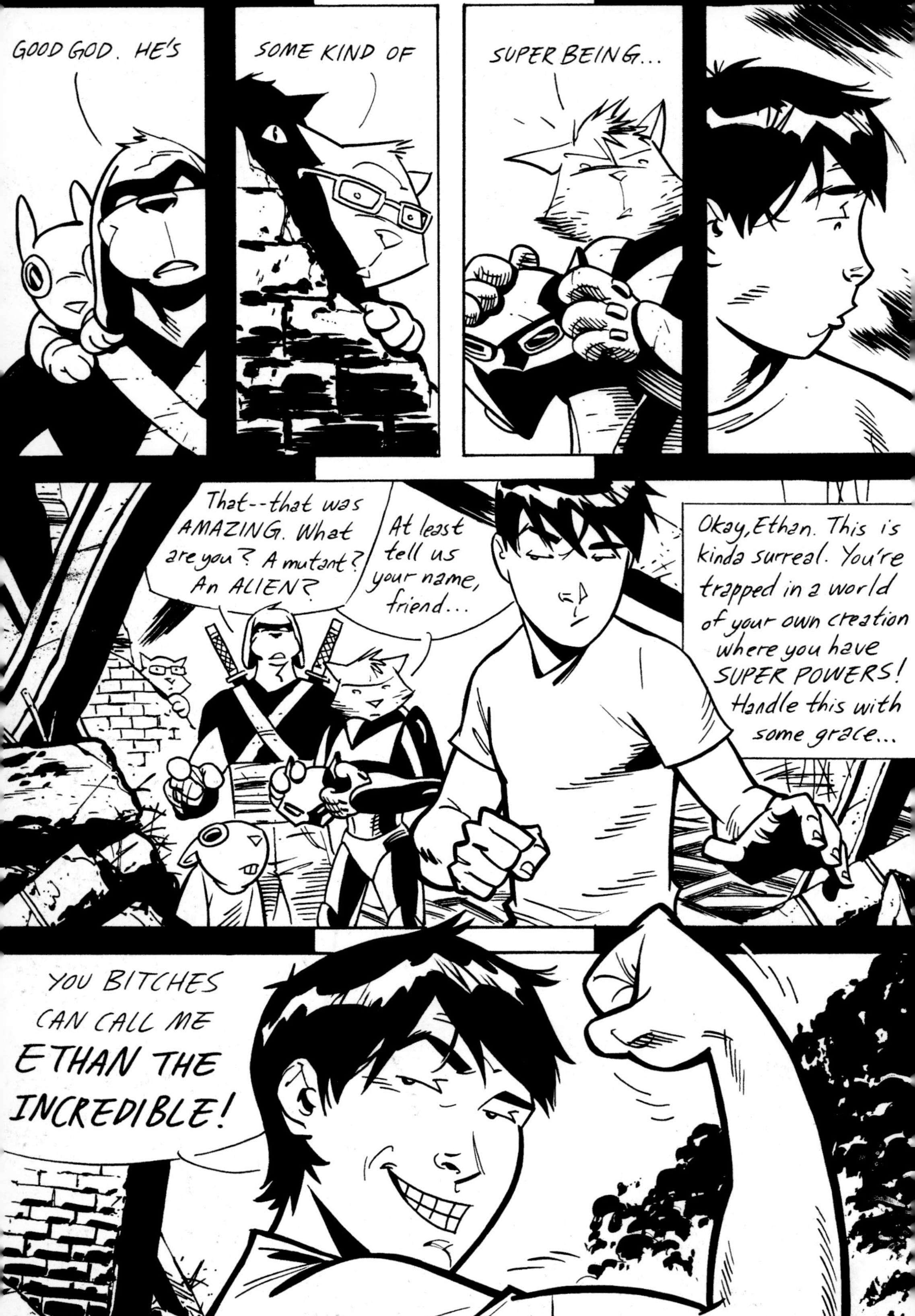
GOOD GOD. HE'S
SOME KIND OF
SUPER BEING...
That--that was AMAZING. What are you? A mutant? An ALIEN?
At least tell us your name, friend...
Okay, Ethan. This is kinda surreal. You're trapped in a world of your own creation where you have SUPER POWERS! Handle this with some grace...
YOU BITCHES CAN CALL ME ETHAN THE INCREDIBLE!

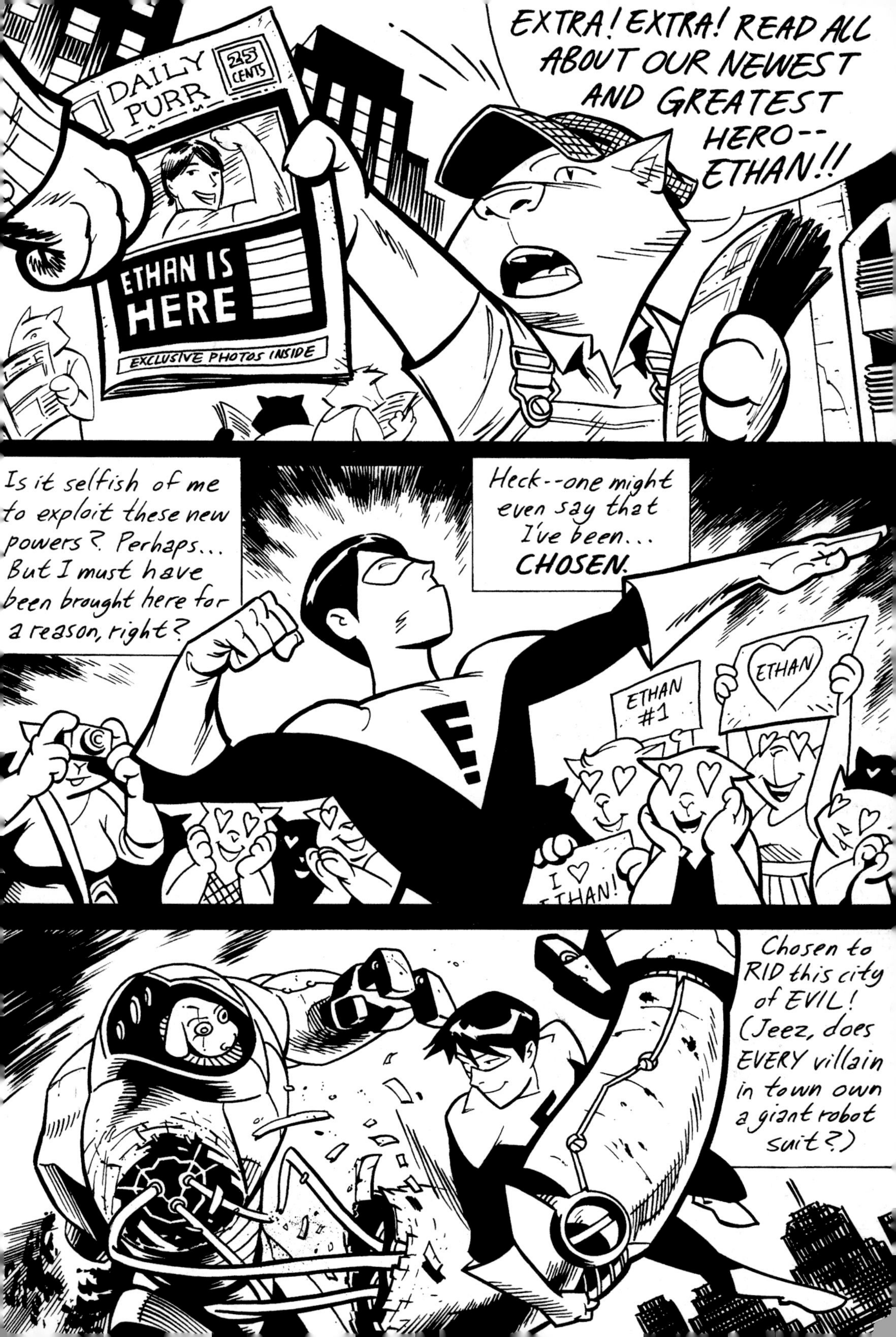

DAILY PURR
25 CENTS
ETHAN IS HERE
EXCLUSIVE PHOTOS INSIDE
EXTRA! EXTRA! READ ALL ABOUT OUR NEWEST AND GREATEST HERO-- ETHAN!!
Is it selfish of me to exploit these new powers? Perhaps... But I must have been brought here for a reason, right?
Heck--one might even say that I've been... CHOSEN.
ETHAN #1
ETHAN
I ♡ ETHAN!
Chosen to RID this city of EVIL! (Jeez, does EVERY villain in town own a giant robot suit?)

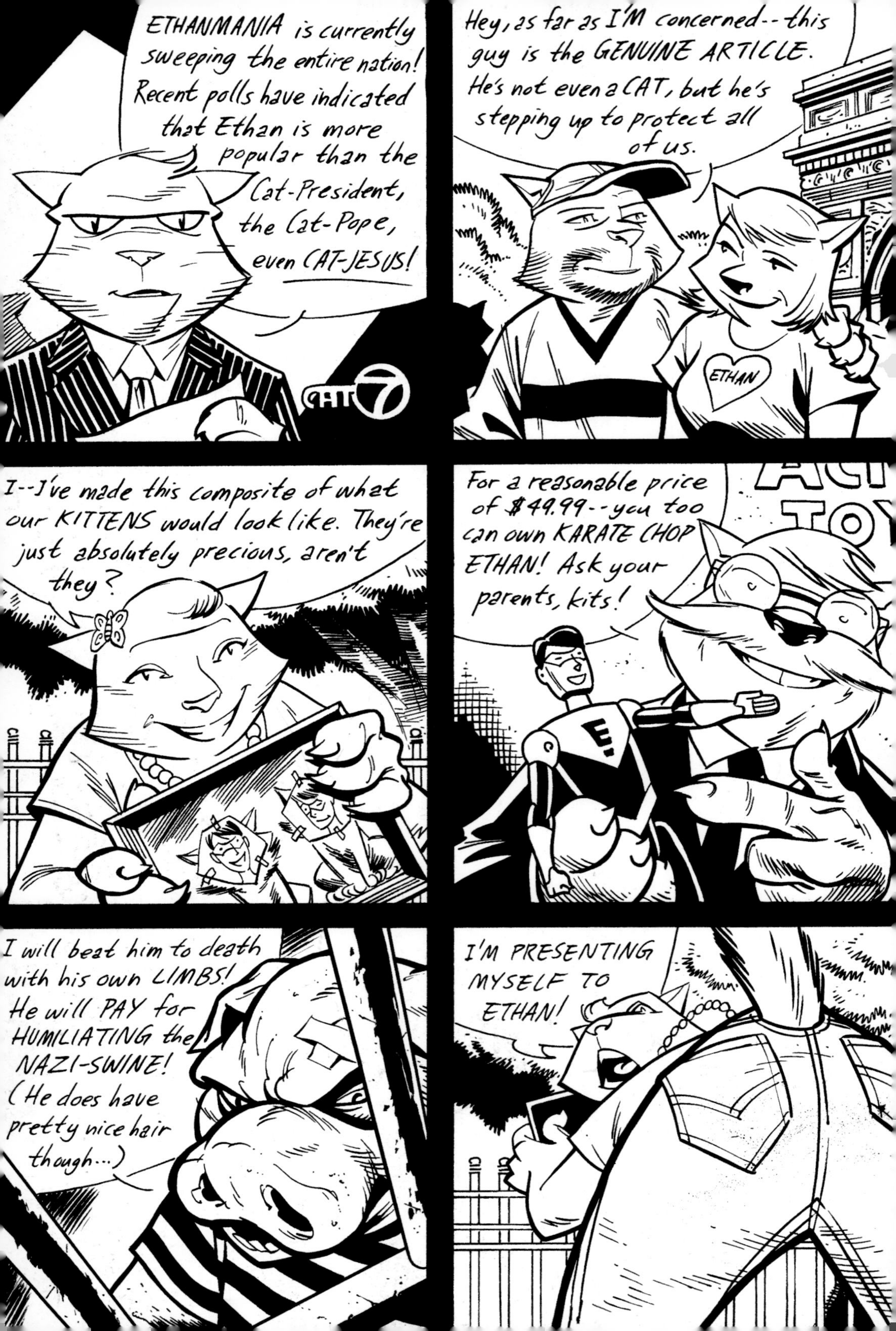
ETHANMANIA is currently sweeping the entire nation! Recent polls have indicated that Ethan is more popular than the Cat-President, the Cat-Pope, even CAT-JESUS!
CHT 7
Hey, as far as I'M concerned--this guy is the GENUINE ARTICLE. He's not even a CAT, but he's stepping up to protect all of us.
ETHAN
I--I've made this composite of what our KITTENS would look like. They're just absolutely precious, aren't they?
For a reasonable price of $49.99--you too can own KARATE CHOP ETHAN! Ask your parents, kits!
I will beat him to death with his own LIMBS! He will PAY for HUMILIATING the NAZI-SWINE! (He does have pretty nice hair though...)
I'M PRESENTING MYSELF TO ETHAN!

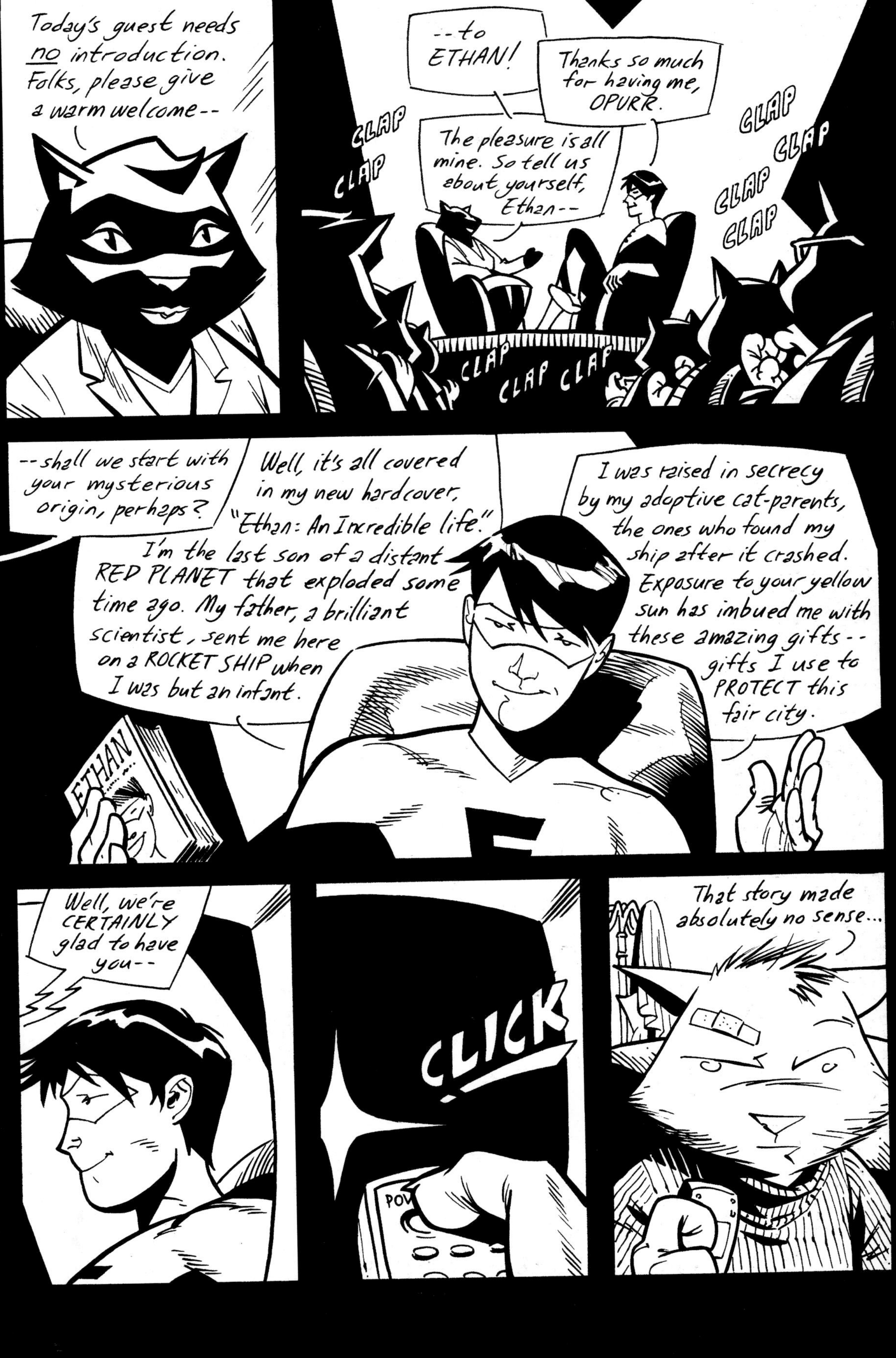
Today's guest needs no introduction. Folks, please give a warm welcome--
--to ETHAN!
Thanks so much for having me, OPURR.
The pleasure is all mine. So tell us about yourself, Ethan--
CLAP CLAP CLAP CLAP CLAP CLAP CLAP CLAP CLAP
--shall we start with your mysterious origin, perhaps?
Well, it's all covered in my new hardcover, "Ethan: An Incredible Life." I'm the last son of a distant RED PLANET that exploded some time ago. My father, a brilliant scientist, sent me here on a ROCKET SHIP when I was but an infant.
I was raised in secrecy by my adoptive cat-parents, the ones who found my ship after it crashed. Exposure to your yellow sun has imbued me with these amazing gifts--gifts I use to PROTECT this fair city.
ETHAN
Well, we're CERTAINLY glad to have you--
CLICK
That story made absolutely no sense...

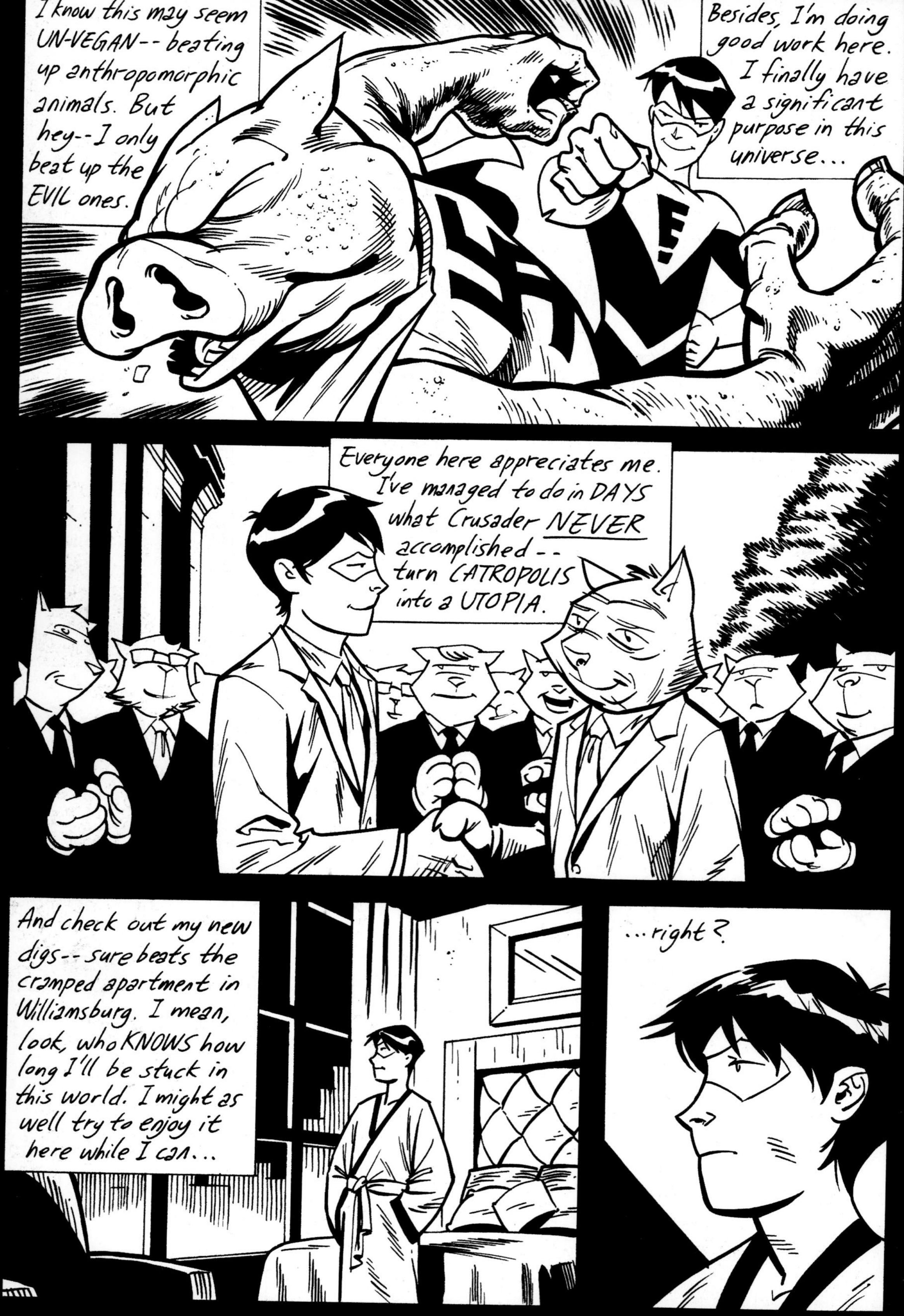
I know this may seem UN-VEGAN-- beating up anthropomorphic animals. But hey--I only beat up the EVIL ones.
Besides, I'm doing good work here. I finally have a significant purpose in this universe...
Everyone here appreciates me. I've managed to do in DAYS what Crusader NEVER accomplished-- turn CATROPOLIS into a UTOPIA.
And check out my new digs--sure beats the cramped apartment in Williamsburg. I mean, look, who KNOWS how long I'll be stuck in this world. I might as well try to enjoy it here while I can...
...right?

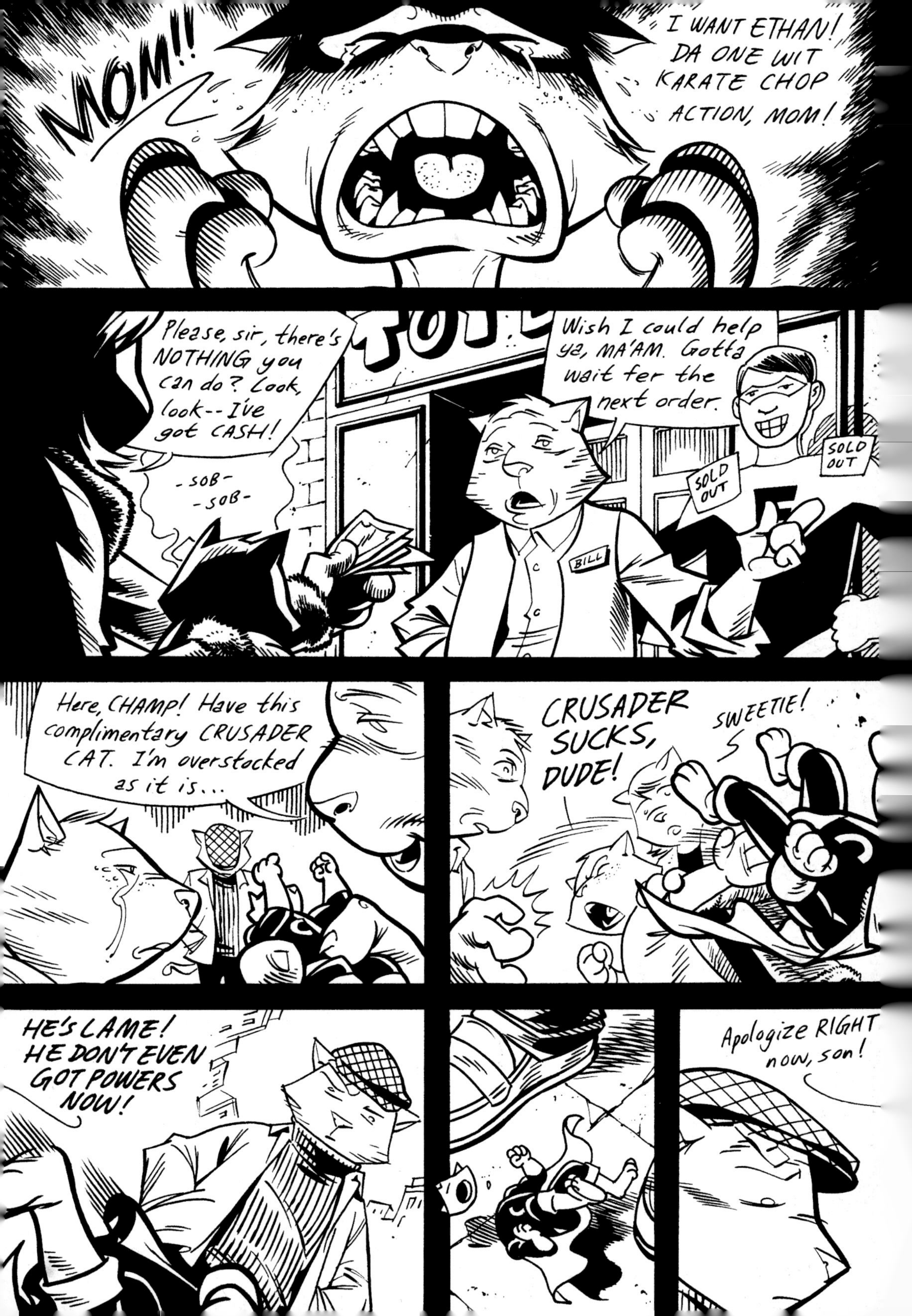
MOM!!
I WANT ETHAN! DA ONE WIT KARATE CHOP ACTION, MOM!
Please, sir, there's NOTHING you can do? Look, look--I've got CASH!
-SOB-
-SOB-
Wish I could help ya, MA'AM. Gotta wait fer the next order.
SOLD OUT
SOLD OUT
BILL
Here, CHAMP! Have this complimentary CRUSADER CAT. I'm overstocked as it is...
CRUSADER SUCKS, DUDE!
SWEETIE!
HE'S LAME! HE DON'T EVEN GOT POWERS NOW!
Apologize RIGHT now, son!

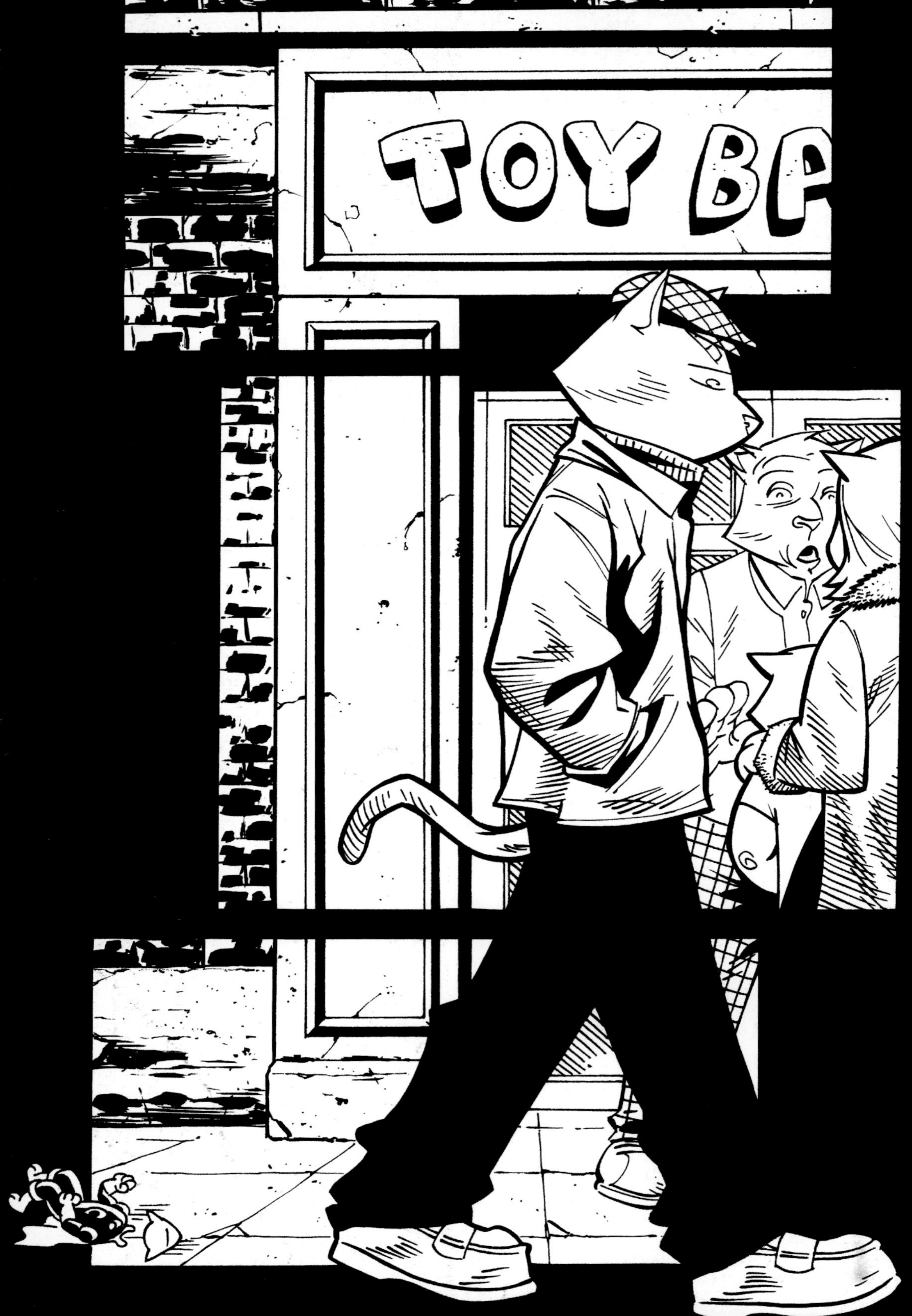
TOY B

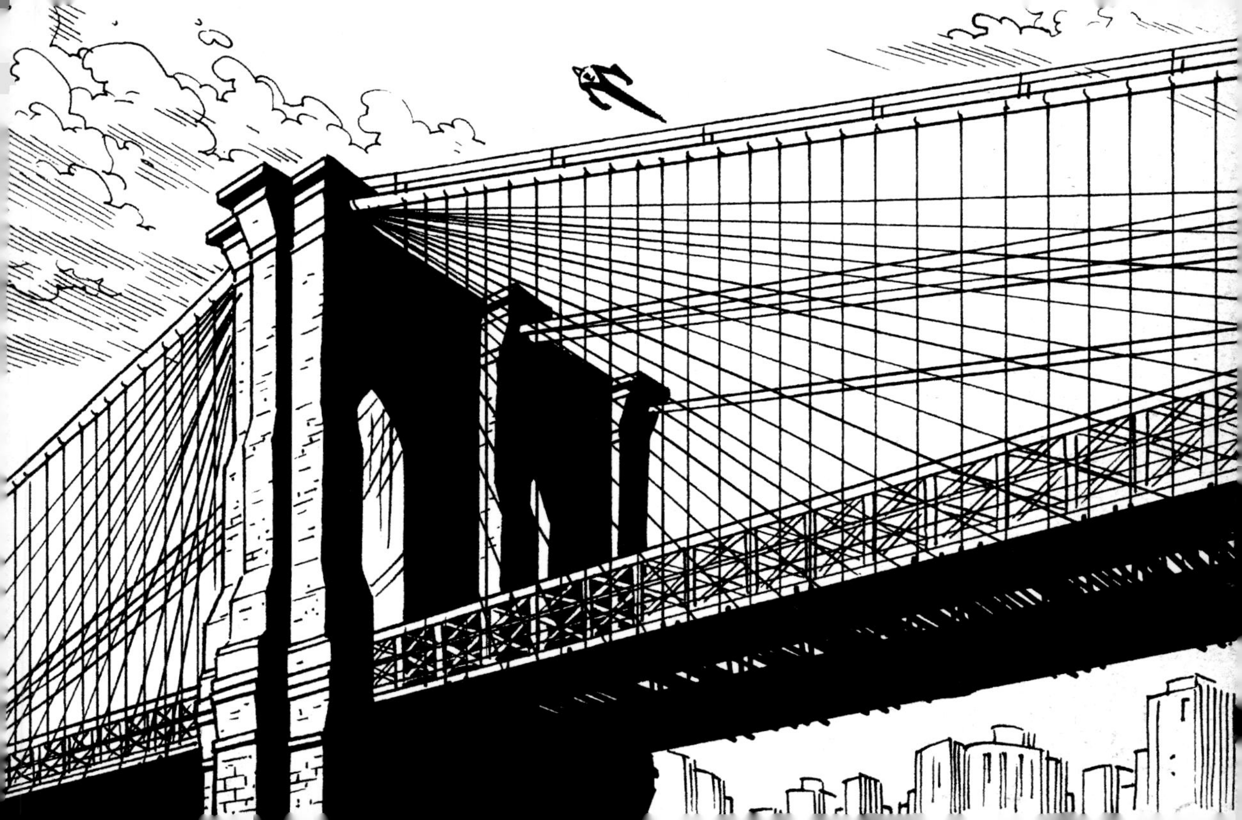

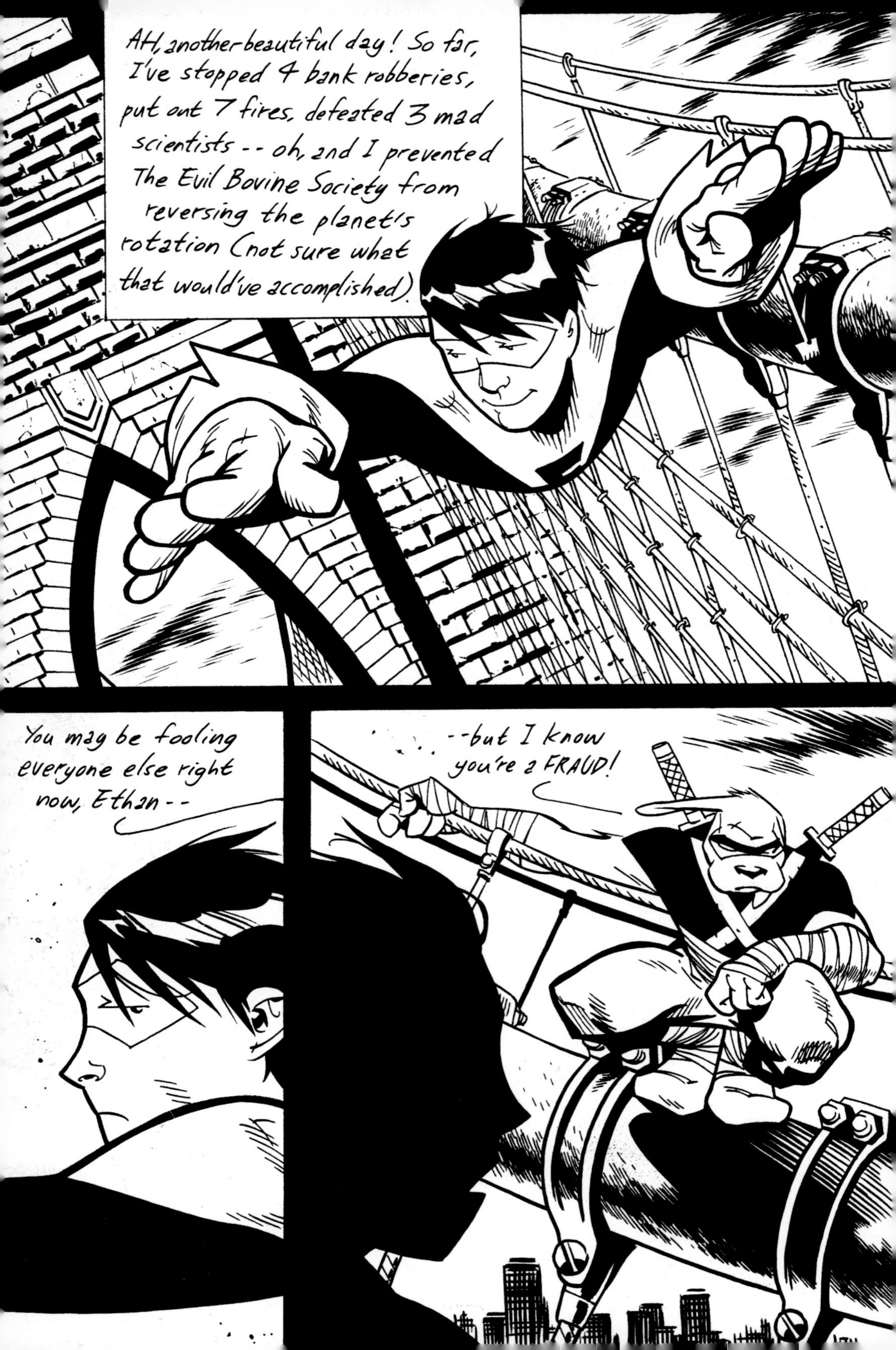
AH, another beautiful day! So far, I've stopped 4 bank robberies, put out 7 fires, defeated 3 mad scientists -- oh, and I prevented The Evil Bovine Society from reversing the planet's rotation (not sure what that would've accomplished).
You may be fooling everyone else right now, Ethan --
--but I know you're a FRAUD!

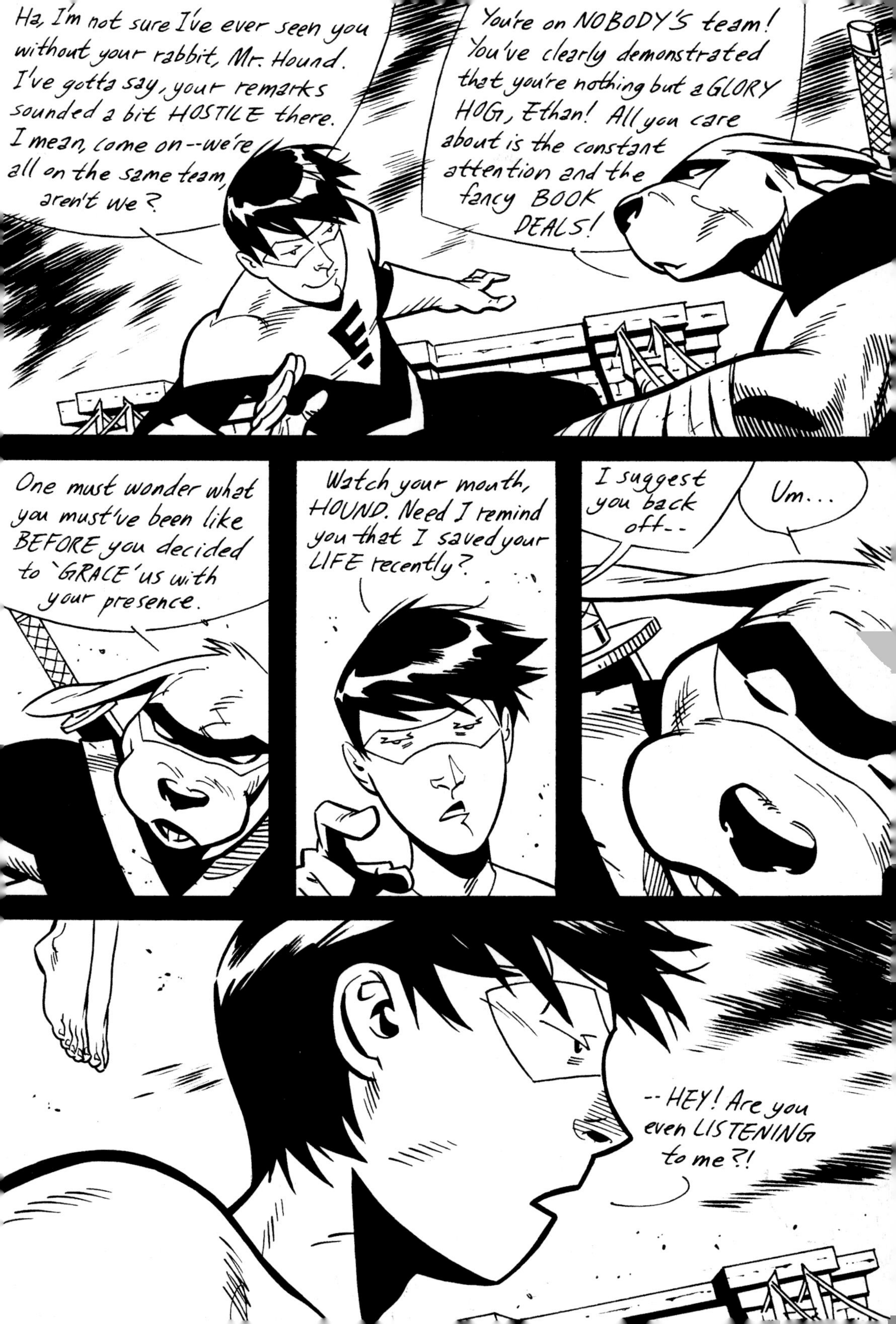

Ha, I'm not sure I've ever seen you without your rabbit, Mr. Hound. I've gotta say, your remarks sounded a bit HOSTILE there. I mean, come on--we're all on the same team, aren't we?
You're on NOBODY'S team! You've clearly demonstrated that you're nothing but a GLORY HOG, Ethan! All you care about is the constant attention and the fancy BOOK DEALS!
One must wonder what you must've been like BEFORE you decided to 'GRACE' us with your presence.
Watch your mouth, HOUND. Need I remind you that I saved your LIFE recently?
I suggest you back off--
Um...
--HEY! Are you even LISTENING to me?!

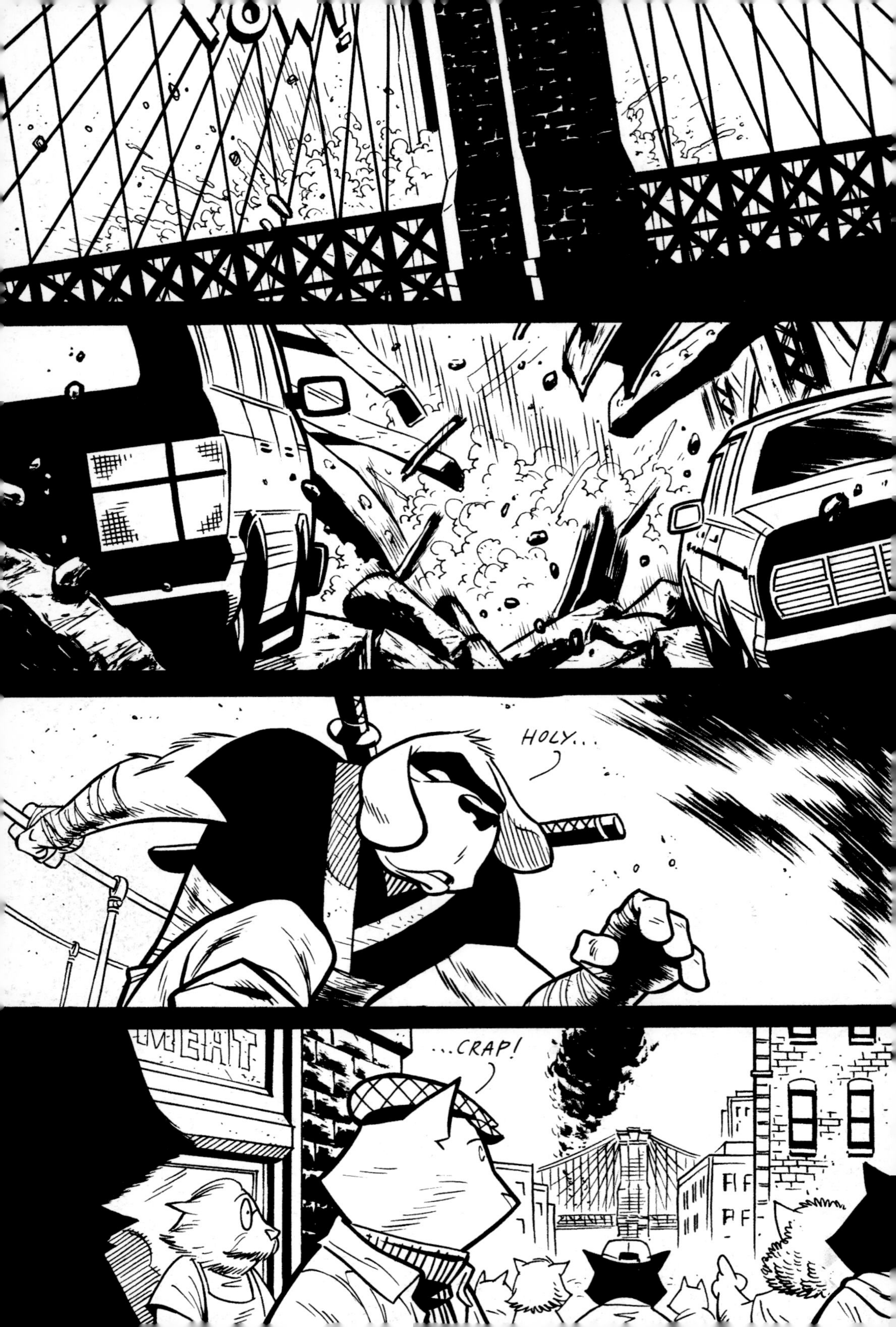
HOLY...
...CRAP!
MEAT

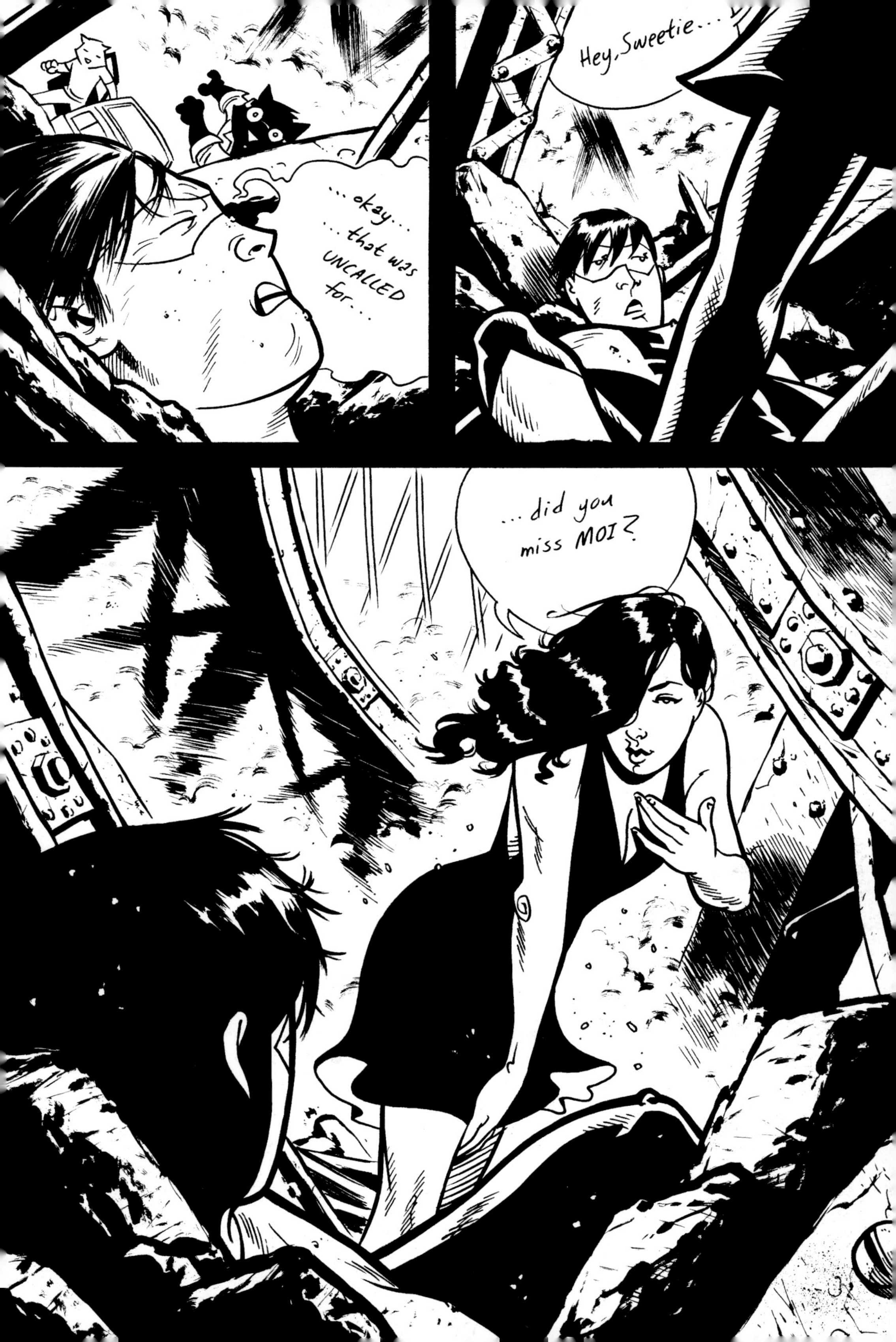
...okay... ...that was UNCALLED for...
Hey, Sweetie...
...did you miss MOI?

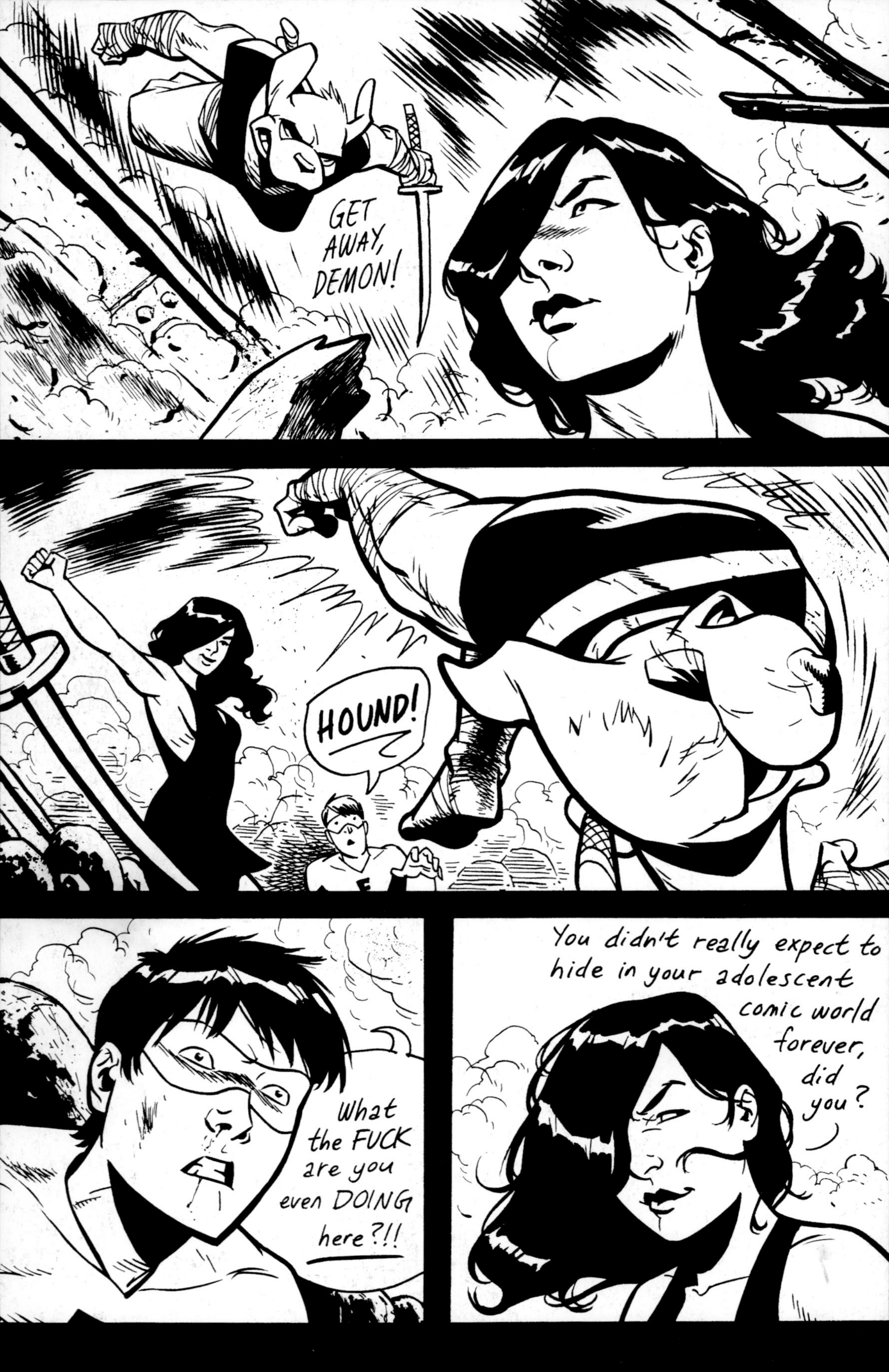
GET AWAY, DEMON!
HOUND!
What the FUCK are you even DOING here?!!
You didn't really expect to hide in your adolescent comic world forever, did you?

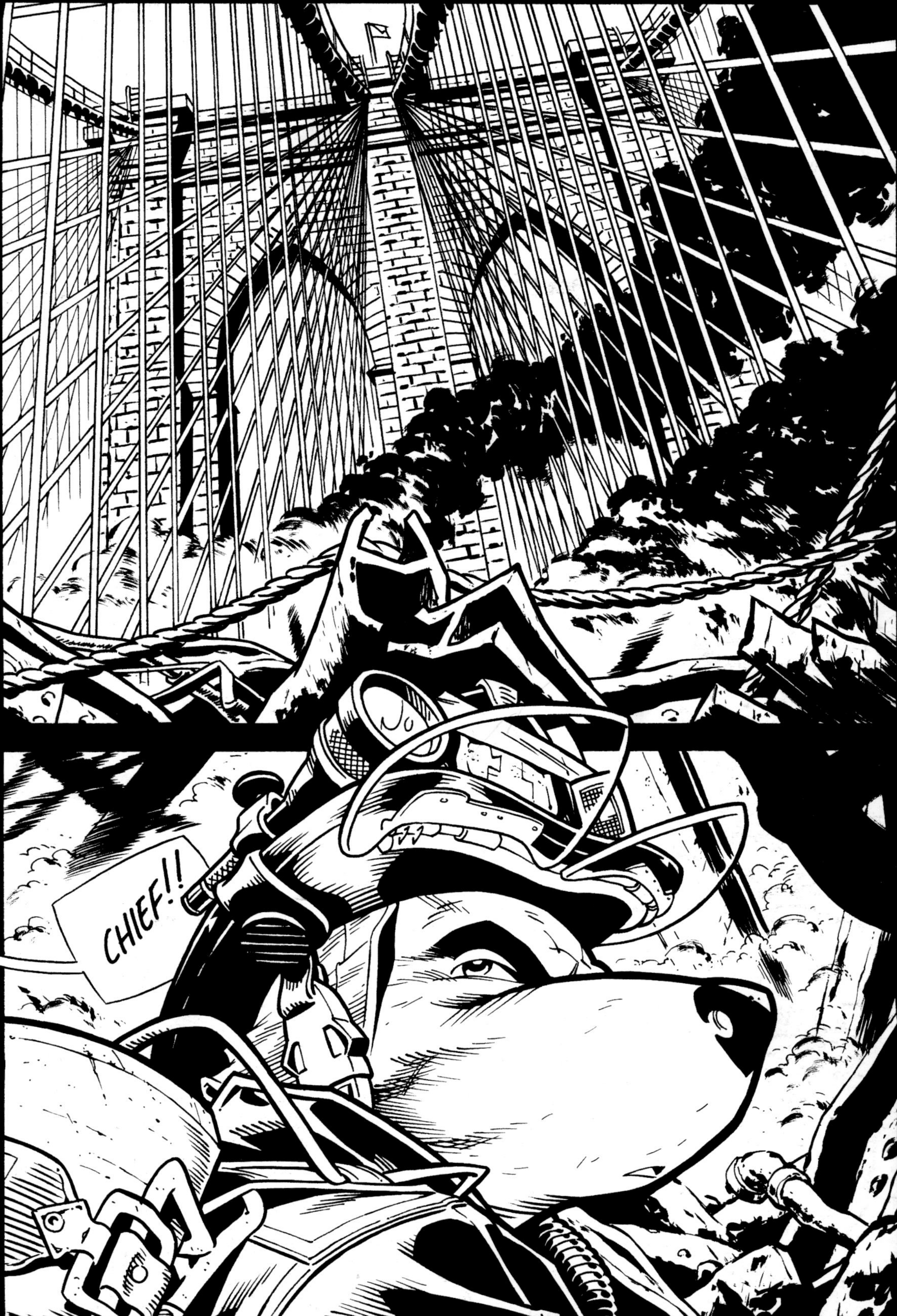
CHIEF!!

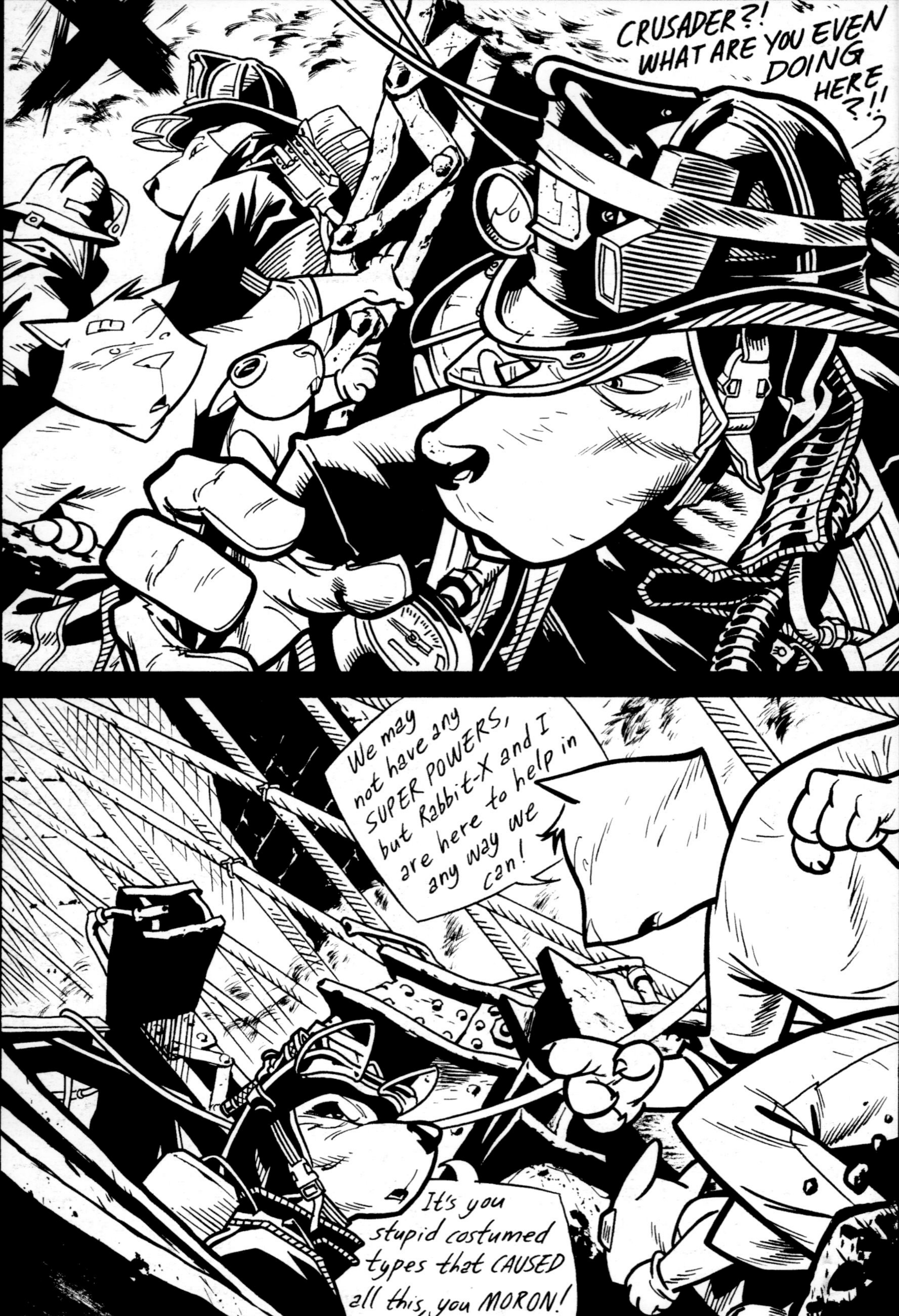
CRUSADER?! WHAT ARE YOU EVEN DOING HERE?!!
We may not have any SUPER POWERS, but Rabbit-X and I are here to help in any way we can!
It's you stupid costumed types that CAUSED all this, you MORON!

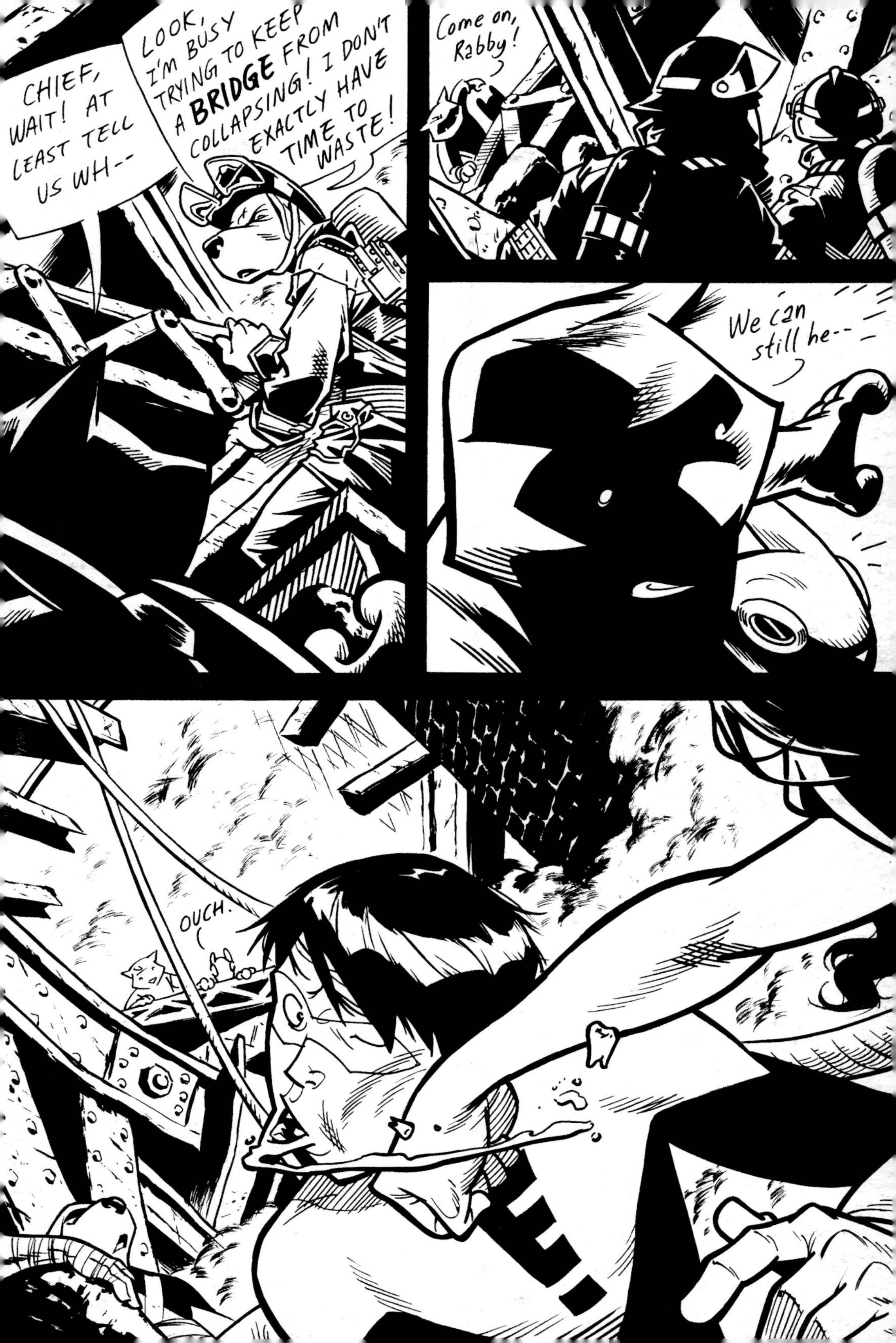
CHIEF, WAIT! AT LEAST TELL US WH--
LOOK, I'M BUSY TRYING TO KEEP A BRIDGE FROM COLLAPSING! I DON'T EXACTLY HAVE TIME TO WASTE!
Come on, Rabby!
We can still he--
OUCH.

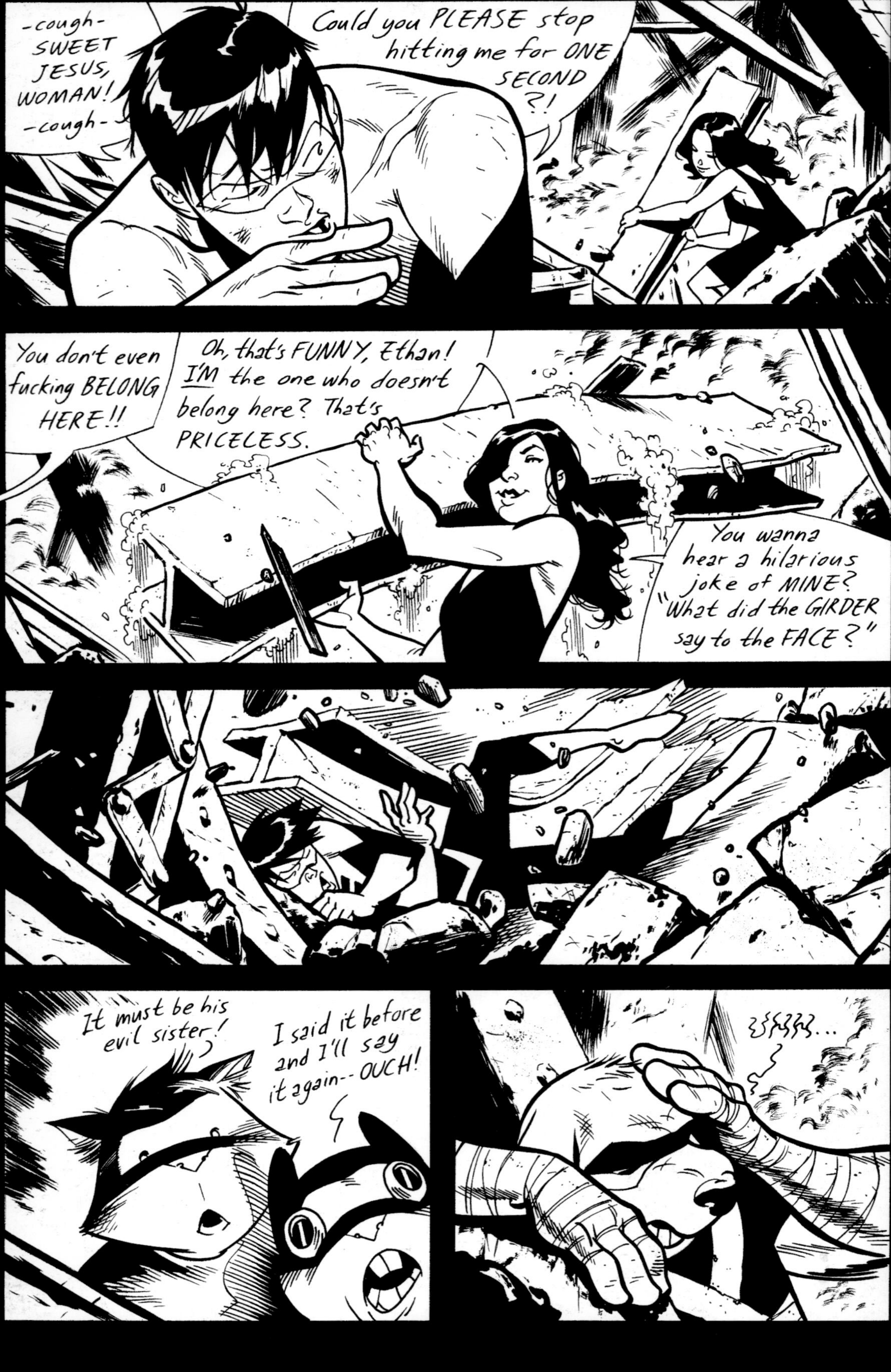
-cough- SWEET JESUS, WOMAN! -cough-
Could you PLEASE stop hitting me for ONE SECOND ?!
You don't even fucking BELONG HERE!!
Oh, that's FUNNY, Ethan! I'M the one who doesn't belong here? That's PRICELESS.
You wanna hear a hilarious joke of MINE? "What did the GIRDER say to the FACE?"
It must be his evil sister!
I said it before and I'll say it again-- OUCH!
zzzzzz...

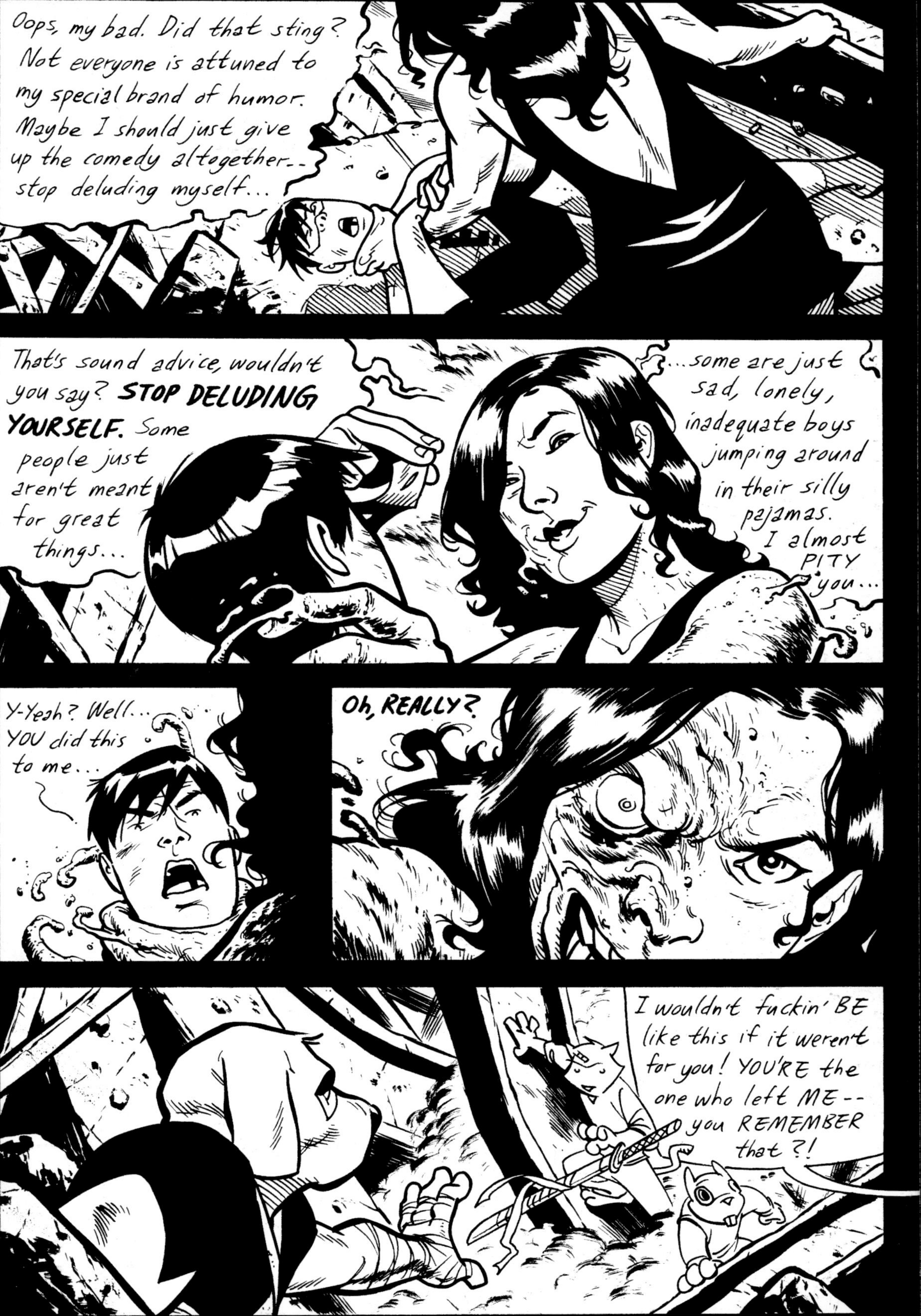
Oops, my bad. Did that sting? Not everyone is attuned to my special brand of humor. Maybe I should just give up the comedy altogether-- stop deluding myself...
That's sound advice, wouldn't you say? STOP DELUDING YOURSELF. Some people just aren't meant for great things...
...some are just sad, lonely, inadequate boys jumping around in their silly pajamas. I almost PITY you...
Y-Yeah? Well... YOU did this to me...
Oh, REALLY?
I wouldn't fuckin' BE like this if it weren't for you! YOU'RE the one who left ME-- you REMEMBER that?!

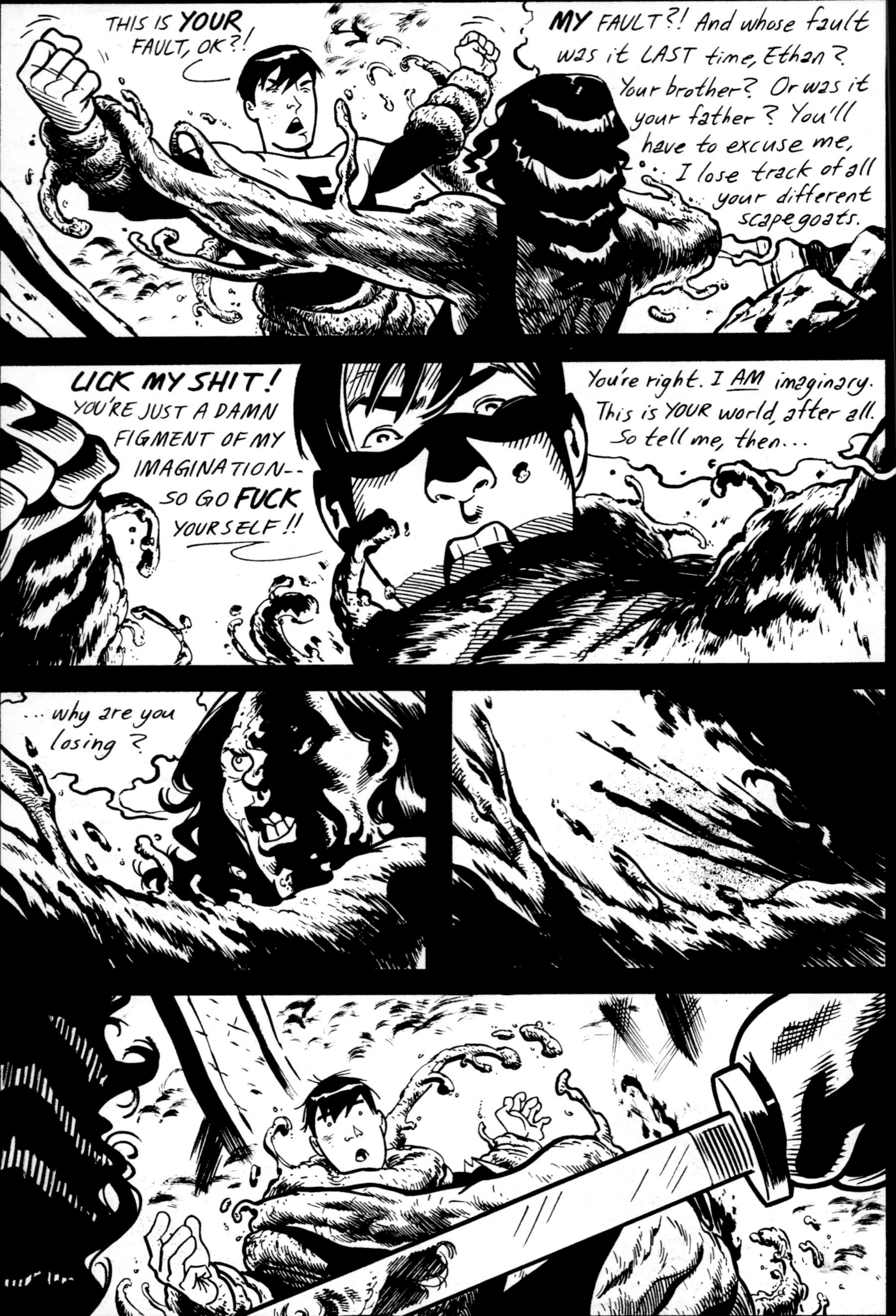
THIS IS YOUR FAULT, OK?!
MY FAULT?! And whose fault was it LAST time, Ethan? Your brother? Or was it your father? You'll have to excuse me, I lose track of all your different scapegoats.
LICK MY SHIT! YOU'RE JUST A DAMN FIGMENT OF MY IMAGINATION-- SO GO FUCK YOURSELF!!
You're right. I AM imaginary. This is YOUR world, after all. So tell me, then...
...why are you losing?

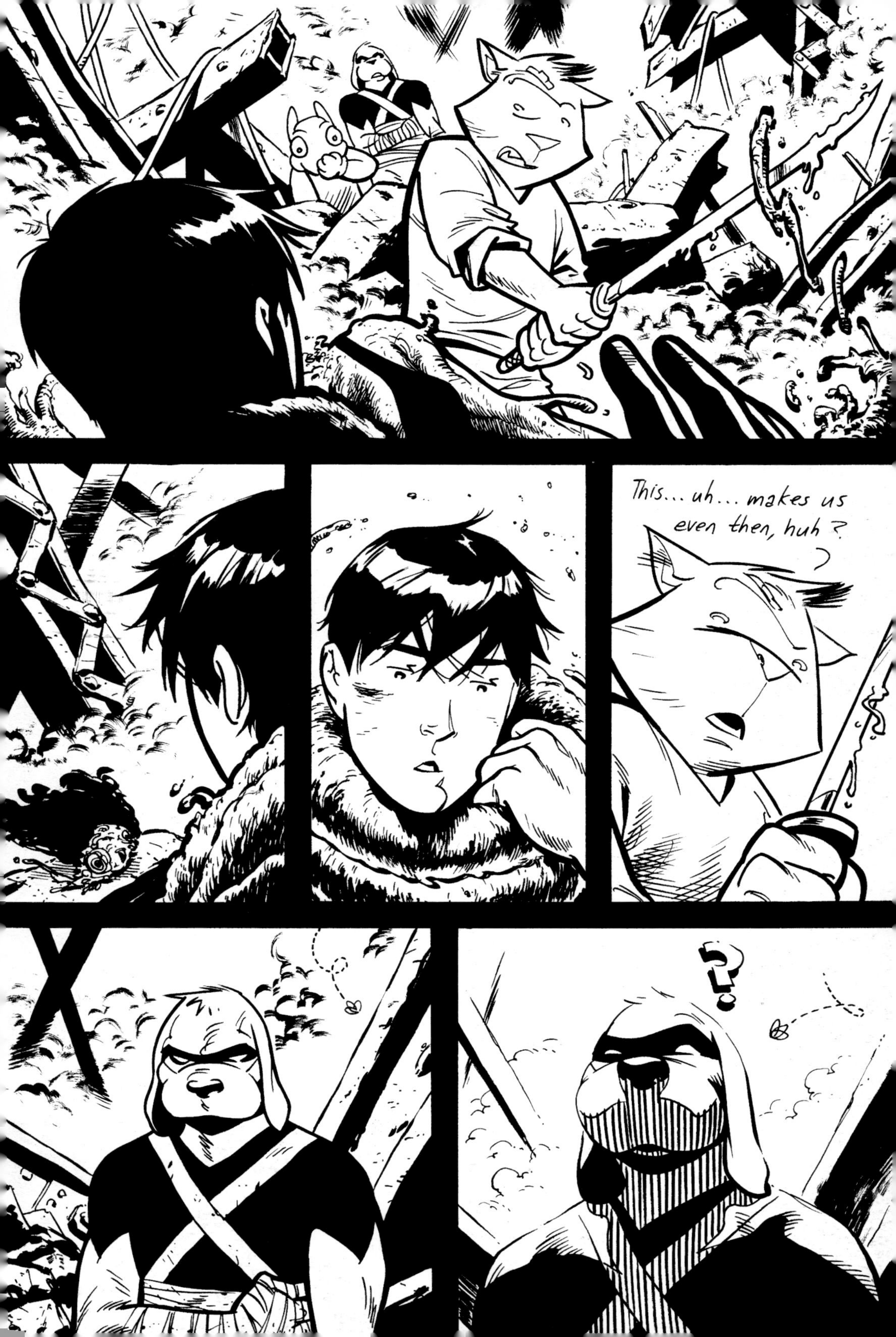
This... uh... makes us even then, huh?
?

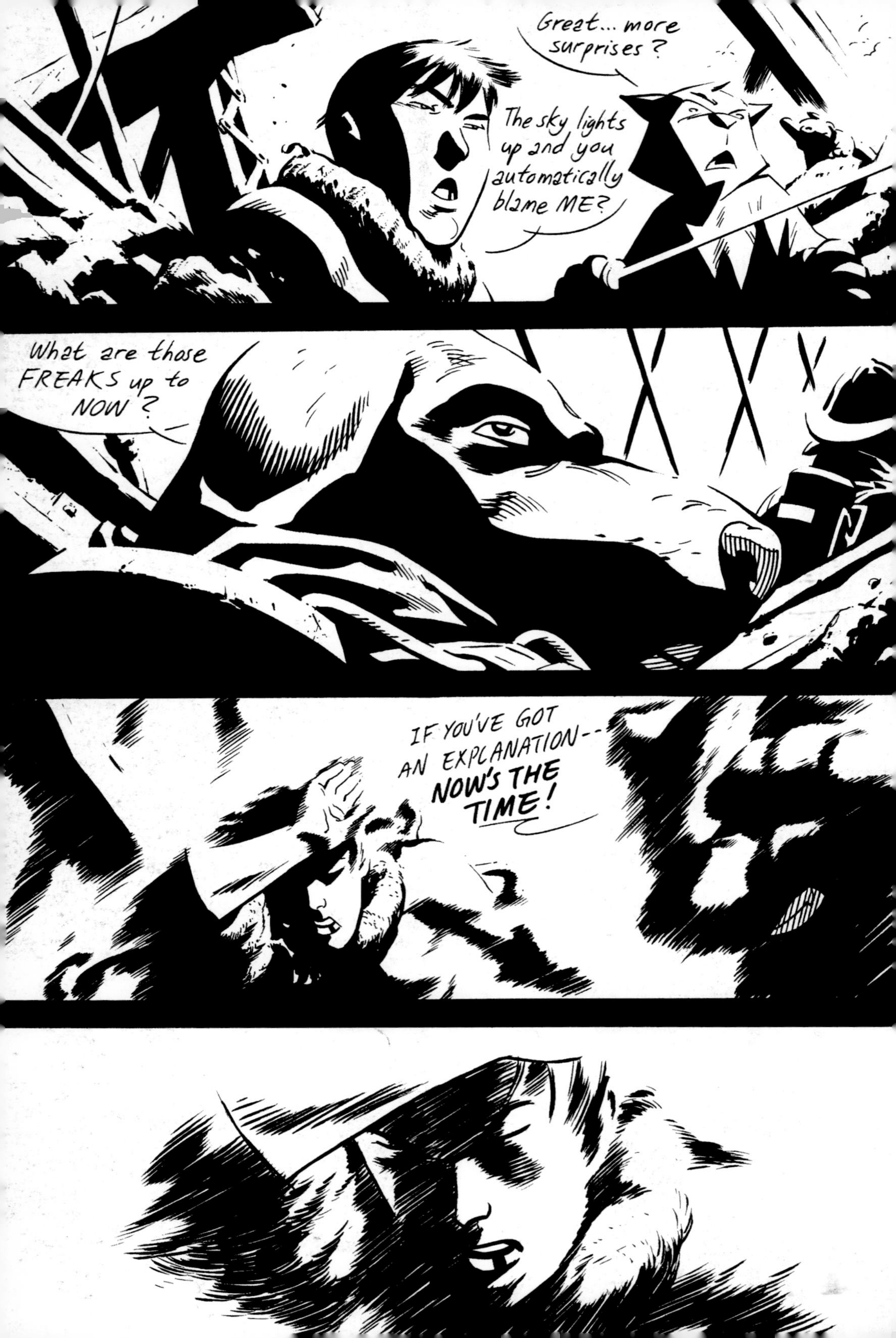
Great... more surprises?
The sky lights up and you automatically blame ME?
What are those FREAKS up to NOW?
IF YOU'VE GOT AN EXPLANATION---
NOW'S THE TIME!

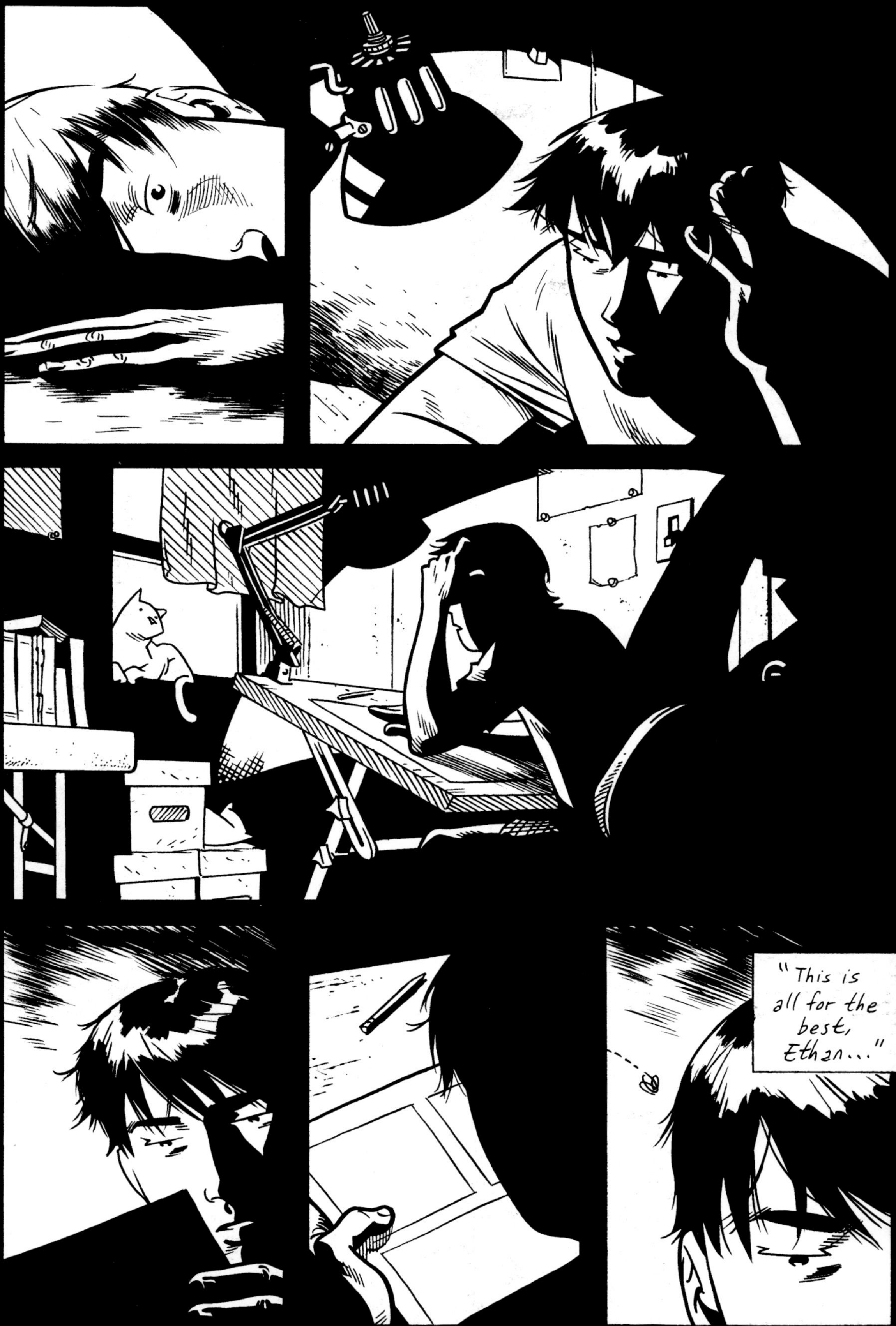
"This is all for the best, Ethan..."

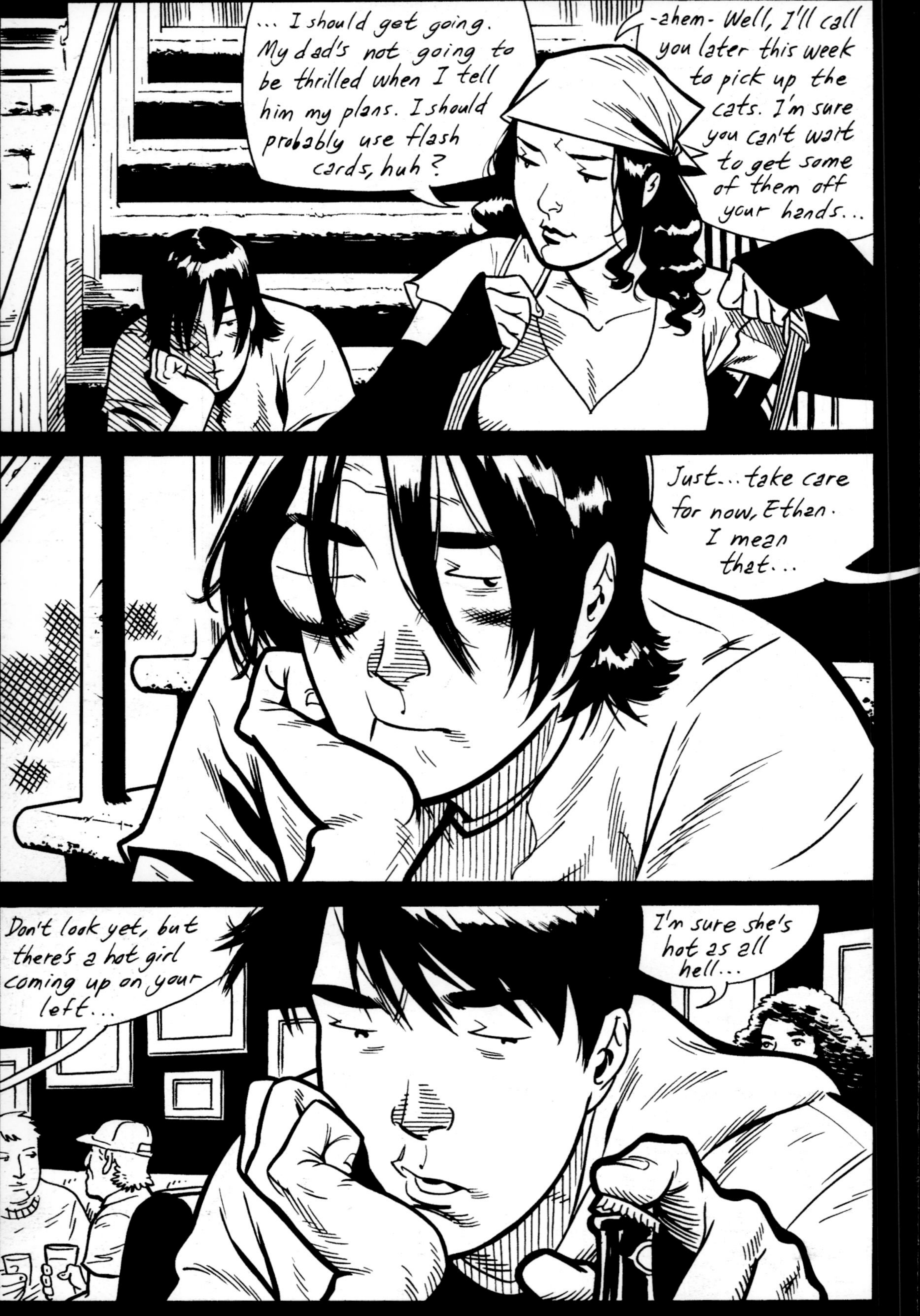
... I should get going. My dad's not going to be thrilled when I tell him my plans. I should probably use flash cards, huh?
-ahem- Well, I'll call you later this week to pick up the cats. I'm sure you can't wait to get some of them off your hands...
Just... take care for now, Ethan. I mean that...
Don't look yet, but there's a hot girl coming up on your left...
I'm sure she's hot as all hell...

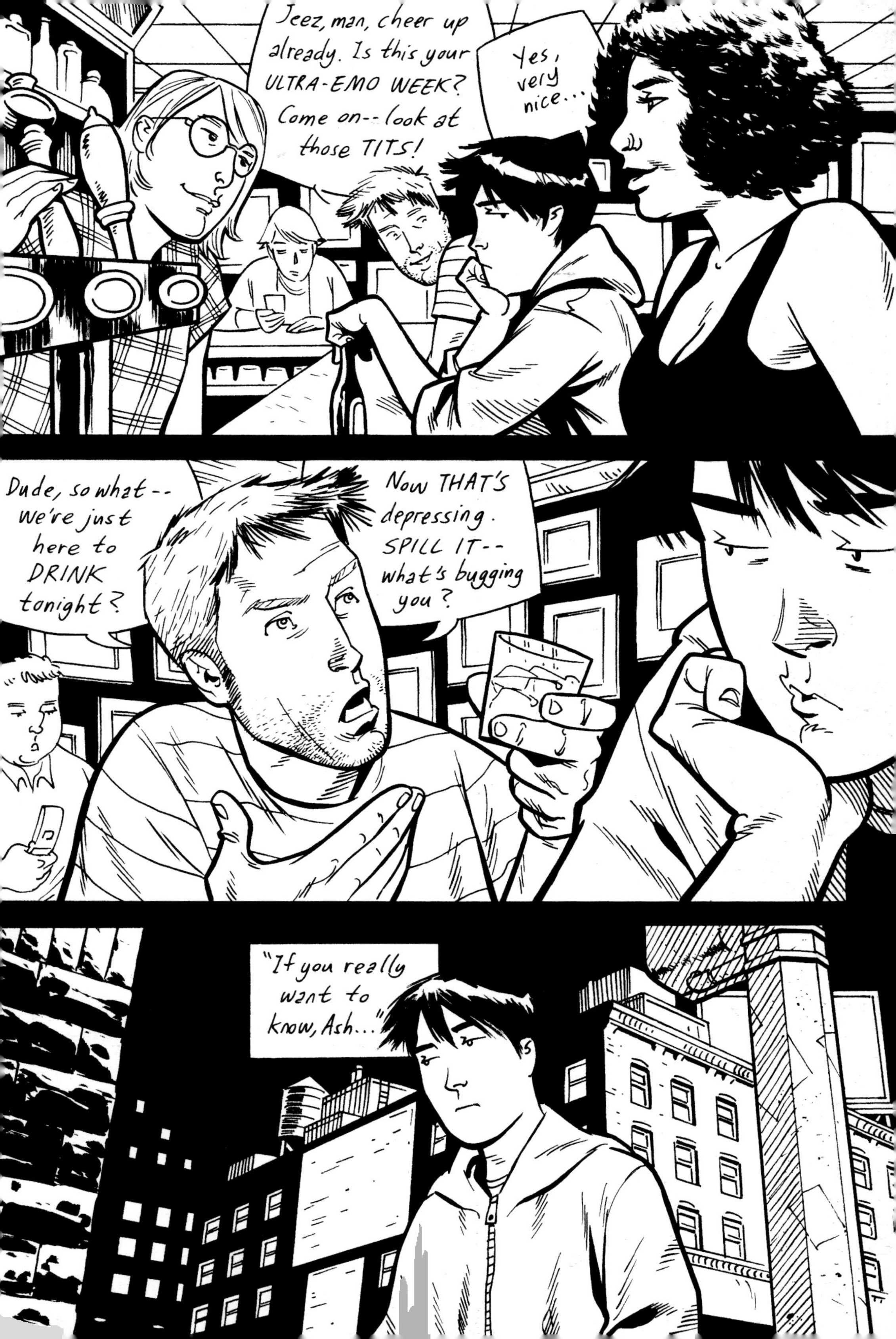
Jeez, man, cheer up already. Is this your ULTRA-EMO WEEK? Come on--look at those TITS!
Yes, very nice...
Dude, so what--we're just here to DRINK tonight?
Now THAT'S depressing. SPILL IT--what's bugging you?
"If you really want to know, Ash..."

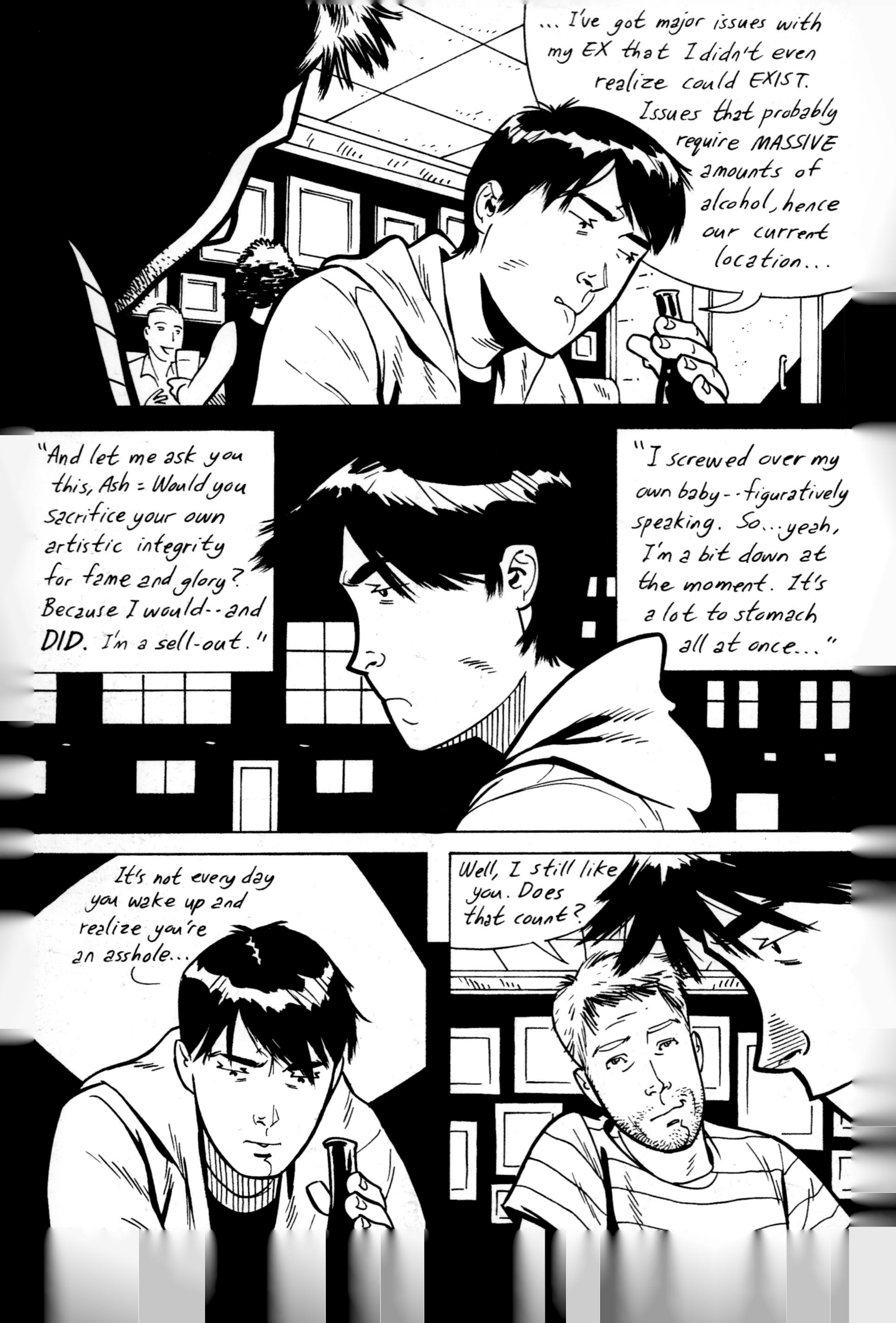
... I've got major issues with my EX that I didn't even realize could EXIST. Issues that probably require MASSIVE amounts of alcohol, hence our current location...
"And let me ask you this, Ash: Would you sacrifice your own artistic integrity for fame and glory? Because I would--and DID. I'm a sell-out."
"I screwed over my own baby--figuratively speaking. So...yeah, I'm a bit down at the moment. It's a lot to stomach all at once..."
It's not every day you wake up and realize you're an asshole...
Well, I still like you. Does that count?

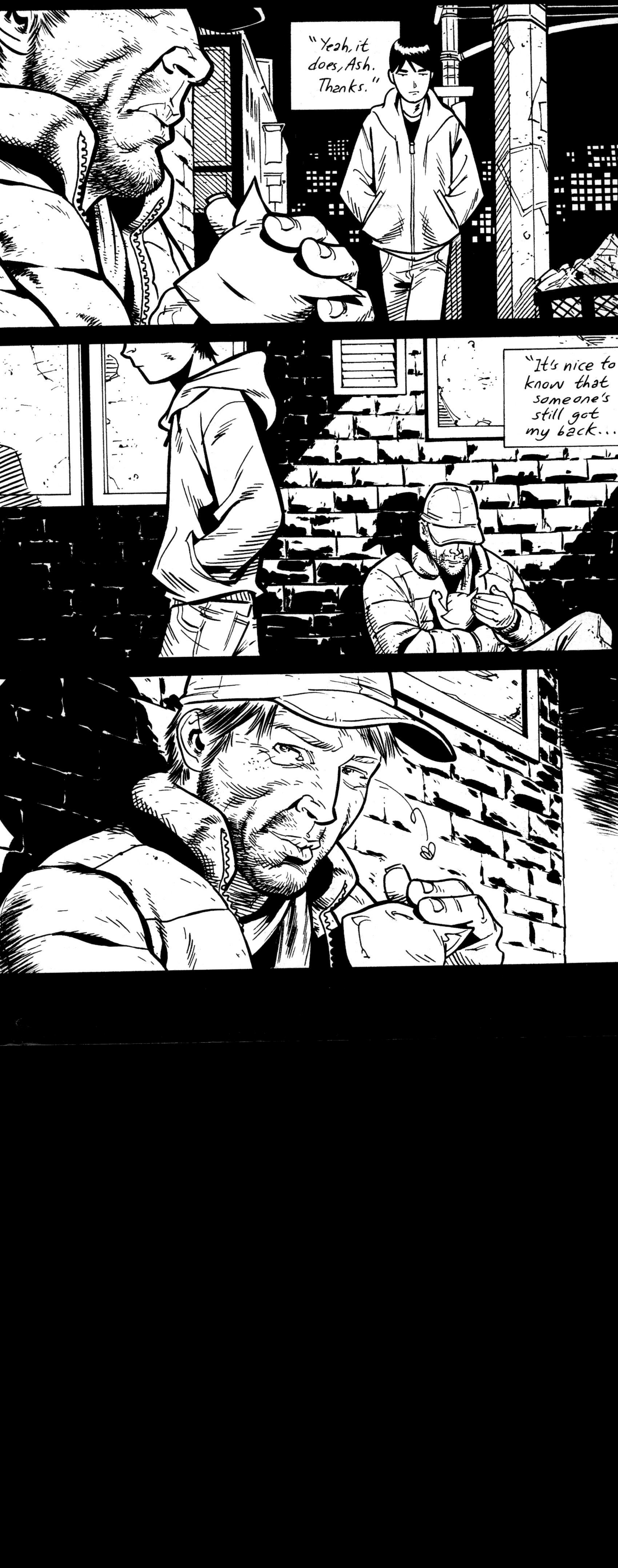
"Yeah, it does, Ash. Thanks."
"It's nice to know that someone's still got my back..."

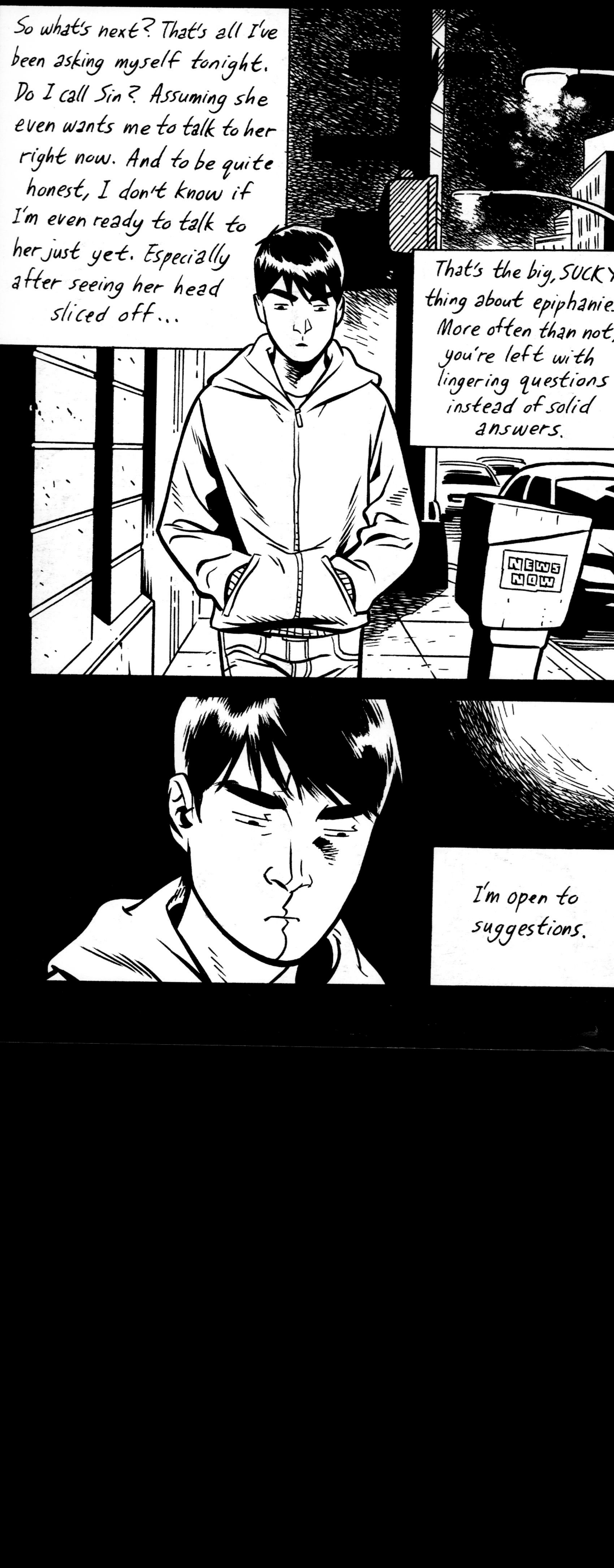
So what's next? That's all I've been asking myself tonight. Do I call Sin? Assuming she even wants me to talk to her right now. And to be quite honest, I don't know if I'm even ready to talk to her just yet. Especially after seeing her head sliced off...
That's the big, SUCKY thing about epiphanies. More often than not, you're left with lingering questions instead of solid answers.
NEWS NOW
I'm open to suggestions.